© 2025 Casey Kim. All rights reserved. No part of this book may be reproduced, stored in a retrieval system, or transmitted in any form or by any means without the prior written permission of the publisher.
First Edition: 2025 Publisher: Dawn Star Publishing
ISBN: 978-1-968249-06-9

For Another Beginning

I feel relieved. No regrets. It is finished.
This is my honest feeling
after completing three volumes
in English and two in Korean.

But why does it feel like my life
is only now beginning
at the age of 63,
even as a homeless man?

As long as my writing can offer someone
hope, joy, and encouragement,
I must not stop.
I've come to accept this path
as my life's calling.

Just as a grain of wheat falls to the ground
and dies to bear much fruit,
I have chosen not merely to live my life—
but to burn it brightly.

If my words can become a candle
to light the way for others,
I will gladly offer up my life
for the harmony, love,
and unity of the world.

Another journey,
shared with my neighbors—
Now, it begins again.

Enlightenment and Eternal Happiness

A journey through the novelized Scriptures,
led by an old man, a young boy, and you.
Along this dramatic path,
we encounter the answers to life's greatest questions.

SJCB Dialogue

At the end of each of the 66 books of Scripture, SJCB Dialogue unfolds— a living circle of conversation among the four great sages of humanity: Socrates, Jesus, Confucius, and the Buddha. Transcending language, religion, ethnicity, and civilization, they gather not to preach, but to share, to listen, and to seek together— rooted only in truth and love. This open forum of awakening dissolves the inner walls of the human soul and reminds us that humanity is one. Here begins the dawn of a new human civilization.

Contents

continue from Volume 2 (Matthew to Revelation)

The New Testament
Chap 1 : The Gospels (Matthew to John)

Volume 2. Mark : Mark testifies of Jesus, who came to give enlightenment to humanity—culminating in the Last Supper and His passion · 8

Volume 3. The Gospel of Luke : Luke, a Gentile and Paul's personal physician, presents Jesus as the perfect human being · 26

Volume 4. The Gospel of John : John testifies to the divinity of Jesus Christ, the Son of God who transcends all · 60

Chapter 2: The Book of History (Acts)

Volume 5. Acts : Continuing from his gospel, Luke records the acts of the apostles following the ascension of Jesus Christ · 99

Chapter 3: The Letters (Romans to Jude)

Volume 6. Romans : Paul writes to the Romans to resolve the conflict between Jews and Gentiles · 126

Volume 7. 1 Corinthians : Paul writes to the Corinthian church with wisdom, eternal life, and the love of God · 141

Volume 8. 2 Corinthians : Paul sends a second letter to the Corinthians, urging love and unity among all humanity · 154

Volume 9. Galatians : Paul encourages the Galatians to live by the grace of Christ, not under the bondage of the law · 164

Volume 10. Ephesians : Paul exhorts the Ephesians to live victorious lives through the grace of God · 171

Volume 11. Philippians : Paul's prison epistle to the church in Philippi · 185

Volume 12. Colossians : Another prison epistle, warning the Colossians against legalism and mysticism · 192

Volume 13. 1 Thessalonians : To the Thessalonians—Europe's first converts—Paul proclaims the gospel of Christ · 198

Volume 14. 2 Thessalonians : Paul's second letter to the Thessalonians, urging them to stay grounded in truth and purity · 201

Volume 15. 1 Timothy : Paul's letters, compiled into Scripture by his disciple Timothy · 204

Volume 16. 2 Timothy : Paul's second prison epistle to Timothy, written before his martyrdom · 209

Volume 17. Titus : Paul writes to his disciple Titus, urging him to pursue a life of holiness as a leader · 213

Volume 18. Philemon : A personal letter from Paul to Philemon, a wealthy man converted through him, pleading for forgiveness · 215

Volume 19. Hebrews : An anonymous author urges faith in Christ as superior to the old covenant · 217

Volume 20. James : James, the brother of Jesus, writes that faith without works is dead—addressed to the twelve tribes · 226

Volume 21. 1 Peter : Peter writes to scattered Jews, offering wisdom for enduring suffering · 236

Volume 22. 2 Peter : Peter warns against deception regarding Christ's second coming and final judgment · 243

Volume 23. 1 John : John's first letter emphasizes love, righteousness, and walking with God · 246

Volume 24. 2 John : A short letter to a chosen lady and her children, encouraging harmony and courage · 251

Volume 25. 3 John : John praises the sincerity of Gaius and Demetrius
· 253

Volume 26. Jude : Jude, the brother of James, urges believers to defend the faith against Gnostic heresies · 255

Chapter 4: The Book of Prophecy

Volume 27. Revelation : From exile on Patmos, John records visions of Christ's return and the creation of a new heaven and new earth
· 259

Volume 2: Mark

"Tell me about Mark," Yesac asked.

"Mark deals with the purpose of Jesus' coming into the world." said the boy.

"Jesus came to serve, not to be served, and to sacrifice himself to pay for the sins of mankind," Yesac said.

"What makes Jesus great is that he overcame all the hardships of hunger and thirst to achieve his goal. He even demonstrated superhuman abilities through prayer and the power of the Holy Spirit," said the boy.

"He was the only righteous man who demonstrated that what he taught was practiced with quick determination."

Yesac flipped to the first chapter of the Gospel of Mark or Jesus.

'The beginning of the gospel of Jesus Christ, the Son of God.
"The words of the prophet Isaiah are fulfilled:
Behold, I send my messenger before thee,
and he shall prepare thy way.

The voice of one crying in the wilderness:
Prepare ye the way of the Lord, make His paths straight."

John the Baptist appeared in the wilderness,
preaching a baptism of repentance for the remission of sins.
All the country of Judea and Jerusalem went out to him,
and they were baptized by him in the Jordan River,
confessing their sins.

Now John was clothed in camel's hair with a leather belt around his waist, and he ate locusts and wild honey.

He preached, saying,
"After me comes one more powerful than I,
the straps of whose sandals I am not worthy to stoop down and untie."

Then came Jesus from Nazareth of Galilee, and was baptized by John in the Jordan.

*And immediately as He came up out of the water, He saw the heavens
opened, and the Spirit descending on Him like a dove.
A voice came from heaven:
"Thou art my beloved Son; in Thee I am well pleased."*

*And the Spirit immediately drove Him into the wilderness.
He was there forty days, being tempted by Satan.
He was with the wild beasts, and the angels ministered unto Him.*

*After John was taken,
Jesus came into Galilee, preaching the gospel of God, saying:*

*"The time is fulfilled, and the kingdom of God is at hand;
repent, and believe in the gospel."*

*And as He walked by the Sea of Galilee,
He saw Simon (Peter) and Andrew, his brother,
casting a net into the sea—for they were fishermen.*

*And Jesus said unto them,
"Follow me, and I will make you fishers of men."'*

"The four gospels have a lot of overlap," said the boy.

"Duplication is review, and review is the best way to enlightenment," Yesac said.

It was the Bible study method taught by Master Yesac. Although many of the tools for enlightenment that the old man taught were repetitive, by repeating and reviewing those tools, one could draw closer to the world of enlightenment.

"When Jesus was baptized by John, Jesus saw something," said the boy.

"What?" asked Yesac.

"He saw heaven being torn open and the Spirit descending on him like a dove," the boy answered.

"And Jesus, who had been anointed by John, heard," added Yesac.

"What?" the boy asked.

"The voice of God says, 'You are my son in whom I delight andlove,'" said Yesac.

"Jesus was tempted by Satan in the wilderness and lived in the wilderness with wild animals for forty days," said the boy.

"So we shouldn't be hard-hearted about the trials we face in life," said Yesac.

"Yes, we must overcome all hardships and become a fisher of men," the boy said.

"Twelve fishers of men preaching the gospel, good," Yesac said and turned the pages of Mark's Gospel.

*'But that ye may know
that the Son of Man hath authority on earth to forgive sins:
I say unto thee— Arise, take thy reward, and go thy way.'
(To the man with the palsy)*

*And when Jesus heard it, He said unto them:
'Laws are useless unto them that are well,
but unto them that are sick, they are profitable.
I am not come to call the righteous, but sinners.'*

*Then the Pharisees said unto Him,
'Behold, what is one thing they cannot do on the Sabbath day?'
And He said unto them: 'The Sabbath was made for man,
and man for the Sabbath: therefore,
the Son of Man is Lord even of the Sabbath.'*

"Christ's teaching is that the Sabbath was made for man, not man for the Sabbath," said the boy.

"That's right. Religion exists for people, not people for religion," Yesac said.

"If it weren't for Jesus, we'd be stuck with a religion that is forever looking up," added the boy.

"Yes. Through Jesus, the Old Testament law was fulfilled," said Yesac.

"So that we could have a participatory faith, a faith that realizes itself by doing what it says," added the boy.

"Jesus is the way, the truth, and the life," said Yesac. The

boy flipped through the pages of Mark's Gospel.

> 'And the Pharisees went out, and soon afterward the Herodians,
> and they conspired together how they might kill Him.
> But Jesus, with His disciples, withdrew to the sea;
> and a great multitude followed Him—
> from Galilee, and from Judea, and from Jerusalem,
> and from Idumea, and from beyond the Jordan,
> and from Tyre and Sidon,
> and from all the surrounding region,
> when they heard of the great works which He had done.'

"He teaches that whoever blasphemes (blasphemes [blæsfi:m]) against the Holy Spirit will not be forgiven forever butwill remain in eternal sin," said the boy.

"Who can blaspheme the Holy Spirit? Who is the spirit of God and Jesus, and who is love? You must be holy yourself and watch out for Satan. Satan cannot drive out Satan," said Yesac.

"It's good to review the great teaching, 'Whoever does God's will is my brother and sister and mother.'"

"That's right. All of us humans are friends, brothers, and sisters with the same father," said the boy.

Yesac flipped through the pages.

> 'Again, Jesus began to teach by the sea,
> and a great multitude was gathered unto Him.
> So He got into a boat and sat down in the sea,
> while all the people were on the land by the shore.
> The crowd that gathered was so great that He sat out on the lake,
> and all the people were along the shore at the water's edge.
> And He said unto them, "He that hath ears to hear, let him hear.
> The farmer soweth the word. The kingdom of God is as if a man should
> sow seed into the ground."
>
> And He said unto them,
> "Where unto shall we liken the kingdom of God?
> Or with what parable shall we compare it?
> It is like a grain of mustard seed, which, when it is sown in the earth,
> is smaller than all the seeds that be in the earth.
> But when it is sown, it groweth up, and becometh greater than all
> herbs, and bringeth forth great branches,
> so that the birds of the air may nestle under the shadow of it."'

"The setting for Jesus is as romantic and wonderful as any: the seashore, the high mountains, the ship at sea, the wilderness, and the people gathered on the land by the sea. It's a scene from a great one-sided drama, a movie," said the boy.

"What does this say, 'He who has ears, let him listen?'" asked Yesac.

"................"

The boy fell silent.

"We must understand that the secret of God's kingdom has already been given to us," said Yesac.

"Yes, we already have the kingdom of God within us as long as we live by walking with Jesus and becoming His Word," the boy commented. The old man was surprised by the boy's realization but hid his expression.

Sunday is always a more relaxed day.
With his daily two-hour routine of stretching, running, and weight training at dawn, and two hours of soccer on Sundays,
Yesac's body is as supple as a woman's, and at 62, he is in top shape.
Even though he is homeless, he is building six-pack abs and triceps.
To him, the body is the temple where Jesus dwells.
That's why regular exercise and Bible study are not hobbies but his sacred life system. He has been deeply influenced by Korea's ancient Hwarangdo tradition— the warrior-scholars of the Silla Dynasty.
They practiced martial arts and followed MuSaDo (무사도, 武士道) in the mountains of Geumgang and Jiri.
Like Jesus who was tested in the wilderness, Hwarangs would visit deep caves, fast, pray, and pursue mystical experiences.
Yesac, inspired by this, always sought to combine the spiritual and the physical. The most representative figure of Hwarangdo is General Kim Yusin, a national hero and an ancestor of Yesac.
The Five Worldly Precepts of Hwarangdo were not unlike the Ten Commandments of Moses.
They included:

- Loyalty to the King (God)– SaGunYiChung (事君以忠 사군이충)
- Filial piety to parents– SaChinYiHyo (事親以孝 사친이효)
- Seeking beautiful mountains and waters– YuOhSanSu (유오산수)
- Practicing Tao and righteousness– SangMaDoYi (상마도의)
- Enjoying music and poetry– SangYulGaRak (상율가락)

These five principles became Yesac's own code of life.
He lives like a modern-day Hwarang —
training his body, sharpening his mind,
and walking with God in the wilderness of this world.
The boy turned the pages of the book that enlightened him.

'And when Jesus had come to the other side of the sea, into the region of Gerasenes, he went out of the boat. And immediately a man possessed with an unclean spirit came out from among the tombs and met him.
For Jesus had already said to him,
"Come out of this man, you impure spirit!"

Jesus said unto her, "Daughter, thy faith hath made thee well; go in peace. Thou art loosed from thy sickness, and be thou well."
Taking her by the hand, he said unto her, "Talitha koum," which is translated, "I say unto thee, girl, arise."
Jesus took much heed of them, that no man should know this thing. And he said unto them, "Give her something to eat."'

"What does it mean that Jesus' healing of the Gerasenes maniac took place in the Decapolis, a Gentile neighborhood?" asked the boy.

"It is a testimony that Jesus did not come to abolish the Old Testament law but to fulfill it," replied Yesac.

"................"

When the boy fell silent, Yesac opened the Old Testament. It was Leviticus 19:34.

'The foreigner residing among you must be treated as your native-born. Love them as yourself.'

"What a great teaching to love a stranger as yourself," the boy said this, recalling Yesac's words that one day, with just this one line of teaching, the world could be unified, and humanity could become one.

"Understanding and appreciating that God is so compassionate that He heals all who are alive, transcending language and culture, nation and ethnicity, religion and space and time, is the path to enlightenment," Yesac responded.

"Those who have the mind-ear, the ear of the heart, will understand," the boy said and recalled the older man's words, which said that differences are not objects of conflict but of understanding, learning, harmony, and love.

"What is the meaning of Jesus' sign that even the wind and the sea obey him?" the boy asked.

"................."

"Jesus is greater and more holy because He does what He saysand teaches," said Yesac.

"Act, act, act(HaengHaengHaeng 行行行 행행행), so does thatmean that going to church or temple doesn't bring about significant change because there is no action based on enlightenment?"

The boy murmured to himself, and the old man, Yesac, remained silent.

"Was told to love, but hate; was told not to judge, but a judge; was told not to worry, but worry; was always told to rejoice and be thankful, but grieve and complain?" the boy repeated to himself again, his eyes resting on Yesac's little note.

'Daughter, your faith has healed you!'

Those were the words of Jesus as he healed the girl with the hemorrhage.

"Faith," the boy said, remembering Matthew 14. It showed Jesus and Peter walking on the water.

'And Peter got out of the boat and walked on the water to Jesus. But when he saw the wind, he was afraid and began to sink. He cried out, "Lord, save me!" Immediately Jesus stretched forth his hand and caught him, and said unto him, "O thou of little faith, why didst thou doubt?"'

After sleeping over at a friend's house at 5 a.m., Yesac and the boy were stuck on the highway for three hours in the sweltering August Dallas weather. Their old car had broken down, but they had the wisdom and strength to get them through the not-so-great times. It was the words of 1 Timothy 6:7, the teaching of free hand to free hand, that enriched their hearts.

'The Pharisees and all the Jews do not eat unless they wash their hands diligently, keeping the tradition of the elders.'
Then the Pharisees and scribes asked Jesus,
"Why do your disciples not walk according to the tradition of the

elders, but eat bread with unwashed hands?"
And Jesus answered, *"You have forsaken the commandment of God and hold to the tradition of men. You are experts at setting aside the commandment of God in order to keep your tradition. For Moses said, 'Honor your father and your mother,' and 'He who speaks evil of father or mother is to be put to death.'"*

"The Pharisees and Jews speak of things seen, and Jesus speaks of things unseen," said the boy.

"Even a boy has the mind's eye to see the invisible," Yesac said.

"Jesus' teaching was not about visible sacrifices, but about invisible love and mercy," said the boy.

Their faces, old man and boy, could not have been more transparent and peaceful than when they spoke of the invisible world. God is love, and love is invisible, but we, humanity, love each other, and it exists.

The boy flipped through the pages of Mark's Gospel and saw a note in Yesac's little notebook summarizing Christ's teachings that overlapped with Matthew's Gospel.

- *InNeungHongDo BiDoHongIn* 인능홍도비도홍인 人能弘道 非道弘人 ; *The Sabbath was made for man, not man for the Sabbath. - Mark 2:27*
- *Cross(十字架 십자가) = MooAh(無我 무아 Jesus): If anyone would come after me, let him deny himself and take up his cross and follow me.- Mark 8:34*
- *PilSangZeukSa PilSaZeukSang* 필사즉생 필생즉사 必死則生 必生則死: *If you try to save your life, you'll lose it, If you lose your life for my sake, you'll gain it.*
- *ChunSangChunHaYuAhDokJon* 천상천하 유아독존 天上天下 唯我獨尊; *For what does it profit a man to gain the whole world, and forfeit his soul? - Mark 8:36*
- *OByungYiEo* 오병이어 五餅二魚 :*And taking the five loaves and the two fish, he looked up to heaven and said a blessing and broke the loaves and gave them to the disciples to set before the people. And he divided the two fish among them all.- Mark 6:41*
- *SaHaeJiNaeKaeHyungJeYa* 사해지내 개형제야 四海之內, 皆兄弟也; *Whoever does the will of God is my brother and sister and mother. - Mark 3:35*

Yesac, who does not have a home, lives in his car or an office at a factory. Just as Jesus was starving in the wilderness, hunger came to him late in the evening. Yesac filled a bowl with water to prepare his ramen.

The boy turned the page of Mark.

"Do you have eyes but fail to see, and ears but fail to hear? And don't you remember?" Jesus said, "If you can? Everything is possible for one who believes."
He replied, "This kind can come out only by prayer."
Sitting down, Jesus called the Twelve and said, "Anyone who wants to be first must be the very last, and the servant of all."
He took a little child and said, "Whoever welcomes one of these little children in my name welcomes me. And whoever welcomes me does not welcome me but the one who sent me."
"Salt is good, but if it loses its saltiness, how can you make it salty again? Have salt among yourselves, and be at peace with each other."

"A man's life becomes what he thinks it should be, and the belief in his thoughts produces miracles," said the boy.

"Faith is stronger than belief, for nothing is impossible for him who believes, and it produces miracles that are not miraculous," Yesac said.

"Just as Jesus came to serve the world and became king, so those who want to serve their neighbors live their best lives," said the boy.

"Jesus' great teaching was that to welcome a child is to welcome Jesus and to welcome Jesus is to honor God," Yesac said.

"Yes. We are to be the salt of the earth, a light of peace and love to our neighbors," the boy said.

The savory smell of boiling ramen noodles whetted the boy's and Yesac's appetites, but they didn't take their eyes off Mark's Gospel. The next Scripture reading was about a rich man seeking to gain eternal life.

'And as Jesus went forth into the street, there came unto him a man, and kneeling down, said unto him, "Good Teacher, what shall I do to inherit eternal life?" And he said unto him, "Thou knowest the commandment:
Thou shalt not kill, Thou shalt not commit adultery,
Thou shalt not steal, Thou shalt not bear false witness,
Thou shalt not defraud, Thou shalt not take intoxicating liquors,

Thou shalt honor thy father and mother."
Jesus saw him, and loved him, and said unto him,
"Thou lackest but one thing: go, sell all that thou hast, and give to the poor, and thou shalt have treasure in heaven: and come, follow me."'

"Jesus teaches a rich man that the way to eternal life is in the Ten Commandments and that the only good one is God," said the boy.

"Not only that, but the way to eternal life is to give everything you have to your neighbor and follow Jesus," Yesac said.

"So Jesus says it's easier for a camel to go through the eye of a needle than for a rich man to enter the kingdom of God," said the boy.

"There is a man who was rich and entered the kingdom of heaven," Yesac said.

"Who's that?" asked the boy.

"Siddhartha."

"Ah, yes. You mean the prince who renounced the world's greatest wealth, honor, and power, left the world, and became enlightened," the boy remembered.

"Yes. Enlightenment is the narrow gate to eternal life," Yesac explained what it meant to be truly enlightened.

"So you would say that the prince was like the man who kept the Ten Commandments of Moses and gave all his wealth to the poor." The boy was curious.

"Certain death brings life; if one is determined to die, one will live. The reward for this is the treasure that comes from heaven, it is eternal life," Yesac said, reflecting on Buddha's ascetic practices and Jesus in the wilderness, prepared to face death.

"Is there also a Ten Commandments in Buddhism?" the boy asked.

"There is something similar to the Ten Commandments called the Ten Virtuous Precepts (*SipSunKye* 십선계 十善戒)."

The old man handed over his small notebook. The green letters were meticulously inscribed.

1. Do not kill (BulSalSang 不殺生 불살생)) - Do not take life. (Exodus 20:13: You shall not murder)
2. Do not steal (BulTuDo 不偸盜 불투도) - Do not steal. (Exodus 20:15: You shall not steal)
3. Do not commit adultery (BulSaEum 不邪婬 불사음) - Do not commit adultery. (Exodus 20:14: You shall not commit adultery)
4. Do not lie (BulMangEou 不妄語 불망어) - Do not bear false witness. (Exodus 20:16: You shall not bear false witness against your neighbor)
5. Do not use frivolous speech (不綺語 불기어) - Do not engage in frivolous or meaningless talk. (Ephesians 4:29: Let no corrupting talk come out of your mouths, but only such as is good for building up, as fits the occasion, that it may give grace to those who hear)
6. Do not speak harshly (BulAkKu 不惡口 불악구) - Do not speak harshly or use abusive language. (Colossians 3:8: But now you must put them all away: anger, wrath, malice, slander, and obscene talk from your mouth)
7. Do not cause discord (BulYangSul 不兩舌 불양설) - Do not sow discord among friends. (Proverbs 16:28: A perverse person stirs up conflict, and a gossip separates close friends)
8. Do not covet (BulTam 不貪 불탐) - Avoid greed and covetousness. (Colossians 3:5: Put to death, therefore, what is earthly in you: sexual immorality, impurity, passion, evil desire, and covetousness, which is idolatry)
9. Do not harbor anger (BulJin 不瞋 불진) - Avoid anger. (Ephesians 4:26: "Be angry and do not sin; do not let the sun go down on your anger.")
10. Do not be foolish (BulChi 不癡 불치) - Avoid foolishness. (Proverbs 14:16: The wise fear the Lord and shun evil, but a fool is hotheaded and yet feels secure)

The boy was amazed by the old man's meticulousness in finding corresponding verses in the Bible and carefully recording them. The tools for enlightenment that the old man had passed on—such as revering heaven and loving people (KyungChunAeIn 敬天愛人 경천애인), penetrating everything as one (IlYiKwanJi 一以貫之 일이관지), and all laws returning to one (ManBupKwiIl 萬法歸一 만법귀일)—flashed through the boy's mind like a beam of light.

The boy seemed to understand why the old man Yesac had emphasized and taught this passage so strongly. The universe, the Earth, and everything in it transcended time and space and became one. Naturally, all humans on this Earth appeared and felt like brothers and sisters, and God was love. Transcending countries, ethnicities, cultures, and religions (Christianity, Islam, Hinduism, Buddhism, Judaism, Sikhism, Taoism, Bahá'í Faith), the boy's heart grew ever more loving, considering everyone better than himself just as they were, without addition or subtraction. This was eternal happiness.

Ignoring the boy's solemn expression, Yesac turned the pages of the Gospel of Mark.

'Jesus said,
"Truly I tell you, no one who has left their home, or brothers, or sisters, or mother, or father, or children, or lands for my sake and for the gospel, will fail to receive a hundred times as much in this present age—homes, brothers, sisters, mothers, children, and lands—along with persecutions, and in the age to come, eternal life.
Many who are last will be first, and the first will be last.
But not so with you. Whoever wants to become great among you must be your servant, and whoever wants to be first must be the slave of all. For the Son of Man did not come to be served, but to serve, and to give his life as a ransom for many."'

"You must pay a price to inherit eternal life."

"What does Jesus mean when he says that he will leave his house, brothers, sisters, parents, children, and possessions?" the boy asked.

"Not only wealth but also possessions and attachments to relationships and follow the Word of Truth. It teaches us to realize the impermanence of life's ties, which are impermanent and will eventually part, and to realize the eternal truth, which is eternal life. If you think about how Abraham tried to sacrifice Isaac to God without delay, it will be easier to understand."

At that moment, the boy remembered Hermann Hesse's words. 'There may be two or three may go with. But the last step must be taken alone.'

All these words were teachings to let go of attachment to impermanent possessions and remain free in eternal truth.

"The statement that many who are first shall be last and many who are last shall be first is a hope for those whose lives are hard," said the boy.

"Eternal life belongs to those who love the Word and endure to the end," Yesac said.

"Yes. The Word is eternal, and if we live as the Word, which is truth itself, that is eternal life," the boy understood what his teacher wanted him to know.

"We should follow in the great footsteps of Jesus, who humbled himself to serve his neighbor and even gave his life as a ransom for mankind."

In the boy's little notebook, he carefully wrote down in English the great teachings of Christ that he had just studied with Yesac, and he meditated on them indefinitely, letting them speak for themselves.

'Truly I tell you, Jesus replied, no one who has left home or brothers or sisters or mother or father or children or fields for me and the gospel will fail to receive a hundred times as much in this present age: homes, brothers, sisters, mothers, children, and fields—along with persecutions—and in the age to come eternal life. But many who are first will be last, and the last first. Not so with you. Instead, whoever wants to become great among you must be your servant, and whoever wants to be first must be slave of all. For even the Son of Man did not come to be served, but to serve, and to give his life as a ransom for many.'

A life of nothingness, of having nothing and needing nothing, is that why Master Yesac was always so steadfast and resolute, no matter what happened to him? The boy thought to himself.

Meanwhile, Jesus had finished preaching in Galilee and was on his way to Jerusalem. He arrives at a place called Bethphage and Bethany on the Mount of Olives.

"Just as life is a gift, so is heaven a gift from God. A gift is something that is given freely, usually against one's will."

"The rest of our life is to be lived in love and mercy, extending God's grace to our neighbors."

"The great thing about the words of Jesus that we learn and study is that they are the epitome of humility, service, and boldness."

The boy opened the Word.

'Jesus saith unto them, Ye misunderstand, because ye know neither the Scriptures, nor the power of God: for when a man is raised from the dead, he is neither married, nor given in

marriage, but is like the angels in heaven. And as for the resurrection of the dead, have ye not read in the book of Moses, in the book of the plucking of thorns, wherein God saith unto Moses, I am the God of Abraham, and the God of Isaac, and the God of Jacob: for God is not the God of the dead but of the living. Ye have greatly misunderstood: for to love God with all one's heart, and with all one's soul, and with all one's wisdom, and with all one's strength, and to love one's neighbor as oneself, is better than all burnt offerings and other sacrifices offered by fire, which are offered by fire: ... And Jesus called his disciples together, and said unto them, Verily I say unto you, This poor widow hath put in more than all that put into the treasury. For they all put in out of their abundance; but this poor widow put in out of her meager possessions, all that she had, even all her living.'

"For God is not the God of the dead, but of the living. the eyes of the mind and the ears of the heart," said the boy.

Those who are present will see and hear this great teaching, and that is enlightenment," the boy continued.

"It is a great enlightenment for us to hear that the teaching of the whole Bible is to love God above all burnt offerings and sacrifices," said Yesac.

"Making the Lord Lord of your life and loving your neighbor asyourself is the noblest, holiest, and best way to live," said the boy.

"In the widow who gives all in spite of her lack, rather than out of her abundance, we see the hope of those who have nothing," said the boy.

"If you will die, you will live, for that is the narrow gate to enlightenment," said Yesac.

"Weak men with faith make history, rather than strong men without faith," said the boy.

The boy had just passed the real estate agent exam andstarted a real estate brokerage. Today, a colleague named Brian Kim treated him to a rich lunch at a Chinese restaurant called Dong Tian Hong to celebrate the closing of the deal. The boy ate gratefully. If the Silla painters were cultured, the boy was living a harmonious life of hard work, study of the Word, and steady exercise. The boy was once surprised to hear that Brian Kim was praying for Master Yesac.

> *'Jesus said unto him, Take heed that ye be not deceived by men. For many shall come in my name, saying, I am he and shall deceive many. Take no thought beforehand what they shall say unto you when they shall take you away, but speak whatsoever they shall give you in that hour: for it is not ye that speak, but the Holy Ghost: ...And ye shall be hated of all men for my name's sake: but he that shall endure unto the end shall be saved: ...For there shall arise false Christs and false prophets, and shall perform signs and wonders, and shall deceive, if it were possible the elect.'*

Before he met his teacher, Yesac, the boy had thin ears, like an athlete's, and was often misled by the words of others, leading to loss of substance and hurt to his heart.

After hearing Yesac say, "Man is not an object of faith, but of love," he learned not to be deceived by people. Standing tall on the Word, the boy gained enlightenment and could live a life of wisdom and grace without being misled by anything.

"I sometimes experience moments when I hear you say to me not as your voice but as the voice of the Holy Spirit," the boy said.

"I also have moments when I realize that what I am saying may not be what I really mean. That's when I realize that the Holy Spirit is speaking God's word through me to the boy."

"It is through longsuffering, the fourth fruit of the Spirit, that we become children of God."

"There is no deception in the Holy Spirit."

It's Friday morning. They were stranded in the office for three days and two nights due to the continuous ordeal of junk cars. Still, they woke up early in the morning with a happy heart and exercised for an hour by stretching and exercise. No amount of unfavorable circumstances could change their ever-satisfied and grateful feelings.

Old man Yesac and the boy opened the last chapter of Mark's Gospel.

> *'And Pilate, desiring to satisfy the crowd, released Barabbas to them, and handed Jesus over to be scourged and crucified. They clothed Him in a purple robe, placed on His head a crown of thorns, and mockingly said, 'Peace be unto Thee, King of the Jews.' They struck Him on the head with a reed, spat upon Him, and knelt in false homage. Then they*

took away His cross and led Him to a place called Golgotha, which means Place of the Skull. It was about the third hour in the morning when they crucified Him. With a loud cry, Jesus breathed His last. And when the centurion, who stood facing Him, saw how He died, he said, 'Truly, this man was the Son of God.'"

"Those who think they have trials in their lives should consider the crucifixion as a testament to Jesus' reality as a perfect servant of humanity," said the boy.

"Let us not forget the terrible suffering of being scourged and spat upon, crowned with thorns and crucified, the Lamb of God who takes away the sins of mankind," said Yesac.

"The disciple Judas betrayed him, and Peter denied him," the boy said.

"Life comes once and goes once, and it is a blessing not to be crucified but to die in peace," the boy continued.

"That is why death is a blessing for the enlightened."

"Surely this man was the Son of God," the boy commented.

The boy's gaze never left Mark's Gospel as he meditated.

'And the young man said unto them, Marvel not: ye seek Jesus the Nazarene, which was crucified: for he is risen, and is not here: behold, where they laid him......After he had risen early in the morning of the first day of the week, he appeared first unto Mary Magdalene, whom he had cast out of seven demons before. ... Afterward, when the eleven disciples were eating, Jesus appeared unto them and rebuked them for their unbelief and hardness of heart because they believed not the word of them that saw him risen from the dead... And said unto them, go ye into all the world, and preach the gospel to every creature.

He that believeth and is baptized shall be saved; but he that believeth not shall be condemned: and these signs shall follow them that believe: they shall cast out devils; they shall speak with new tongues; they shall take up serpents; if they drink any deadly thing, it shall not hurt them; they shall lay hands on the sick, and they shall recover. And when the Lord Jesus finished speaking, he was received up into heaven, and sat down on the right hand of God. And the disciples went forth, and preached everywhere: and the Lord was with them, and confirmed the word with signs which followed.'

"Jesus has risen from the dead. He has risen," said the boy.
"And now our job is to go into all the world and preach the gospel to all creation," said Yesac.
"Yes. Those are the first words of the risen Jesus," said the boy.
"We can do it because Jesus is with us," the boy added.

And so Yesac and the boy lived a blessed life of being words to each other.

Jesus was crucified on a Friday, the greatest event in human history and the most painful death ever suffered by a human being. Jesus rose from the dead three days later on Sunday.

"After work today, prepare the Gospel of Luke," Yesac was ready to move to the Gospel of Luke.

"Okay," the boy said.

Yesac and the boy didn't need to prepare breakfast. They had recently changed their eating pattern to eating only two meals a day. It saves them money and time, and best of all, they feel much lighter. The boy was whistling and getting ready for work.

SJCB Dialogue - The Gospel of Mark

"Jesus came to serve, and He is the embodiment of love in the form of a servant. True leadership is humility and sacrifice. Act immediately—those who are awakened do not delay. Truth is not proven by thought, but by action." Said the Buddha through action.

"We must awaken to Jesus' words that the Kingdom of God is already within us. Heaven is not far away, but exists in a life that loves others. The Word is life and the Kingdom itself, and when that seed grows, one's entire life bears fruit." Said Socrates, speaking from the heaven on earth.

"The first shall be last, and the last shall be first. Long for the Word and the Truth, and take rest when needed. God is not the God of the dead, but of the living. Heaven is here and now, in a life that walks with God as a living being." Said Confucius with the heart of Anbin-nakdo(finding joy in a simple, humble life).

"A life where truth and the Word become life itself—that is true faith. Resurrection is the fulfillment of truth, and the end of suffering is not death, but resurrection. All humanity is included in the promise of this resurrection." Said Jesus through His resurrection.

"The Gospel of Mark is the gospel of life that reveals the way: through the humble and faithful servant Jesus, we learn to live with humility and faith. Act immediately, serve willingly, and for those who believe to the end—there is resurrection." Said Old Man Yesac as he opened the Gospel of Luke.

Volume 3: Luke

"The book of Luke was written by a doctor named Luke who traveled with the apostle Paul on his evangelistic journeys," said the boy.

"Luke presents Jesus as the only righteous one who extends grace to all of humanity without discrimination," said Yesac.

'The only righteous one who bestows grace upon all humanity without discrimination!' The boy whispered to himself, bowing his head like a hermit meditating deep in the mountains.

"Yes. Matthew presents Jesus as a king, and Luke presents Jesus as a man," said the boy.

The boy thought of the image of Jesus as the King in Matthew, as the Servant in Mark, as the Man in Luke, and as Love in John, and he spoke.

"Luke's gospel is a beautifully written literary gospel about Jesus coming as a fully human being to atone for human sin. We too must live our lives like Jesus, as a king ruling the world, as a servant serving our neighbors, as a person resembling God, and as someone living in the love of Christ," the old man said in a voice that was both holy and filled with love.

The thought that enlightenment provided by religion might not have been easily attained without Jesus existing between God and humans flashed through the boy's mind. Loving one's neighbors and becoming like God through Christ might be the hope of humanity. Ultimately, if we achieve such enlightenment, regardless of whom we believe in, all humankind will transcend time and space, become one before God, and meet each other in love. The boy's eternal happiness through enlightenment was unfolding in this way. The path was to regard everyone as better than oneself and to love one's neighbor as oneself, just as they are.

The boy turned the pages of the Gospel of Luke with a thoughtful expression.

'There are many among us who have taken up the pen to write an account of the facts as they were told to them by those who were eyewitnesses of the Word from the beginning, and who have been in the ranks of the army; and I, too, who have studied

the whole matter from the beginning, have thought it good to write to your Excellency, Deobillo, in order that you may know the certainty of what I have learned.'

"From the very first chapter, Luke's sense of mission to write a gospel about Jesus is overwhelmingly solemn," said the boy.

"Luke has carefully examined all the works of Jesus Christ and has become a witness for himself so that he may be able to give you certainty," said Yesac.

"Who is His Excellency Deobillo?" the boy asked.

"The most excellent Theophilus, which means all mankind. It's a little hard to understand because the Korean Bible translates most excellently as His Excellency and keeps the word Theophilus, which means friend of God, friend of Jesus, or people whom God loves," said Yesac.

'Theophilus means friend of God and be loved by God.'

"It means that they wrote the Gospels to make all the facts about Jesus clear to all mankind," the boy said while looking at the words written in the old man's small notebook.

"It's that simple," Yesac finished.

"Isn't that your life, Master?" the boy inquired.

"----------"

Yesac was silent at the boy's words.

But the boy knew. The hope that humanity will gain enlightenment, reach eternal happiness, and become one through love, expressed in the great book, the Bible, the world's best-seller with over 6 billion copies sold, proves that Master Yesac was sent to this world.

Perhaps that's why his name is Yesac, with "Yes" meaning "Yes" and "ac" meaning "Always Christ?" The boy thought this to himself and smiled alone. In fact, Yesac was simply Casey spelled backward, which was the exact name recorded on the old man's driver's license.

The boy turned the pages of Luke.

'In the days of Herod king of Judea, there was a priest of the order of Abijah, whose name was Zechariah, and his wife was of the seed of Aaron (Moses' brother), whose name was Elizabeth. And they were both righteous before God, walking blamelessly in

all thy commandments and statutes.

And the angel said unto them, Fear not, Zachariah: for thy supplication is heard. And thy wife Elizabeth shall bear thee a son, and thou shalt call his name John, and thou shalt rejoice and be glad, and many shall rejoice in him: for he shall be great in the sight of the Lord, and shall drink neither wine nor strong drink, but shall be filled with the Holy Ghost from his mother's womb, and shall convert many of the children of Israel unto the Lord, even unto the Lord our God. '

"Zacharias and his wife Elizabeth were blameless and righteous before God, having kept the Ten Commandments of Moses," said the boy.

"Elizabeth was a descendant of Moses and Aaron," said Yesac.

"It is also amazing that John was a descendant of Moses," said the boy.

"Elizabeth, the mother of John, is a beautiful name," said Yesac.

"Elizabeth II was the queen of England," said the boy.

"Many people rejoiced at John's birth," said the boy.

"John was a great man, called and chosen by God. Before he was born, he was filled with the Holy Spirit from his mother Elizabeth's womb," said Yesac.

"The Bible says that John did not drink wine or soju," the boy was confused.

"In the English Bible, it doesn't say 'soju' but 'fermented drink,' which is a clear liquor that has been fermented," Yesac cleared the boy's doubts.

"There was no such thing as soju back then, like Chamisul or Chueumchurum for the first time," the boy thinks of Korean Soju (a fermented drink) and comments innocently.

Yesac looked at the boy and smiled slightly.

"Even now, monks and priests like John don't drink alcohol."

"Then can sentient beings and believers drink alcohol?" the boy asked.

"The Bible says they may drink. It says to give wine to those who are sad and strong drink to those who are dying," Yesac replied.

"Oh? But I read a verse about not getting drunk," the boy was surprised and said.

"In fact, the first miracle Jesus performed when he came to earth was making wine." Remembering the words of John 2, Yesac said,

"'Give wine to those who are sad and strong drink to those who are dying,' Ah, so when you go to a wedding hall or funeral home, there's always alcohol." the boy nodded and said.

"Solomon said that wine makes life merry," said Yesac.

"Yes. Solomon said that there is nothing better for a person under the sun than to eat and drink and be glad," the boy said, remembering Ecclesiastes 8:15.

"A life in harmony, in the middle, without leaning to the right or the left, is a beautiful thing," said Yesac.

"Confucius is the one who put it so beautifully: don't get drunk. Faith in proportion, alcohol in proportion, life is mostly case-by-case," the boy said, thinking of the Analects of Confucius he had read with the old man.

'Yujumuryang Bulgeupran (유주무량불급란 唯酒無量不及亂)
: The essence lies not in the quantity of alcohol consumed, but in the practice of moderation, for it is in this balance that true enjoyment is found.'

"Your misunderstanding of alcohol is due to the fact that you don't base your standards on the Word but on yourself," the old man said.

In his small notebook, Yesac had written down a passage about alcohol from the book ChaeGeunDam(菜根譚 채근담), written by Hong Jia Sheng during the Ming Dynasty in China.

'Hwaganbangae Jueummihun Chajungdaeyugachui
화간반개 주음미훈 차중대유가취
花看半開 酒飲微醺 此中大有佳趣
When the flowers are half-bloomed,
enjoying them with a little intoxication brings great joy.'

"What kind of book is the ChaeGeunDam?" the boy asked.

"It's a book about relationships with people, enjoyment of nature, and how to handle life, and it was a favorite of Hyundai Group's founder, Chairman Chung Ju-young."

ChaeGeun(菜根 채근) refers to a life of eating unadulterated foods such as herbs and roots and enjoying a life of leisure. It's a classical Eastern teaching that fuses ideas from Confucianism, Taoism, and Buddhism but is easily understood by those who have studied the Bible.

"ChaeGeunDam shows the kind of life that is like being in theworld and not being in the world," Yesac said, flipping to Luke's Gospel.

>*'In the sixth month, the angel Gabriel, sent by God, came to a certain city called Nazareth, a town in Galilee, to a virgin betrothed to a man named Joseph, of the seed of David; and her name was Mary. And he entered unto her, and said unto her, Hail, thou that art favored: the Lord is with thee: and when the virgin heard him, she was astonished, and thought, What mannerof greeting is this? Behold, thou shalt conceive and bear a son, and shalt call his name Jesus; for he shall be great, and shall be called the Son of the Highest: and the Lord God shall give unto him the throne of his father David: and he shall reign over the house of Jacob forever, and his dominion shall be great.'*

"This is the moment when Mary, favored by God, conceived and gave birth to Jesus, the Son of the Most High God," said the boy.

"God will give Jesus the throne of David, the ancestor of Christ, and as descendants of Jacob, the kingdom of Christ will endure forever," Yesac said and turned the page of Luke's Gospel.

>*'And the angel answered and said unto him, The Holy Ghost shall come upon thee, and the power of the Most High shall overshadow thee: therefore shall that holy one which shall be born be called the Son of God. Behold, thy kinswoman Elizabeth also hath conceived a son in her old age, and she that was barren is now six months old: for all the word of God is not without power... Mary said, My soul hath praised the Lord, and my heart hath rejoiced in God my Savior: for he hath considered the lowliness of the handmaid. Behold, now therefore, shall all*

generations call me blessed. For the mighty one has done great things unto me, holy is his name... and Elisabeth conceived a son when she was past her due time, and her neighbors and her kinsmen rejoiced when they heard that the Lord had great compassion on her.'

"I know that the Holy Spirit will come on the boy, and the power of the Most High Jesus Christ will overshadow you," said Yesac.

"That the Holy and Mighty One is doing great things for me?" the boy asked and the Holy Spirit was sensitizing the boy.

"All the words of God are not impossible. For no word from God will ever fail."

Yesac's voice sounded holy to the boy's ears.

The boy remembered 1 Peter 1.

'Be holy, because I am holy.'

John was born, and Luke records the great prophecy of John's father, Zacharias.

'And Zacharias his father was filled with the Holy Ghost, and prophesied, saying, Praise be to the Lord, the God of Israel, that he hath turned his face toward his people, and hath raised up for us a horn of salvation in the house of his servant David; salvation from our enemies, and from the hand of all them that hate us, as thou hast spoken by the mouth of thy holy prophet of old, saying, Have mercy on our fathers, and remember thy holy covenant, which thou swarest unto Abraham our father.

For thou, hast had compassion on our fathers, and hast remembered thy holy covenant, which thou swarest unto Abraham our father. To deliver us out of the hand of our enemies, that we may serve thee fearlessly in holiness and righteousness all the days of our life. And thou, child, shalt be called a prophet of the Most High, to go before thee, and to prepare the way before thee, that thy people may know salvation through the forgiveness of sins; because of the mercies of our God. For the sun shall rise upon us from on high, to give light to them that sit in darkness and in the shadow of death, and to guide our feet in the path of peace. And the child shall grow, and be strong in heart, and shall be in the empty field until the day of his appearing unto Israel.'

Yesac and the boy represented a beautiful meeting of the Old and New Testaments and meditated on Luke's gospel over and over again. There was a timeless meeting between David and Abraham, John and Jesus Christ.

"What do you think makes the rising sun come to us from heaven to shine on those living in darkness and the shadow of death to guide our feet into the path of peace?" Yesac suddenly asked.

"The tender mercy of our God, yes," the boy answered without hesitation.

"Jesus was in the wilderness, and John was in an empty field." said the boy.

"It's just a difference in the translation of wilderness, but it's a wilderness like an empty field." Yesac and the boy smiled as if it didn't matter.

"Just as all roads lead to Rome, great leaders had to walk the paths of the wilderness." Yesac's words struck the boy's ears, and any ordeal became a time of training and gratitude for the boy.

*'The angel said to them, 'Do not be afraid, for behold—
I bring you good news of great joy for all people.
Today in the city of David, a Savior has been born to you.
He is Christ the Lord. And this will be a sign to you:
you will find a baby wrapped in swaddling clothes,
lying in a manger.' Mary and Joseph found the babe
just as the angel had said.
And when eight days had passed, they circumcised him
and gave him the name Jesus. When the days of purification were
completed, according to the Law of Moses,
they brought the child to Jerusalem to present him to the Lord.
And there it was said, "My eyes have seen your salvation,
which you have prepared in the sight of all nations—
a light for revelation to the Gentiles, and the glory of your people
Israel."*

*Afterward, they returned to Galilee, to their hometown of Nazareth.
The child grew and became strong, filled with wisdom,
and the grace of God was upon him.
When he was twelve years old, they went up to Jerusalem for the Feast.
After the celebration, as they were returning,
the boy Jesus stayed behind in Jerusalem.*

*Three days later, they found him in the temple,
sitting among the teachers, listening to them and asking questions.
All who heard him were amazed at his understanding and his answers.
When his parents asked why he had stayed behind,
Jesus replied,
"Why were you searching for me?
Did you not know I had to be in my Father's house?"
Then he returned with them to Nazareth, and was obedient to them.
His mother treasured all these things in her heart.
And Jesus grew in wisdom and stature,
and in favor with God and man.'*

"Jesus was born in humble circumstances, not in a place of splendor," said the boy.

"Swaddled in swaddling clothes and laid in a trough, God creates history from the smallest of things," said Yesac.

"The Holy Spirit came upon Simeon, a Jerusalemite who was righteous and devout and favored by God, and said, 'Jesus is a light for revelation to the Gentiles,'" said the boy.

"We should imitate Jesus, who is so merciful and loving that he loves all mankind and extends grace to them," said Yesac.

"Yes. Differences are proof of coexistence, not contradiction," said the boy.

"All humanity under heaven is one," said Yesac and continued to educate the boy.

"Mary and Joseph didn't even realize what their son, Jesus, was saying," said the boy.

"It is possible not to understand the will of the Father on earth and the Father in heaven," said Yesac.

"Jesus was already fully human and fully divine at the age of 12, keeping the Ten Commandments," said the boy.

"He went to his hometown of Nazareth and was obedient to his parents," said Yesac.

"When he was 12 years old, people were amazed at his understanding and his answers. Everyone who heard him was amazed at his understanding and his answers," Yesac told the boy.

"God was already present with Jesus, who mostly asked and listened," said Yesac.

"God and men loved Jesus more and more as he grew in wisdom and stature, and in favor with God and man," said the boy.

"Adam and Jesus, two men who came into this world without sin, but Jesus is the only one who exists as a perfect righteous man," said Yesac.

"Yes. He suffered all the trials we would have suffered and ascended to heaven," as the boy said, Yesac turned the pages of the book.

> *'And it came to pass in the days of Annas and Caiaphas,*
> *the high priests, that the word of God came to John,*
> *the son of Zechariah, in the wilderness.*
> *John went throughout the region around the Jordan,*
> *preaching a baptism of repentance for the forgiveness of sins.*
> *'Even now,' he cried,*
> *'the axe is laid at the root of the trees. Every tree that does*
> *not bear good fruit will be cut down and thrown into the fire.'*
> *To all the people he said,' I baptize you with water,*
> *but one more powerful than I is coming.*
> *I am not even worthy to loosen the straps of his sandals.*
> *He will baptize you with the Holy Spirit and with fire.'*
> *And when all the people were being baptized,*
> *Jesus also came to be baptized.*
> *As he prayed, the heavens opened, and the Holy Spirit descended upon*
> *him like a dove in bodily form.*
> *And a voice came from heaven, saying,*
> *'You are my beloved Son; in you I am well pleased.'*
> *Jesus was about thirty years old when he began his ministry.*
> *And the people knew him as the son of Joseph—*
> *Joseph, the son of Heli, the son of Enosh, the son of Seth,*
> *the son of Adam, the son of God.'*

'John emphasized the need to move beyond outward religious rituals such as sacrifices to heart repentance and practical life changes.'

"John ministered near the Jordan River, preaching a baptism of repentance for the forgiveness of sins," said the boy.

"John himself baptizes with water, but he says that the

coming Jesus will baptize with the Holy Spirit and fire," Yesac added.

"Yes. John is confessing that he is not worthy to untie the straps of Jesus' sandals," said the boy.

"Now Jesus is going to start teaching," said Yesac.

"Right. Jesus was 30 years old, and he died at 33, so it was only three years that he did all those things, although some say he died at 37," said the boy.

"God only took six days to create this world, so that's the power of God and Jesus," Yesac said.

Jesus' main stage of activity was in Capernaum, where the site of Peter's house was found, where he chose 12 disciples and ministered for two years, preaching the gospel.

It's the seventh day of being stuck in the office because Yesac's old car broke down. But Yesac's expression did not show the slightest sign of discomfort. "Is your teacher truly a man who lives by the Word? Or does he have a secret way of living life?" The boy pondered quietly. But Yesac, a man who never skips a workout, picked up his master after he finished his three-wall stretch and headed to the soccer field. Mind, body, and spirit are one, and for Yesac. The body he needed to keep in tip-top shape was the temple where Jesus dwelled. It was the first week of September 2023.

Returning from the soccer field, Yesac flipped through the pages of Luke's Gospel.

'And Jesus, being filled with the Holy Spirit, returned from Jordan, and wandered forty days in the wilderness, led by the Spirit and tempted by the devil. And in all these days he was tempted by the devil: and when the days were fulfilled, he gave him up.'

"What did Jesus use to overcome the devil's temptations while starving in the wilderness for forty days?" the boy asked.

"The Bible," replied Yesac.
"What?" The boy was confused.
"The Word," replied Yesac.
Yesac turned to Psalm 119.

'I have put Your Word in my heart, that I might not sin against You.'

"Oh, I see. Jesus defeated the demons by quoting Scripture," said the boy.

Jesus actually resisted the devil's sweet temptations on three occasions with the following words from Deuteronomy 6 and 8.

'Know that man does not live by bread alone, but by every word that comes from the mouth of the LORD. Do not put the Lord your God to the test, that you may know that if you go after other gods, and serve them, and bow down to them, I will testify unto you, that you shall surely perish.'

The Word was so great that God created the world with it, and Jesus defeated Satan in the wilderness with it. That's the Bible.

"I was surprised to learn that it was the Word of God, rather than any special miracle or power, that enabled Jesus to endure and overcome Satan in the wilderness after forty days of starvation," the boy commented.

"The Word is a special miracle and power," said Yesac.

"That's why the Bible is a book that all human beings should love to read," Yesac added.

After overcoming all of the devil's temptations, such as telling him to turn into a loaf of bread, bow down to me, and jumping off the top of the temple, Jesus returns from the wilderness to Galilee and preaches the gospel. When Jesus arrived in Nazareth, where he grew up, he read the Bible in the synagogue on the Sabbath. The Bible verses he read were as follows:

'The Spirit of the Lord is upon me, because he has anointed me to proclaim good news to the poor; he has sent me to preach freedom to the captives and recovery of sight to the blind, to set at liberty those who are oppressed, to proclaim the acceptable year of the Lord's favor.'

"Just imagining Jesus reading the Bible is moving," said the boy.

"....................."

Yesac was silent for a moment, as if moved.

"Jesus, the one who preaches the Good News to the poor by the Holy Spirit, the one who heals and frees all of us from our trials and suffering, is the truth, the way, and the life," Yesac added.

"Yes. He is gracious to us who are crushed under the weight of life, who do not see even though we have eyes to see and do not hear even though we have ears to hear," said the boy.

The faces of both men, Yesac and the boy, shone with grace, mercy, love, and realization.

'Truly I tell you, no prophet is accepted in his hometown.'

These words set the boy free from the hatred and love of all those around him. He accepted that no one was righteous and that he himself could never be perfect. The best he could do was to honor God and love his neighbor.

Meanwhile, Jesus is fishing in Simon's boat on the shore of Lake Gennesaret, and he catches so many fish that his nets tear, astonishing Simon, James, and John.

"Jesus fishing, how romantic," the boy said.

"Simon, James, and John, who left everything they owned and followed Jesus, are also brave and wonderful people who practiced non-possession," Yesac said.

> "And Jesus stretched out his hand, touched me, and said,
> 'Be thou cleansed, if you will.'
> And at that moment, the leprosy left me."
> The word of Jesus spread all the more,
> and great crowds gathered to hear Him
> and to be healed of their diseases.
> But He often withdrew to secluded places and prayed.
> Levi held a great feast for Jesus in his house,
> and many tax collectors and others sat with them.
> For no one drinks old wine and suddenly desires new;
> the old is good.

> Then Jesus went up into the mountain to pray.
> All night He prayed to God, and when morning came,
> He called His disciples to Him and chose twelve,
> whom He also named apostles: Simon, whom He also called Peter,
> Andrew his brother, James and John, Philip and Bartholomew,
> Matthew and Thomas, James the son of Alphaeus,
> Simon who was called the Zealot, and Judas Iscariot,
> who would become the one to betray Him.'

"Jesus went up on a mountain and spent the night in vigil. Spent the night praying to God," said the boy.

"Then he chose the twelve disciples," said Yesac.

"Now we come to Jesus' Sermon on the Mount and Sermon on the Plain," the boy blushed and said.

'And Jesus lifted up his eyes and saw his disciples, and said unto them, Blessed are you that are poor, for yours is the kingdom of God; blessed are you that are hungry, for you shall be filled; blessed are you that weep, for you shall laugh; blessed are you when men shall hate you, and shall revile you, and shall use all manner of reproach against you, and shall persecute you, and shall call your name evil But I say unto you that hear me, Love your enemies, do good to them that hate you, bless them that curse you, and pray for them that despitefully use you. Turn the other cheek to him that smites you on the other cheek, and withhold not your garment from him that robs you of your coat. And give to him that asketh you, and whatsoever thou hast that is thine. Give to him that asketh you, and ask not again of him that taketh from you.'

The old man and the boy drank bottled water at the same time as they drank Word.

'Do unto others as you would have them do unto you. For if ye love them that love you, ye shall be praised: for even sinners love them that love them. For if ye do good to them that do good to you, ye shall be praised. For even sinners do this. For if ye lend unto men, expecting to receive, ye shall be commended: for even sinners lend unto sinners, expecting to receive.

But love your enemies, do good, expect nothing, and lend, and your reward shall be great; and you shall be the sons of the Most High. Son of the Most High, for he is merciful even to the ungrateful and the wicked. Be merciful, even as your Father is merciful to you. Judge not, and you will not be judged; condemn not, and you will not be condemned; forgive, and you will be forgiven.'

In the boy's little notebook, Jesus' teachings were carefully written in English.

"What a great teaching to bless and pray for those who hate, curse, and insult you, when life is full of love and hate. May I be holy like Jesus and merciful like God," the boy commented.

"We also need great courage to give all that I have to my neighbor. A heart that does not judge, does not condemn, and forgives all, what a great teaching," said Yesac.

The boy flipped through the pages of Luke's Gospel.

'Why seest thou the mote that is in thy brother's eye, and perceivest not the beam that is in thine own eye. there is no good tree that bringeth forth bad fruit, and no bad tree that bringeth forth good fruit: for every tree is known by its own fruit: you cannot pluck a fig from a thorn, or a grape from a briar. For out of the treasure of the heart a good man bringeth forth good, out of the treasure of his heart good; and an evil man bringeth forth evil out of the treasure of his heart evil: for out of the abundance of the heart the mouth speaketh.

Ye call upon me, Lord, Lord, and yet do not do what I say: for every one that cometh unto me, and heareth my words, and doeth them, I will shew him the same thing. He that heareth, and doeth not, is likeunto a man that built a house, and dug it deep, and laid the foundation upon a rock: and the rushing waters came up, and the

torrents beat upon it, and it was not able to be moved because it was well built: but he that heareth, and doeth not, is like unto a man that built his house upon the rock of the earth, without a foundation: and the torrents beat upon it, and it fell, and was destroyed.'

Even before he knew the Bible, the boy had learned from Yesac not to judge others, to have eyes and a heart that saw his neighbor as he was, without adding to or subtracting from his own ideas, and to treat him with mercy and love. But the dissonances that come with living life as a non-righteous person are not so easily avoided, and it was the teaching of Jesus Christ in the parable of the chaff and the beam that eventually brought some closure. Yesac and the boy mulled over the words in the boy's little notebook once more.

'Why do you look at the speck of sawdust in your brother's eye and pay no attention to the plank in your own eye?'

These were the words of Jesus Christ, who taught him to always look inward and examine himself and to see and treat his neighbor with positivity, love, and compassion.

"Words reveal who a person is," said Yesac.

"Yes. People are loved by their words and hurt by their words," said the boy.

As the boy studied the Bible with Yesac, he learned how to examine his own heart and speak to his neighbors in a way that would benefit them and give them courage and hope. Blessed are the peacemakers. The boy was living such a blessed life.

"Jesus emphasizes doing, doing, doing, not just saying Lord, Lord," said the boy.

"Faith without acts is dead," said Yesac coolly.

"Then faith without love is also dead." said the boy more coolly. The boy was learning wisdom, cool-headedness, and mercy together.

"Faith with acts teaches us that when a flood comes, and the rushing waters crash against a house, it will never be shaken because it is well built," Yesac said.

Yesac and the boy were learning to live by the Word, to become the Word themselves. For enlightenment by acts!

'At that very time Jesus cured many who had diseases, sicknesses and evil spirits, and gave sight to many who were blind. And he said unto them, Go ye, and tell John what ye have seen and heard, that the blind receive their sight, and the lame walk, and the lepers are cleansed, and the deaf hear, and the dead are raised, and the poor have the gospel preached unto them; and blessed is he that shall not be offended because of me. I tell you, among those born of women there is not one greater than John; but in the kingdom of God one who is least is greater than I. Therefore I tell you, my many sins are forgiven, because I love much: for he who loves much loves little.'

"The more we love, the more our sins are forgiven," said the boy.

"Because God is love," said Yesac.

"Love is light, and sin is darkness," Yesac continued.

"Love is heaven, and sin is hell," the boy said with an expression of realization.

"There's no way to get rid of sin, only love," said Yesac.

Yesac and the boy read and read and read and meditated on the Word. So that the Word would become them and they would become the Word.

'Their many sins have been forgiven—as their great love has shown. But whoever has been forgiven little loves little. The one who is least in the kingdom of God is great.'

The boy read the old man's little notebook and turned the page of Luke.

'After these things, the twelve disciples were with Him
as He traveled through towns and villages,
proclaiming the Kingdom of God and preaching the good news.
'The seed,' He said, 'is the Word of God.
Those by the wayside, on the rocks, among thorns,
or in good soil— they are those who hear the Word.
What is hidden will not remain hidden;
what is concealed will be brought into the light.
He answered them, 'My mother and my brothers are those
who hear the Word of God and do it.'

And they came into the region of the Gerasenes,
which is opposite Galilee.
Then He called the twelve disciples to Him
and gave them power and authority over all demons,
and over all sickness.
He sent them out to preach the Kingdom of God,
to lay hands on the sick, and to heal them.
'Whoever seeks to save their life will lose it,
but whoever loses their life for My sake will save it.
What does it profit a man to gain the whole world,
lose his own soul?' Then He said, 'I tell you the truth
—there are some standing here who shall not taste death
before they see the Kingdom of God.'

About eight days later, Jesus took Peter, John, and James,
and went up into a mountain to pray.
As He prayed, His appearance changed,
and His garments became dazzling white, shining with brilliance.
Suddenly, two men appeared—Moses and Elijah
—speaking with Him in glory.
They spoke of the suffering and death He would face
in Jerusalem in the days to come. And Jesus said,
'Foxes have holes, and birds of the air have nests,
but the Son of Man has nowhere to lay His head.'

"Jesus' statement that those who hear the word of God and do it are my mother and my brother gives me a lot to think about," said the boy.

"I, too, have learned and realized from Jesus' great teaching to love widely, with an open heart and unrestricted," said Yesac, and opened his small notebook.

It was the 21st chapter of the Analects of the Confucius Institute.

'GunJa KeungYiBuJang KunYiBuDang (군자 긍이부쟁 군이부당 君子 樂而不爭 群而不黨); The righteous have compassion for their neighbors and do not quarrel; they group together, but do not play favorites or collude.'

"Do you remember 'GunJa HwaYiBuDong, SoIn DongYiBuHwa (군자 화이부동 소인 동일화 君子和而不同 小人同而不和)'?"

"Yes. It means righteous men live in harmony but do not assimilate, and unrighteous men assimilate but do not live in harmony."

The boy recalled the Zaro (子路)section of the Analects of Confucius that he had studied with Yesac.
The boy's small notebook contained writings from the section on government in the Analects of Confucius.

"A righteous man is friendly to all but does not conspire, and an unrighteous man is not friendly to all but does collude."

"You also remember the importance of impartiality to all (SaBulPyunBuDang 사불편부당 士不偏不黨), right?"

"Yes. Righteous men should not be biased toward one side and should not form narrow-minded groups," the boy said, remembering a history book from the Spring and Autumn Chronicles of China.

"A righteous person is gentle on the outside but full on the inside," said Yesac.

"We learn that being from Christ's great teaching not to take personal interests but to love all," said the boy.

"All laws return to one," said Yesac.

There is a saying 'SangJunByukHae 桑田碧海 상전벽해', As the mulberry fields changed to become the blue sea, the world passed by, and so did Yesac's life, day by day and year by year. A year after leaving the bitter Willy Wilderness behind, Yesac was on his way to Oklahoma. It was a beautiful vacation spot three hours from Dallas.

'*After this, the Lord appointed seventy others and sent them out two by two to every town and place where He Himself was about to go.*
He said to them,
'The harvest is plentiful, but the laborers are few.
Ask the Lord of the harvest, therefore,
to send out laborers into His harvest field.
Go on your way—I am sending you out as lambs among wolves.
Carry no purse, no bag, no sandals, and greet no one on the road.
Whatever house you enter, first say, "Peace be to this house."
I tell you, it will be more bearable for Sodom on that day than for that town. Woe to you, Chorazin! Woe to you, Bethsaida!
If the miracles performed in you had been done in Tyre and Sidon, they would have repented long ago in sackcloth and ashes.
It will be more bearable for Tyre and Sidon at the judgment than for you."
"But do not rejoice that the spirits submit to you,"
He said, "Rather, rejoice that your names are written in heaven."
Then a certain lawyer stood up to test Jesus and said,
"Rabbi, what shall I do to inherit eternal life?"
Jesus replied, "You have answered well. Do this, and you will live."
But wanting to justify himself, the man asked,
"And who is my neighbor?"
And Jesus answered him with the story
of the one who showed mercy to his neighbor.
Later, He came to a village, and Martha welcomed Him into her home.
But she was anxious and troubled about many things.
Jesus said to her,
"Martha, Martha, you are worried and upset about many things, but only one thing is needed. Mary has chosen the better part, and it will not be taken from her."

"Jesus sent his disciples out in twos and threes to preach the gospel everywhere," said the boy.

"The harvest (gospel) was plentiful, but the laborers (disciples) were few, so he used the most effective method," said Yesac.

"Even though He commands them to leave for nothing, He expresses the same tender feelings of sending a lamb to the flock," said the boy.

"Who can fathom the heart of a leader, and we should pay attention to the teaching that the secret to eternal life is to be a devotee of God," said Yesac.

"Yes. The whole Bible teaches us to fear God and love our neighbor," the boy responded.

He who shows mercy to his neighbor is his brother; do the deed, do the deed, do the word, and you shall live! These were the great teachings of Jesus. In the boy's little notebook, the secret to eternal life was written in English.

'What must I do to inherit eternal life? Love the Lord your God with all your heart and with all your soul and with all your strength and with all your mind; and, Love your neighbor as yourself.'

Yesac turned to the book of Luke's Gospel.

'And when Jesus had prayed in one place, one of his disciples said unto him, Lord, teach us also to pray, as John taught his disciples to pray. Jesus said unto him, When ye pray, pray this manner: Our Father, hallowed be thy name; thy kingdom come; give us this day our daily bread; and forgive us our trespasses, as we forgive all that trespass against us; and lead us not into temptation. And I say unto you, Ask, and it shall be given you; seek, and ye shall find; knock, and it shall be opened unto you: for everyone that asketh receiveth; and everyone that seeketh findeth; and it shall be opened unto him that knocketh. For ye that are evil, even as ye know how to give good things unto your children, how much more shall not your Father which can give the Holy Ghost to them that ask him? Jesus saith unto them, Blessed are they that hear the word of God, and keep it.

When they were gathered together, Jesus said unto them, This is an evil and wicked generation: they shall seek a sign, and shall not find it, except it be a sign of Jonah: for as Jonah was a sign unto the Ninevites, so shall the Son of man be unto this generation. And in the day of judgment the queen of the south shall arise and condemn the men of this generation because she came from the ends of the earth to hear the wise words of Solomon: but greater than Solomon is here; and in the day of judgment the men of Nineveh shall arise and condemn the men of this generation, because they heard the preaching of Jonah, and repented: but greater than Jonah is here. No man lighteth a lamp and putteth it not in a hole, nor under a vessel, but upon a lampstand, that he that goeth in may see the light. The lamp of thy body is the eye: if thine eye is good, thy whole body shall be light: but if it is bad, thy body also shall be dark.'

"Here comes the Lord's Prayer, the Lord's Prayer of Jesus," said the boy, recalling Jesus' teaching on prayer engraved on his heart tablet.

"If you pray and do the word, ask and you shall receive, seek and you shall find, knock and the door shall be opened to you," said Yesac.

"Jesus is talking about the sign of Jonah," said the boy.

"Do you remember Jonah, the one we studied?" asked Yesac.

"Yes. It's the 32nd book of the 39 books of the Old Testament. Jonah came out of the fish's belly after three days, and Jesus rose from the ground after three days," the boy answered.

The study method of the old man and boy, teaching and learning by connecting the Old and New Testaments, was their wisdom in easily understanding difficult things.

"The Ninevites were converted after hearing Jonah's proclamation of judgment, and mankind was enlightened and brought to the truth through the death and resurrection of Jesus Christ," said Yesac.

"Yes. The Old Testament is the testimony of the Messiah to come, and the New Testament is the record of the Messiah who has come," the boy commented.

"The Old Testament was fulfilled by the New Testament and Jesus Christ," said Yesac.

"We humans saw imperfection in all the laws, prophets, and kings of the Old Testament and saw perfection in Jesus Christ," said the boy. Yesac's eyes widened at the boy's words. His expression was one of gratitude and emotion for the boy who was coming to enlightenment.

"Jesus" salvation and healing ministry, which transcends time and space and seeks to heal all of humanity, including the Gentiles, was also fulfilled by his disciples after Pentecost," said

Yesac.

"Pentecost?" the boy asked.

"Pentecost commemorates the descent of the Holy Spirit on the disciples 'gathering on the 50th day after Jesus' resurrection.'" Yesac answered.

The boy test-drove the car after a two-day trip to MRG Real Estate Company MT. Realizing that they could live without a house but not without a vehicle, Yesac and the boy looked at each other's faces as they drove the second-hand SUV that they had purchased through people through God's protection. It was a look that said, "Are we allowed to drive a car like this?" Like people who have been given a favor they can hardly afford.

The old man turned the pages of Luke's Gospel.

'Do not be afraid, for even the hairs of your head have been numbered. When they bring you before synagogues, rulers, and authorities, do not worry about how you will defend yourself or what you should say. You are more precious than many sparrows.
The Holy Spirit will teach you at that very hour what you should say.
He also told us: 'Beware of all covetousness, for a man's life does not consist in the abundance of his possessions.

Life is more than food, and the body is more than clothing.'
Consider the ravens: they neither sow nor reap, they have no storeroom or barn, yet God feeds them.
How much more valuable are you than the birds?
And who of you by worrying can add a single inch to your height? If you cannot do even such a small thing,
why do you worry about the rest?
Consider the lilies of the field, how they grow:
they neither labor nor spin, yet I tell you,
not even Solomon in all his glory was arrayed like one of these.

If God so clothes the grass of the field,
which is here today and tomorrow thrown into the fire,
how much more will He clothe you— O you of little faith!
Do not be anxious about what you will eat or drink,
and do not be troubled.
For the people of the world seek after these things,
but your Father knows that you need them.
To whom much is given, much will be required;

*and from the one who has been entrusted with much,
even more will be demanded.'*

Yesac saw that Christ's teaching on defeating greed was written in the boy's little notebook. It was written in English.

'Watch out! Be on your guard against all kinds of greed; life does not consist in an abundance of possessions.'

At the same time, the boy also saw a passage in Yesac's little notebook about the three poisons of humans.

'The three poisons of man are greed, anger, and foolishness (ignorance).'

"Isn't the Three Poisons a Buddhist doctrine?" the boy recalled the TamJinChiSamDog(貪瞋癡三毒 탐진치삼독) he studied with the old man, Yesac.

"Yes, from the teaching of James that greed begets sin and sin begets death, from the words of Proverbs to be slow to anger, and from Solomon's teaching that the fear of God is the root of wisdom, we can awaken from ignorance and folly," answered Yesac

The boy recalled the meaning of the Manbupkwiil (萬法歸一 만법귀일), which he had studied with his teacher. Just as all lawsreturned to one, all humanity became one to the boy as timepassed.

"Human misery comes from disharmony, from too much emphasis on one thing over another, so we must awaken from the folly of materialism and lead a life of harmony with the studyof the mind," said Yesac.

"Yes. I can hear the thunder of Jesus' teaching that life does not consist in the abundance of possessions, so let go of greed," said the boy.

"Pope John Paul II should be reminded of why he drove the most frugal car when he visited Korea," said Yesac thoughtfully.

"What a metaphor for materialism: a nice car, clothes, nice house," said the boy, agreeing with his teacher, Yesac.

At first, the boy admired Yesac simply for being the Word and living willfully, not worrying about what to eat or wear, even when he was in the midst of pain and hunger.

However, as the years passed and he realized the Word with

Yesac, the boy truly understood his teacher. The words of Psalm 119, 'The unfolding of your words gives light; it gives understanding to the simple,' had opened up the boy's world. He learned not to worry as he watched the ravens that God raised, neither sowing nor reaping, neither alcoves nor storehouses.

"I, too, have learned not to worry from Christ's teaching: Who of you, by worrying, can add a single hour to your life?" Yesac declared.

Yesac's words had hit the boy in the ear with another realization.

"Yes. Even the wild chrysanthemum by the side of the road grows well alone, even though no one else tends it," said the boy, his words thoughtful and measured.

"The things and honors that men seek so much, they are no better than a single wildflower," Yesac spoke, pleased at his student's understanding.

"Yes. The only thing that endures is the truth, the Word." The boy nodded.

"Seek ye first the Word and the truth, and that is the kingdom of God, and all other things necessary shall follow." Yesac finished.

As the sun was setting in the evening, Yesac was tidying up his car outside the office when he ran into an old friend from soccer, a man by the name of Zidane. The friend was an honest car mechanic and a good soccer player, and he was grateful for that. There may have been a 25-year age gap between him and Yesac, but Yesac called him just a friend, all the same.

The boy turned the pages of the textbook of life. It was a holy book.

'Therefore, he said, what shall the kingdom of God be like unto me, except it was a grain of mustard seed which a man took and sowed in his field, and it grew into a tree, and the fowls of the air nestled in its branches; and he said, what shall the kingdom of God be like unto me, except it were leaven, which a woman took, and sifted, and put into the lard, and made it all leavened. And it came to pass, as he went about, teaching in all the villages, that he came to Jerusalem: and some said unto him, Lord, is it possible that so few there be that shall find salvation?

And he said unto them, strive ye to enter in at the strait gate:

forI say unto you, there shall be many that shall seek to enter in, andshall not be able: and behold, not all that shall be last shall be first, but all that shall be first shall be last. And Jesus answered and said unto the experts in the law, and unto the Pharisees, whether it be lawful to heal on the Sabbath day, or not? When thou art invited, go thou rather and sit down at the head of the table, and he that invited thee shall come and beseech thee to come up and sit down with him as a friend; and then shall thou be glorified before all that sit with thee.

For whosoever exalted himself shall be humbled, and whosoever humbled himself shallbe exalted: and whosoever cometh to me, and hateth not fatherand mother, and wife, and brethren, and sisters, and even his own life, cannot be my disciple: and whosoever will not take up his cross, and follow me, cannot be my disciple: and whosoever will not forsake all that he hath, and come after me, cannot be my disciple: and in like manner, whosoever will not forsake all that he hath, and come after me, cannot be my disciple. Salt is good, but if it has lost its savor, with what shall it be salted: it is good for nothing, neither for the earth nor for the manure; but he that hath ears to hear, let him hear.'

"How sweet are the words of Jesus, who gives humility to those who are first and hope to those who are last," the boy said with a thankful face.

"The truth is sweeter than chocolate." Yesac nodded.

The boy spoke further. "Another question that comes up is whether it's okay to work on the Sabbath. There is a lot of repetition in the writings of the apostles who preached the gospel—Matthew, Mark, Luke, and John."

Yesac responded by saying, "Repetition is a good thing, and many people don't realize that if you say something once or twice, it doesn't stick, which is why Jesus repeats himself: 'Whoever has ears to hear, let them hear.'"

"I've read André Gide's Strait is the Gate, but Jesus' words, 'Enter through the narrow gate,' are a new discovery," said the boy.

André Gide, who won the Nobel Prize in Literature in 1947, was a French novelist who began writing at the age of 19 after dropping out of school due to ill health.

"André Gide believed that God allowed humans to live life to the fullest, enjoying all its pleasures," says the boy.

Yesac nodded, "Solomon said something similar in the book of Ecclesiastes."

"It is not God who suppresses human happiness, but the morals and ethics that men themselves have imposed on themselves," said the boy.

In André Gide's The Narrow Gate, the protagonist, Jerome, is in an unrequited love with his cousin's sister. But they both choose the narrow gate because they see it as infinitely pure and holy.

"Jesus is asked by the scribes and Pharisees whether it is lawful to work on Sunday," the boy pointed out.

Yesac nodded. "Jesus' wise answer and great teaching was that if your own oxen or children were drowning, would you not save them because it was the Sabbath?"

"Yes. Jesus taught that love and mercy are better than sacrifice," the boy said agreeably and then continued, "Jesus came to set us free from the law and sin."

Yesac took the opportunity to impart some knowledge.

"By participating, realizing, and acting on our faith, rather than just watching, we become Christ's apostles to take the gospel to the ends of the earth. Through the New Testament, Jesus completed the Old Testament, whose teachings were love of God and humility. The way to humility is found in the words of Jesus Christ: 'For all who exalt themselves will be humbled, and those who humble themselves will be exalted.'"

Later on, the boy meditated, copying the notes from Yesac's little notebook into his own. He began to read out the words out loud, attempting to memorize them.

'If anyone comes to me and does not hate father and mother, wife and children, brothers and sisters—yes, even their own life, such a person cannot be my disciple.'

'And whoever does not carry their cross and follow me cannot be my disciple. In the same way, those of you who do not give up everything you have cannot be my disciples;

Muah Musoyoo PilsaZeukSang
(無我무아, 無所有무소유, 必死則生필사즉생.'

"Whoever has ears to hear, let them hear." The boy whispered to himself in a holy voice.

Yesac turned the page of Luke's Gospel.

'With devotion in his heart, he continued reading, "For I say unto you, that if one sinner repented, there is more joy in heaven over ninety-nine righteous, who do not need repentance. For he that is faithful in the least is faithful also in the greatest, and he that is unjust in the least is unjust also in the greatest; and if ye be unfaithful in unrighteous riches, who shall be faithful to you in that which is true? For a servant cannot serve two masters: for either he will hate the one, and love the other; or he will honor the one, and despise the other: for you cannot serve both God and mammon.

The Pharisees, being lovers of money, heard all these things, and scoffed at them: but Jesus said unto them, Ye justify yourselves before men, but God knoweth your heart: for that which is exalted among men is hated of God. For the law andthe prophets fulfilled till John: but after that, the gospel of the kingdom of God is preached, and breaketh in upon every man: but it will be easier for heaven and earth to pass away, than for one stroke of the law to fall.'

"The story of the Law and the Prophets in the Old Testament was told until the time of John when the Law and the Prophets were fulfilled by our Lord Jesus Christ, who came after John and set all men free. The good news of the kingdom of God is being preached, and everyone is forcing their way into it," said the boy.

"It is easier for heaven and earth to disappear than for the least stroke of a pen to drop out of the Law," said Yesac.

"Jesus' Galilean ministry ended, and now it is prophesied that the gospel will be spread to the ends of the earth, centered on the disciples," said the boy.

"Not just the 12 apostles and the 70, but all of humanity, all of us, are Jesus' little disciples," said Yesac.

Meanwhile, a short distance from the office was Whataburger, where Yesac often stopped to read or write. Today, it had been a while since he'd been there, so it felt fresh. He smiled compassionately at the beautiful neighborhood that still haunted him.

The boy turned the page of the book.

*'And Jesus said, "If a man sins against you seven times in a day,
and seven times returns to you saying, 'I repent,'
you shall forgive him." Then the Pharisees asked Him,
"When will the Kingdom of God come?"
Jesus replied,
"The Kingdom of God does not come with visible signs.
You cannot say, 'Look, here it is,' or 'There it is,'
for behold, the Kingdom of God is within you."
He continued, "As it was in the days of Noah—
people were eating and drinking, buying and selling,
marrying and being given in marriage,
until the day Noah entered the ark—
and the flood came and destroyed them all.*

*So also shall it be in the days of Lot.
They ate and drank, bought and sold, planted and built.
But on the day Lot left Sodom, fire and brimstone rained
from heaven and destroyed them all.
It shall be just like this on the day the Son of Man is revealed.
Then, a tax collector stood at a distance.
He would not even lift his eyes to heaven,
but beat his breast and cried,
"God, be merciful to me, a sinner!"
Jesus said,
"I tell you, this man went home justified, rather than the other.
For all who exalt themselves shall be humbled,
and those who humble themselves shall be exalted."
And He added, "Truly I say to you, whoever does not receive the
Kingdom of God as a little child shall never enter it."'*

The boy then recorded in his little notebook the verse that brought his teacher to enlightenment himself when Jesus read and meditated on the Bible on the Mount.

'And the Pharisees asked him, when shall the kingdom of God come? Jesus answered and said unto them, the coming of the kingdom of God is not something that can be observed, nor will people say, here it is or there it is because the kingdom of God is in your midst.'

"The Pharisees are asking when the kingdom of heaven, which has already come among them, will come," said the boy.

"A long time ago, a man named Siddhartha attained enlightenment through six years of penance and decided not to teach, thinking of the living beings who would notunderstand him even if he spoke to them," said Yesac.

"Yes. Even modern people in this age of civilization struggle tounderstand Jesus' words, and so they are misled by false prophets," said the boy.

"Jesus is clear: the kingdom of God does not come to be seen, the kingdom of heaven is not here or there, the kingdom of God is in your midst, very simply and clearly," said Yesac.

"Yes. Wherever you walk with the Lord Jesus is the kingdom of heaven, and he who has ears to hear will understand." Yesac thought it was great that the boy realized so early and didn't waste his life.

"The motto of General Yi Sun-sin, 'Pilsazeuksang Pilsangzeuksa(필사즉생 필생즉사 必死則生 必生則死),' is repeated again and again in Luke's gospel," said the boy.

Repetition meant doing, doing, doing.

"This meek general had early on realized the teachings of Jesus Christ. 'Whoever tries to keep their life will lose it, and whoever loses their life will preserve it; Pilsazeuksang Pilsangzeuksa(필사즉생 필생즉사 必死則生 必生則死),'" said old man, Yesac.

"There's a big teaching about humility that's re-emerging," said the boy.

"Enlightenment comes from studying with a clear focus rather than wandering around in confusion," Yesac noted.

"Yes. The Old Testament teaching is to know and serve God in humility," the boy agreed and looked at the old man's little notebook.

'Those who exalt themselves will be humbled, and those who humble themselves will be exalted.'

"I am alive today because Jesus taught me to 'always pray and not give up,'" Yesac said.

"What does it mean that whoever does not receive the kingdom of God as a little child will not enter it?" asked the boy, with a hint of confusion and fear in his voice.

"If your mind is clouded with thoughts and complications, you will never see the kingdom of God. As the Sermon on the Mount teaches, one must be poor and pure in heart, like a child, to experience the kingdom of God." Yesac explained patiently before continuing on.

The boy turned the pages with a poor and pure expression.

'They put in an offering out of their abundance, and this widow out of her poverty, all that she had for her living." ..... Therefore, resolve not to study beforehand for an excuse, and you will be hated by all men for my name's sake, but not a hair of your head will suffer. For by your patience shall your souls be saved. and then shall men see the Son of man coming in the clouds of heaven with power and great glory. For when ye see the bud, ye know naturally that the summer is at hand; so likewise, when ye see these things coming to pass, ye know that the kingdom of God is at hand.

Verily I say unto you, all these things shall be fulfilled before this generation passes away. Heaven and earth shall pass away, but my words shall not pass away. Take heed to yourselves, or else your hearts will be dulledby debauchery, drunkenness, and the cares of life, and that day will come upon you unexpectedly, like a snare. And that day willcome upon all who dwell on the face of the whole earth. Therefore, watch and pray always, that ye may be ready toescape all these things that shall come, and to stand before the Son of man: for Jesus taught in the temple by day, and went outby night, and rested on a mountain, which is called the garden ofOlives; and all the people came to the temple early in the morning to hear him.'

"Jesus teaches, 'Stand firm, and we will win life,'" said the boy.

"Because heaven and earth will pass away, but his words will never pass away, for the words of truth are eternal law," said Yesac.

"How is it that Jesus is so holy that he teaches in the temple by day and goes out at night to rest on a mountain called the Mount of Olives?" the boy said with a grateful expression.

"Even a boy can do it, Jesus says," Yesac answered.

Yesac opened his little notebook. It opened on John 14,

and the boy began to read it out loud,

> *'Whoever believes in me will do the works that I have been doing, and they will do even greater things than these because I am going to the Father.'*

Yesac was teaching the boy both positivity and humility by telling him that he could do anything and that everything was possible because Christ went to God. Christ was the only one who carried the cross and went to God.

Then the boy flipped to the last page of Luke's Good News and began to meditate.

> *'Now the festival of unleavened bread,*
> *called the Passover, drew near,*
> *and the chief priests and scribes were seeking a way to kill Him,*
> *for they feared the people.*
> *Jesus went out, as was His custom, to the Mount of Olives,*
> *and His disciples followed Him.*
> *When He came to the place, He said to them,*
> *"Pray that you do not enter into temptation."*
> *Then He withdrew from them about a stone's throw,*
> *knelt down, and prayed,*
> *"Father, if it be Your will, remove this cup from me.*
> *Yet not my will, but Yours be done."*
>
> *And a messenger from heaven appeared to Him, strengthening Him.*
> *As He labored and prayed more earnestly,*
> *His sweat became like drops of blood falling to the ground.*
> *Then they brought Him to a place called the Skull,*
> *and there they crucified Him—with two evildoers also,*
> *one on His right, and the other on His left.*
> *Then Jesus said,*
> *"Father, forgive them, for they know not what they do."*
> *And Jesus cried out with a loud voice,*
> *"Father, into Your hands I commit my spirit."'*

"As God has entrusted a kingdom to Jesus, so Jesus has entrusted a kingdom to us," said the boy.

"The way to rule well in the kingdom we have been given is to live our lives according to the Word only," said Yesac.

"The image of Jesus on his knees in prayer is both desperate and holy," said the boy.

"How solemn it is to hear Jesus pray, even in the face of death, that His will be done, not His own, but the will of His Heavenly Father," said Yesac.

'Father, if you are willing, take this cup from me; yet not my will, but yours be done.'

"It is pitiful to see Jesus praying so earnestly, striving and struggling, that his sweat was like drops of blood falling to the ground," the boy remarked in awe.

"What is even more remarkable is that he said to those who were crucifying him, 'Forgive them, Father, for they do not know what they are doing.'" Yesac pointed out.

"Jesus' prayer was a living teaching for all of humanity to follow and learn from," Yesac continued.

"So, we have no neighbor in our lives whom we cannot forgive," said the boy.

"The two things Jesus left behind when he died were forgiveness and the entrustment of his soul to God the Father," said Yesac and showed his little notebook to the boy.

'Father, into your hands, I commit my spirit.'

"Yes," the boy nodded.

When Jesus had said this, he breathed his last. That's how Jesus died.

Yesac and the boy looked solemn in silence.

'At dawn on the first day after the Sabbath, these women, with the spices they have prepared, will go to the tomb and when they saw that the stone had been rolled away from the tomb, they went in and found the body of the Lord Jesus not there. And as they were in sorrow, suddenly there appeared unto them two men in glorious apparel stood by them. And the women were afraid, and fell on their faces: and they said unto them, why do ye look for the living among the dead? He is not here; he has risen! Remember how He spoke unto you when He was in Galilee. Saying, The Son of man must be delivered into the hands of sinners, and be crucified, and on the third day rise again the third day: and

they remembered his words, and returned from the sepulcher, and told all these things to the eleven apostles, and to all the others. (These women were Mary Magdalene, Joanna, and Mary the mother of James, and the other women who were with them, who also told these things unto the apostles.) And Peter arose, and went to the sepulcher, and stooped down, and looked in, and saw nothing but the linen cloths: and he marveled at what had happened, and went home. And it came to pass the same day that two of them went from Jerusalem unto a village called Emmaus, which is about twenty and five miles from Jerusalem, and they told one another all these things that had happened. And while they were talking and inquiring one another, Jesus drew near and walked with them: but their eyes were blinded, and they recognized him not. '

"Jesus is risen," said the boy.

"Jesus had already said in Galilee while he was still alive that the Son of Man must be delivered over into the hands of sinners, be crucified, and on the third day rise again," said Yesac.

Mary Magdalene and Mary, the mother of James, witnessed Jesus' resurrection at dawn on the first day of the week.

The boy turned the page of the book.

'Then Jesus began with Moses and all the Prophets and explained to them what was said in all the Scriptures concerning himself... "The Lord has indeed risen and has appeared to Simon." Then, the two told what had happened on the way and how they recognized Jesus when he broke the bread. While they were still discussing this, Jesus stood among them and said, "Peace be with you." They were startled and frightened, thinking they saw a ghost. He asked them, "Why are you troubled, and why do doubts rise in your minds? Look at my hands and my feet. It is I! Touch me and see; a ghost does not have flesh and bones, as you see I have." He told them, "This is what I told you while I was still with you: Everything must be fulfilled that is written about me in the Law of Moses, the Prophets, and the Psalms." Then, he opened their minds so they could understand the Scriptures. He told them, "This is what is written: The Messiah will suffer and rise from the dead on the third day, and repentance for the forgiveness of sins will be preached in his name to all nations, beginning at Jerusalem. You are witnesses of these things.'

"Jesus opens our minds to understand the scriptures," the boy said.

In Yesac's little notebook, Jesus' teachings about opening our minds to understand the Scriptures were written in green letters.

'This is what I told you while I was still with you: Everything must be fulfilled that is written about me in the Law of Moses, the Prophets and the Psalms.'

The boy slapped his knee with the palm of his hand, belatedly realizing that the 66th book of the Old Testament was about Jesus Christ.

"Because God is love, and Jesus is love."

Yesac's low voice rumbled in the boy's ear.

"Jesus living in us, then the Bible is the story of all of us, all of humanity," the boy whispered to himself.

"Let's prepare the Gospel of John, the last book of the Gospels," Yesac said.

"Yes," said the boy.

On Saturday mornings, after doing laundry and exercising, Yesac and the boy replaced breakfast with sandwiches and coffee. At 62 years old, Yesac's body has only gotten stronger and more radiant.

"I wonder what is the secret to the health of the old man Yesac, who is stronger and fitter than me." The boy tilted his head in wonder and whispered.

Diligence of mind and body, regular exercise that became a habit, a clean mind, and the right food: that's what he saw in Yesac.

SJCB Dialogue – The Gospel of Luke

"The Gospel of Luke is one of the Gospels that records the life and teachings of Jesus, bearing a profound message for all humanity. It emphasizes that God's love is open to everyone, as Jesus spent time even with tax collectors and sinners. We must pay attention to the fact that God's love and the path of salvation are offered not to a select few, but to all humankind." Said the Buddha, with a heart embracing all people.

"God draws near to the poor and the humble. That is why Jesus said it is harder for a rich man to enter the Kingdom of Heaven than for a camel to go through the eye of a needle. Jesus was born in a manger in Bethlehem—a majō (마조 馬槽), a trough for animals to eat or sleep. This signifies that God began His work from the lowest and poorest of places, delivering the message that He draws near to those with humble hearts." Said Socrates, with a spirit of humility.

"Jesus taught, 'As I have forgiven you, so also must you forgive one another.' He emphasized the importance of forgiveness in human relationships and taught that repentance and forgiveness lie at the heart of a life aligned with God's will. 'Love your neighbor as yourself' is one of the most important lessons in the Gospel of Luke. Jesus showed this love not merely in words, but through action, teaching that true love must be demonstrated through deeds." Said Confucius, highlighting the power of forgiveness and love.

"The Gospel of Luke declares that the Kingdom of God is already here on earth. Jesus revealed that God's kingdom was realized in Him, and that it first takes root within the hearts of people. He clearly stated that He came not to be served, but to serve. True wealth is not material, but spiritual. Jesus paid attention to the outcast, the poor, the sick, and the foreigners— proving that the Kingdom of God is not for a privileged few, but for all people." Said the boy, with a heart of service.

"The Gospel of Luke delivers the hope of resurrection and eternal life through the resurrection of Jesus. By rising from the dead, Jesus opened the possibility of resurrection to all humanity. Anyone who awakens through His word can transcend death and enjoy eternal happiness." Said the old man, turning the page to the Gospel of John, as he spoke of the meaning of resurrection.

Volume 4: John

"What is the book of John?" Yesac asked.

"This is the Gospel written by John, one of the three closest to Jesus, like Peter and James. John was the faithful apostle who lived with and cared for Jesus' mother," the boy replied.

"What we should note here is that Jesus' death was not the taking of his life, but the laying down of his life of his own free will, and that his death was not a humiliation but a glory and a source of life," added Yesac.

"A distinctive feature of John's Gospel is that it deals with the divinity of Jesus, unlike the Synoptic Gospels of Matthew, Mark, and Luke, which deal with the same subject," Yesac continued.

Yesac and the boy simultaneously opened the Gospel of John with expressions of love and mercy.

'In the beginning was the Word, and the Word was with God, and the Word was God; he was in the beginning with God, and all things were made through him, and without him was not anything made that was made. In him was life, and this life was the light of men. The light shines in the darkness, and the darkness does not understand. And there was a man sent from God, whose name was John. He came to bear witness, that he might testify of the light, and that every man might believe that he was the light; and he was not this light, but the light that came to testify of him.

And there was a light, the true light, which was in the world, and shineth in every man; and the world was made, and the world was made by him; and the world knew him not, because he came into the world, and his own people did not receive him, but to them that received him, to them that believed on his name, he gave power to become the children of God, to them that were born, not of blood, nor of the will of the flesh, nor of the will of man, but of God. And the Word became flesh, and dwelt among us, and we beheld his glory, glory as of the onlybegotten of the Father, full of grace and truth.'

"This is the first chapter of the Gospel of John, which brought great enlightenment to you, teacher," the boy said with a gentle expression.

"You may remember the first verse of Genesis 1:1 when we first started studying the Bible," Yesac added.

"Yes. 'In the beginning God created the heavens and the earth,'" the boy recalled the words and said.

"So the first teaching of the Gospel of John is that God created the heavens and the earth, and the God who created the heavens and the earth is the Word," Yesac said.

"The Word, then the Bible is God," the boy said.

"Good, you understand quickly. The creation of heaven and earth was done through the Word," the old man said with a joyful expression.

"And in the Word was life, and this life was the light of men," said Yesac.

The boy saw the phrases in Yesac's small notebook, which had been repeatedly read and meditated upon to the point of wear and tear.

'In the beginning was the Word, and the Word was God. There was life in the Word, which is the light of men.'

In the beginning was the Word, and the Word was God, and in the Word was life, and this life was the light of men. People? Was God, after all, so compassionate and loving of people, of neighbors, of humanity, that he gave us the greatest teaching of all: love your neighbor as yourself? The boy pondered the question.

"Because God is love."

Yesac's voice weighed heavily on the boy's ears.

Ah. God is fearfully and wonderfully mysterious, coming to usnot in one form but in many. God is Jesus, the Holy Spirit, the Word, the Truth, and the Love! The boy's heart was pierced. Unblocked!

"Jesus, the Word made flesh, came to us, so that we might not live by visible bread alone, but by the invisible Word," said Yesac.

Yesac's voice still pierced the boy's ears.

John 1 was the love and the Word that led the boy to

enlightenment. The thought crossed the boy's mind that without the enlightenment from the truth of the Word, he too would have held an idolatrous faith, no different from the 39 kings of Northern Israel and Southern Judah who were divided.

The old man turned the page with a peaceful expression.

> *'And John testified of Him, and cried out, saying,*
> *"This is the one I spoke about:*
> *He who comes after me has surpassed me,*
> *because He was before me."*
> *From His fullness we have all received, grace upon grace.*
> *For the law was given through Moses,*
> *but grace and truth came through Jesus Christ.*
> *No one has ever seen God, but the one and only Son,*
> *who is Himself God and is in closest relationship with the Father,*
> *He has made Him known.*
>
> *This is the testimony of John: When the Jews sent priests and Levites from Jerusalem to ask him, "Who are you?" He confessed freely, "I am not the Christ." They asked him, "Are you Elijah?"*
> *He said, "I am not." "Are you the Prophet?"*
> *He answered, "No." So they said to him,*
> *"Then who are you? Why do you baptize,*
> *if you are neither the Christ, nor Elijah, nor the Prophet?"*
> *John answered them,*
> *"I baptize with water. But among you stands one you do not know—*
> *He who comes after me, the straps of whose sandals I am not worthy to untie." This all took place in Bethany, beyond the Jordan,*
> *where John was baptizing.'*

"You also can live as the protagonist of the voice crying out in the wilderness, 'Make straight the way of the Lord,'" said Yesac.

"Yes. God calls us all, but He gives us the freedom to choose," the boy agreed.

Yesac looked at the Bible verses written in the boy's small notebook. They were from Philippians and John's Gospel.

> *'Whoever believes in me will do the works that I have been doing, and they will do even greater things than these.'*
>
> *'I can do all things through him who gives me strength.'*

"Can I do the works that Jesus did and even greater things? Can I do everything? Does that mean nothing is impossible?"

Theholy book that gives the power of possibility and positivity in all things is the Bible, which contains all the secrets of life.

However,the boy does remember the more important advice from the oldman, Yesac. The one who gives such power is Christ, and the secret to doing even greater things is the teaching of humility and selflessness, which is that Christ went to God the Father by beingcrucified.

Watching the boy gain enlightenment, Yesac turned the pages of the Gospel of John with a satisfied smile.

'The next day, John saw Jesus coming toward him and said, Behold, the Lamb of God, which taketh away the sin of the world. This is the one to whom I spoke before, saying, There is one coming after me, but he is before me. And I knew him not: but I came and baptized with water, that he might be manifested unto Israel. John also bore witness, and said, I saw the Spirit descending from heaven like a dove, and remained upon him. I knew him not: but he that sent me to baptize with water said unto me, If ye see the Holy Ghost descending and abiding on anyman, know that it is he that baptizeth with the Holy Ghost: and Ihave seen him, and have borne witness that he is the Son of God. .....One of the two that heard John, and followed him, was the son of Zebedee.

The next day John saw Jesus coming toward him, and said, Behold, the Lamb of God, which taketh away the sin of the world. And when I said before, There is one coming after me, and he is before me, this is he that is before me. And I knew him not: but I came and baptized with water, that he might be manifested unto Israel. John also bore witness, and said, I saw the Spirit descending from heaven like a dove, and resting on him. I knew him not: but he that sent me to baptize with water said unto me,If ye see the Holy Ghost descending and abiding upon any man, ye know that it is he that baptizeth with the Holy Ghost: and I have seen him, and have borne witness that he is the Son of God.

..... One of the two that heard John, and followed him, was Andrew the brother of Simon Peter. And he sought first his brother Simon, and said unto him, We have seen the Messiah (Christ): and he brought him unto Jesus: and when Jesus saw him, he said unto him, Thou art Simon the son of John: but thou shalt be called Gebba (Peter). The next day, as Jesus went out into

Galilee, he met Philip, and said unto him, Follow me: and Philip was of Bethsaida, of the same city with Andrew and Peter. And Philip found Nathanael, and said unto him, We have found him of whom Moses wrote in the law, and the prophets spake, Jesus of Nazareth, the son of Joseph. Nathanael said unto him, What good thing can come out of Nazareth? Jesus answered and said unto him, I saw thee when thou wast under the fig tree, before Philip called thee. Nathanael answered and said unto him, Rabbi, thou art the Son of God, and thou art the King of Israel. Jesus answered and said unto him, Because thou sayest, I saw thee under the fig tree, believe me, thou shalt see greater things than these: and he said unto him, Verily, verily, I say unto you, Thou shalt see heaven opened, and the messengers of God ascending and descending on the Son of man.'

"Jesus gave Simon, one of the twelve disciples, a new name, Peter," the boy said.

"Philip was from Bethsaida, a town in the same region as Andrew and Peter," the old man recalled and listed the twelve disciples of Jesus: Peter, Andrew, James, John, Philip, Bartholomew, Thomas, Matthew, James, Thaddaeus, Simon (the Zealot), and Judas Iscariot.

The boy turned the pages of the Gospel of John with a calm, ocean-like expression.

*'On the third day, there was a wedding at Cana in Galilee, and the mother of Jesus was there.
Jesus and His disciples had also been invited to the wedding.
But when the wine ran out, the mother of Jesus said to Him, "They have no wine."
The host tasted the wine—though he did not know where it had come from—but the servants who had drawn the water knew.
Jesus had turned the water into wine.
This was the first of His signs, performed in Cana of Galilee, revealing His glory.
And His disciples believed in Him.
Later, when Jesus went to the temple,
He saw oxen and sheep and doves being sold,
and the money-changers seated at their tables.
He made a whip of cords, and drove all the sheep and oxen out of the temple. He poured out the coins of the money-changers,
and overturned their tables. To those who sold doves He said,*

"Take these things away. Do not make My Father's house a house of merchandise!"
For Jesus did not entrust Himself to them, for He knew all men, and He knew what was in their hearts.
He had no need for anyone to testify about man.'

"So the first miracle Jesus performed in this new town was to make wine at an invited wedding feast, but the people in the church say you can't drink, don't drink," the boy said.

"Do not add or subtract from the word, whether it is faith or alcohol. Live according to your measure. You must know how to live life proudly like the horn of a rhinoceros, taking the word as your companion."

"But I've read the Scriptures several times, and though there are passages that say to drink wine, there's no verse saying not to drink," the boy whispered to himself, recalling Proverbs 31.

In the boy's small notebook, Bible verses about alcohol were recorded. They read as follows:

'Give strong drink to the one who is perishing, and wine to those in bitter distress.' - Proverbs 31:6

'So I commend the enjoyment of life, because there is nothing better for a person under the sun than to eat and drink and be glad. Then joy will accompany them in their toil all the days of the life God has given them under the sun.' - Ecclesiastes 8:15

"How ironic. If drinking alcohol was really forbidden, why did Jesus perform his first miracle by making wine when he came to this world? Is life case by case, to be lived according to one's measure? Without swaying to the left or right, just according to the word?" the boy continued to ponder alone.

"In his gospel, Luke writes that John's parents, Zacharias and Elizabeth, did not drink wine or spirits," said Yesac.

"How could John drink alcohol while in the womb?" the boy asked.

"Buddhism says not to drink alcohol," said the boy.

"The life portion of monks or clergy differs from that of ordinary people. People need to learn from Solomon's enlightenment and wisdom," the old man said calmly.

"In fact, even Siddhartha was wary of seeking too much Tao and indulging in too much pleasure," the boy said, recalling what he had studied with the old man, Yesac.

"Moderation and temperance are the answers," the old man replied briefly.

Since coming of age, the boy has occasionally shared a drink with his master, but he has never seen him disheveled or drunk. The only difference was that his face became slightly childlike and innocent.

"Even Jesus spills when he gets angry. He spills people's money. He scatters the coins of the money changers and overturns their tables," said the boy.

"Because people were doing business in the temple, God's house. Shouldn't turning Father's house into a market! That's the kind of behavior of Jesus that brings us closer to God," Yesac said.

"Yes. Jesus was the Word made flesh and came to us," said the boy.

"God was so hard on sin that he destroyed the entire human race, leaving only Noah's relatives," said Yesac.

The conversation between the old man and the boy, who both longed for the truth and wished to live by the Word, flowed seamlessly like a passing breeze and running water.

"The Word is here to teach us that people are not objects of will but of love," the boy said.

> *'Jesus would not entrust himself to them, for he knew all people. He did not need any testimony about mankind, for he knew what was in each person.'*

The boy glanced at Yesac's little notebook.

> *'There is no will, so there is no hurt, but only compassion and love.'*

"Nicodemus was a Pharisee, a legalist, a teacher, and a man of power, but he was darkened in the truth," the boy said.

"The truth of salvation is a gift that comes from revering God and loving your neighbor as yourself, but they tried to obtain salvation through their righteousness."

Yesac's face shone as he spoke, though he seemed unaware of it.

"Yes. Salvation is a precious gift from God, the Holy Spirit, andChrist," the boy said and flipped through the pages of the Gospels.

Before meeting the old man Yesac, someone had once said, "If you believe in Jesus and receive salvation, you'll go to heavenwhen you die." The boy came to realize how foolish and selfish that misleading notion was. No matter how often the boy read and re-read the Bible, he could not find such a message anywhere. Salvation and going to heaven alone? The boy recalled whenhe was confused about religion and smiledcompassionately at himself. The old man taught what people found difficult so quickly. The boy was grateful for the old man'steaching that living a life of revering God, loving one's neighbors,walking with Christ, and following the Word is salvation and the Kingdom of God, which can be experienced while living in this world. As he recalled their study of Matthew 22, the boy turned the pages of the Gospel.

'God is not the God of the dead but of the living.'

'Verily, verily, I say unto thee, Except a man be born again, he cannot see the kingdom of God.'.....Jesus answered, 'Verily, verily, I say unto thee, Except a man be born of water and of the Spirit, he cannot enter into the kingdom of God; for that which is born of the flesh is flesh, and that which is born of the Spirit is spirit. For no man hath ascended into heaven but he that came down from heaven, even the Son of man; and as Moses lifted up the serpent in the wilderness, so must the Son of man be lifted up, that whosoever believeth in him should not perish, but have everlasting life. For God so loved the world, that he gave his only begotten Son, that whosoever believeth in him should not perish, but have everlasting life. For the Father so loved the Son, that he gave all things into his hands: and whosoever believeth on the Son hath everlasting life: and whosoever obeyeth not the Son shall not see life, but the wrath of God abideth on him.'

"It says they cannot see the Kingdom of God unless they are born again. What is the way to be born again?" the boy asked.

"Being born again is not a one-time event, but a journey of constant meditation on the Word. By practicing it, understandingit, and repeating this understanding, we can truly become the Word ourselves. This transformation allows us to love our neighbors, inviting the Holy Spirit into our lives and leading us to the Kingdom of God where Christ resides within us."

Yesac's words, taught with love and simplicity, always came to the boy's heart as enlightenment.

Sundays were soccer days, and Yesac started his day with 45 minutes of stretching as soon as he woke up. Playing soccer three times a week was taking its toll, so he skipped his early morning strength training. Dawn is always fresh in the mind and heart. Yesac flipped through the pages of John's Gospel with a smile on his face.

'No one has ascended into heaven except the one who came down from heaven—the Son of Man.
Just as Moses lifted up the serpent in the wilderness,
so must the Son of Man be lifted up, that whoever believes in Him shall not perish, but have eternal life.
For God so loved the world that He gave His one and only Son, that whoever believes in Him shall not perish,
but have everlasting life. God did not send His Son into the world to condemn the world, but that the world through Him might be saved.
For the Father loves the Son, and has given all things into His hands.
Whoever believes in the Son has life, but whoever rejects the Son
—on him the wrath of God remains.'

"Confucius seems to have truly loved the Bible. He expressed its teachings beautifully," the boy said this while looking at the phrase in Yesac's small notebook.

"MiJiSaeng UnJiSa(미지생 언지사 未知生 焉知死); I have spoken to you of earthly things and you do not believe; how then will you believe if I speak of heavenly things?"

"'MiJiSaeng UnJiSa(미지생 언지사 未知生 焉知死)?' This is a short but big teaching of Jesus: We try to know the things of heaven when we don't even know the things of this world," the boy said.

"You can't know heavenly things until you know earthly things," said Yesac. The old man's words flowed like water, never meeting any obstacles.

"Some say the world is coming to an end, but God so loved the world that he gave his one and only Son, Jesus." the boy said.

"Let us not be deceived by false prophets, for we have learned clearly that no one knows the times, only God does, and that God's purpose in sending Jesus to us was that we might have eternal life, that whoever believes in him should not perish but have everlasting life," said Yesac.

"How can I have eternal life?" the boy asked.

"Eternal life is God's gift to us if we repent of our sins and believe in the Lord Jesus, who died for our sins and rose again on the third day," replied Yesac.

"So eternal life isn't something that continues after death, but an ongoing world that already exists within us," the boy commented.

The boy thought. It was a great realization to realize that eternal life does not begin at death.

"For the enlightened, death has no meaning; we have already conquered death by being crucified with Jesus."

"So when you talk about no-self, transcending birth and death, etc, do you mean a life of eternal life with Jesus, the Truth, and the Word?" the boy inquired.

"That is what the Bible teaches," Yesac's answers were always as simple and clear as his words. After all, truth and leaders should always be honest and transparent; that's what the boy thought.

"It is also the hope of humanity that Jesus did not come to judge the world but to bring salvation to all of us," said the boy.

"God is a God of affirmation, not negation," Yesac added.

"What does it mean that judgment is not something we receive when we die, but that we have already been judged by not believing in Jesus Christ?" the boy asked.

"That's a very good question. We have already learned that God is not a God of the dead, but of the living, and the wages of judgment is eternal life, which we receive by repenting of our sins and believing that the Lord Jesus died for our sins and rose from the dead on the third day." Yesac was happy the boy asked sucha question.

"Ah, yes. You mean that those who did not accept Jesus were judged for not knowing this sweet world of the Word," said the boy with a smile.

"The price of judgment for not knowing this world of joy and happiness, of living a life of eternal life by becoming the Word themselves, is enormous," Yesac said.

"Yes. That is, you always live a life of joy, happiness, and gratitude, no matter the circumstances," the boy commented.

Indeed, what the boy saw was a man who, even in the face of death, lived as the Word himself with unwavering resolve.

"We need to remember the clear truth we learned from the Gospel of Matthew: if we do not know Jesus, God will not recognize us." As he spoke, Yesac turned to Matthew 7.

'I never knew you. Away from me, you evildoers!'

The boy realized in an instant that only through Jesus could he have eternal life. The law was a sacrifice, but Christ was compassion, mercy, and love.

The old man turned the pages of the Gospel.

'For the Lord knows that the Pharisees have heard that there are more disciples of Jesus and more baptizers than John. Jesus himself did not baptize, but his disciples did. And he departed out of Judea, and went again into Galilee, and must pass through Samaria. And he came to a city of Samaria, called Sychar, which is near the land which Jacob gave to Joseph his son, and there was Jacob's well. And it was about the sixth hour, when Jesus was weary of the way, and sat down by the well. And a Samaritan woman came to draw water: and he asked her to give him some: for his disciples were gone into the city to buy food.

And the Samaritan woman said unto him, Thou art a Jew, why askest thou me, a Samaritan woman, for water: for a Jew hath no fellowship with a Samaritan. Jesus answered and said unto her, If thou hadst known the gift of God, and who it was that asked thee for a drink of water, thou wouldest have asked of him, and he would have given thee living water: He that drinketh of the water that I shall give him shall never thirst: but the water that I shall give him shall be in him a well of water springing up into everlasting life:

..... The hour cometh, and is now, that they that worship the Father truly shall worship him with the Spirit. For the Father seeketh such to worship him: for God is a Spirit, and they that worship him worship the Father in spirit and in truth. Jesus saith unto them, My food is to do the will of him that sent me,

and to finish his work perfectly.'

"Jesus and His disciples traveling through Judea, Samaria, and Galilee, baptizing people—how beautiful they are," said the boy with a happy face.

"Even you are a disciple of Christ, who has eternal life, loves the Word, and preaches the gospel," the old man Yesac said with the hope that the boy would not just be a passive observer of faith but become the Word himself and live accordingly.

"How human it is to see the disciples of Jesus going into the neighborhood to buy food," said the boy.

"Jesus came in a human form. He shed tears like us and felt hunger when He was hungry," Yesac said.

"Why didn't the Jews get along with the Samaritans?" the boy asked.

"As we studied in the Old Testament, there is a long history of conflict between the two peoples, with the idol-worshiping Samaritans helping Alexander's army and sabotaging the Jews' efforts to return from Babylonian captivity and rebuild Jerusalem. Jesus' great love for even the Samaritans should inspire us to remember the Old Testament command to love the stranger as yourself," Yesac replied.

"Yes. Jesus is indeed a man of unbounded compassion," said the boy.

"That is why whoever drinks of the water that Jesus gives will never thirst," said Yesac.

"Yes. Indeed, the water Jesus give them will become in them a spring of water welling up to everlasting life." The boy looked at the words written in the old man's small notebook and spoke.

'Whoever drinks the water I give them will never thirst. Indeed, the water I give them will become in them a spring of water welling up to everlasting life.'

Yesac stopped looking at the boy's small notebook.

'God is spirit, and his worshipers must worship in the Spirit and in truth.'

The boy flipped through the pages of John's Gospel.

'Therefore the Jews persecuted him because he did these things on the Sabbath day. Jesus saith unto them, As my Father

worketh, so work I: and for this cause the Jews sought the more to kill him, because he transgressed not only the Sabbath day, but made himself equal with God, calling God his own Father. Therefore Jesus saith unto them, Verily, verily, I say unto you, The Son can do nothing of himself, except he see the works of the Father: for whatsoever the Father doeth, that doeth he the Son also: that all men may honor the Son, even as they honor the Father. He that honoureth not the Son honoureth not the Father that sent him.

Verily, verily, I say unto you, He that heareth my word, and believeth on him that sent me, hath everlasting life, and shall not come into condemnation; but hath passed from death unto life. Verily, verily, I say unto you, The hour cometh, and is coming, in which the dead shall hear the voice of the Son of God: and they that hear shall live. For as the Father hath life in himself, even so hath he given to the Son to have life in him; and because he is the Son of man, he hath given him power to judge: Marvel not at this: for the hour cometh, when all that are in the graves shall hear his voice: they that have done good, unto the resurrection of life; and they that have done evil, unto the resurrection of judgment.'

"Jesus' answer, 'As my Father works all the days of the week, so I work on the Sabbath,' is a great teaching that leads us to open faith," said the boy.

"Following the truth of Jesus, who combines law, mercy, and love, is the way to eternal life," Yesac said.

"We were not alive, but when we repent of our sins and believe in Jesus' death and resurrection and have eternal life, we are given a new life, passed from death to life without judgment," said the boy.

The following Sunday afternoon, Yesac and the boy bought a vegetable kit at Costco. They plan to make a lunch of vegetables and mustard greens and head to the soccer field. It's the day of the NTPSA soccer tournament, and Yesac's face is flushed from the early morning hours, like a child on a picnic. The boy is excited to see how many goals he will score today because his teacher is very good at soccer and has great stamina.

"Jesus said that even the dead will live again if they hear the voice of God," the boy said.

"Even if you were alive, you were not alive, but if you have eternal life and new life, you have been raised from the dead," Yesac said.

"Sometimes the mysterious and unsearchable works of God are beyond our ability to fathom," the boy said.

The boy looked at his teacher's small notebook.

KwonSunJingAk(勸善懲惡권선징악): This four-character idiom appears in the Chunqiu Zuo's Commentary(春秋左氏傳 춘추좌씨전) authored by Confucius and means to encourage good deeds and punish evil ones. This principle is a common teaching across all religions, emphasizing that despite differences in nations, ethnicities, and cultures, humanity is one community pursuing the same values. That is goodness, the sixth fruit of the Holy Spirit.

"Confucius was indeed a great evangelist of the Bible, and how well he was able to express the Bible and convey its teachings to Eastern cultures," the boy said, recalling the teachings he had studied from old man Yesac.

'IlYiKwanJi, ManBupKwiIl(一以貫之 일이관지 萬法歸一 만법귀일); the enlightened one penetrates all things as one, and all the laws of truth return to one.'

"Confucius clearly expressed Jesus' words, 'Those who have done what is good will rise to live, and those who have done what is evil will rise to be condemned,'" the boy said, looking at the old man's little notebook.

"We should be diligent to become the Word ourselves, knowing that the Scriptures not only bear witness to Jesus, but that we have eternal life by reading, meditating, and practicing them," the old man looked at the notes recorded in the boy's small notebook and said.

'You study the Scriptures diligently because you think that in them you have eternal life. These are the very Scriptures that testify about me.'

"Yes. Moses also wrote about Jesus who was to come." The boy looked at John Chapter 5 and said.

'If you believed Moses, you would believe me, for he wrote about me,'

the old man turned the page.

'Afterward Jesus went into the sea of Galilee, which is beyond the sea of Tiberias, and a great multitude followed him, to see the signs which he did with the sick. And Jesus went up into a mount, and sat down with his disciples: and it was near the festival of the Passover, which is a Jewish feast. And when Jesus lifted up his eyes, and saw a great multitude coming unto him, he said unto Philip, where shall we buy bread, that these men may eat?" And there was plenty of grass there: and they sat down, and were about five thousand in number. And when Jesus had taken the loaves, and had blessed them, he gave them to them that sat down: and the meat also he gave them according to their desire. And when his disciples had rowed about ten leagues, they saw him walking on the sea, and drawing nigh unto the boat, and were afraid: but he said unto them, Fear not: and they received him into the boat with gladness: and the boat came into the land whither they were going Jesus answered and said unto them, Verily, verily, I say unto you, ye seek me, not because ye saw a sign, but because ye did eat of the loaves, and were filled. Labor not for food that perisheth, but for food that endureth unto everlasting life: for the Son of man shall give you this food: for the Son of man is the Son of God the Father. And they said unto him, what shall we do that we may do the works of God? Jesus answered and said unto them, It is the work of God to believe on him that sent him: Jesus said unto them, I am the bread of life: he that cometh to me shall never hunger; he that believeth on me shall never thirst.'

"We need to do the work of God, and God says that the work of God is to believe in Jesus Christ whom He has sent."

The boy noted in his small notebook and said, 'The work of God is this: to believe in the one he has sent.'

"Jesus is the bread of life, whoever comes to Christ will never go hungry, and by believing in Christ we will never be thirsty in life."

The old man meditated on the Word once more.

'I am the bread of life. Whoever comes to me will never go hungry, and whoever believes in me will never be thirsty.'

"Happy indeed are those of us who do not labor for food that perishes, but for food that endures to eternal life, the Word and the truth." The boy also meditated on the Word and said.

'Do not work for food that spoils, but for food that endures to eternal life.'

"How holy is the sight of Jesus, ascending the mountain on the other side of the sea in Tiberias, performing miracles with Philip and Andrew and preaching the gospel."

Yesac flipped through the pages of the Gospels and said.

'For I have come down from heaven, not to do my own will, but the will of him who sent me; and the will of him who sent me is that I should lose none of those whom he has given me, but should raise them up on the last day. Verily, verily, I say unto you, he that believeth hath everlasting life: I am the bread of life: your fathers ate of the manna in the wilderness, and died: but this is the living bread that cometh down from heaven, that man may eat of it, and not die: I am the living bread that cometh down from heaven: if any man eat of this bread, he shall live forever.

The Jews, therefore, disputed among themselves, saying, how can this man give us his flesh to eat? Jesus saith unto them, Verily, verily, I say unto you, except ye eat the flesh of the Son of man, and drink his blood, ye have no life in you. He that eateth my flesh, and drinketh my blood, hath everlasting life, and I will raise him up again at the last day: for my flesh is true food, and my blood is true drink. He that eateth my flesh, and drinketh my blood, abideth in me, and I in him: for the living Father hath sent me, and as I live by the Father, so he that eateth me shall live by me. Jesus answered and said unto them, Have I not chosen you twelve, but one of you is a devil: and this is Judas, the son of Simon Iscariot. He is one of the twelve to sell Jesus.'

After suffering a bruise during a soccer match on Sunday, Yesac's gait seemed a little off. The team won 4:1 against Vietnam, but Yesac was injured and played the role of goalkeeper. As the boy looked at him, he realized that a poor diet could lead to injury and that he should eat well while playing sports.

'Jesus answered and said,
"*My teaching is not my own, but comes from Him who sent me. If anyone desires to do God's will, he will know whether my teaching is from God or if I speak on my own. He who believes in me, as the Scripture has said, 'Out of his innermost being will flow rivers of living water.'*"

And Jesus went up to the Mount of Olives.
In the morning, He returned to the temple,
and all the people gathered around Him.
He sat down and began to teach them.
Then the scribes and Pharisees brought before Him a woman
caught in the very act of adultery.
They said, "Teacher, this woman was caught in the act.
Moses commanded us to stone such women.
What do you say?"
They said this to test Him, hoping to find grounds to accuse Him.
But Jesus stooped down and wrote on the ground with His finger.
When they continued to ask, He straightened up and said,
"Let the one among you who is without sin
be the first to cast a stone at her."
Then Jesus said to them,
"I am the light of the world. Whoever follows me shall not walk in
darkness, but shall have the light of life."
"You judge according to the flesh; I judge no one.
But even if I do judge, my judgment is true,
for I am not alone—He who sent me is with me."
And Jesus said to them, "You are from below; I am from above.
You are of this world; I am not of this world."

"The kings of the Old Testament sought God, but when things got good, they forgot about God and sought their own glory, which led to their own destruction. But Jesus is God whose very life is God," said the boy.

"Jesus' words, 'My teaching is not my own. It comes from the one who sent me,' become his own words, and we can learn a lot from the fact that he always lived his life centered on God," Yesac added.

"The teaching 'Stop judging people by mere appearances' and 'Whatever you did to the least of these, you did to Christ' changed my life. It took away the confusion that comes from foolish judgments and gave me the grace to see the little Jesus in everyone," The boy said with a look of realization on his face.

"You learned compassion," Yesac said.

"Compassion?" the boy asked.

"It's not hard to love people we like, but the power to love our enemies comes from learning compassion," Yesac responded.

"...................."

The boy remained silent.

"Mercy(KeungHyool 矜恤 긍휼 love) is the feeling of pity and care. When we see in a passerby the preciousness of life and see in our neighbor the desire to protect that life, we feel boundless love, mercy, and camaraderie," said Yesac.

"......................"

The boy kept silent, but his face radiated peace.

"When we experience compassion in its true form, all conflict and hatred in our relationships will disappear. There is nothing but forgiveness, love, and mercy, as you are granted the grace to see the Lamb in all your neighbors," Yesac added.

"How holy is the image of Jesus teaching on the Mount of Olives and in the temple courts." The boy said with an expression as calm as a gentle wave.

"The teachers of the law and the Pharisees said that according to the law of Moses, a woman caught in adultery should be stoned. When they asked Jesus what he would do, Jesus said, 'Let any one of you who is without sin be the first to throw a stone at her,'" the boy said.

"The teaching, 'Let any one of you who is without sin be the first to throw a stone at her,' was very enlightening to me as well. By meditating on these words, I learned to be tolerant of the sins of others and hard on my own, which was a blissful narrow gate to enlightenment," said Yesac.

"Yes. Jesus fulfilled the Law of Moses with such teachings," said the boy.

"With Jesus, the light of the world, we have the light of life," Yesac said.

"Jesus, who judges no one, is truly holy." The boy spoke as he looked at the old man's small notebook.

'You judge by human standards; I pass judgment on no one.'

"What makes Jesus even greater is that he is always with God," said Yesac.

"Yes. Jesus was never alone; God was always with him." The boy jotted down notes in his small notebook as he spoke.

> *'The one who sent me is with me; he has not left me alone,*
> *for I always do what pleases him,'*

"If we think like Jesus, God is always within us," said Yesac.

"Thank you, Master, for teaching me a faith that goes beyond the faith of looking to the faith of participation and realization," the boy thanked Yesac.

"Not me, thank Jesus!" said Yesac.

The boy turned to the Gospel of John with a grateful expression on his face.

> *'Then Jesus said to the Jews who had believed in Him,*
> *"If you abide in my word, you are truly my disciples.*
> *And you shall know the truth, and the truth shall make you free."*
> *For whoever commits sin is a slave to sin.*
> *But if the Son sets you free, you shall be free indeed.*
> *"But you seek to kill me, because my word has no place in you.*
> *I have told you the truth, that I heard from God—*
> *Abraham did not do this."*
> *"There is but one Father—God.*
> *If God were truly your Father, you would love me,*
> *for I have come from God.*
> *I did not come of my own accord, but He sent me."*
> *"Why do you not understand my words?*
> *I do not seek my own glory,*
> *but the One who seeks and judges is with me."*
> *"Truly, truly, I say to you, if anyone keeps my word,*
> *he shall never see death—ever."*
> *Jesus answered them,*
> *"If I glorify myself, my glory is nothing. It is my Father who glorifies me,*
> *the one you call your God."*
> *And then Jesus said to them,*
> *"Truly, truly, I say to you: Before Abraham was, I AM."'*

"What is the purpose of people having religion?" the boy inquired.

"The purpose of life, finding psychological stability and comfort, spiritual experiences, curiosity about the afterlife, discovering one's identity and self-awareness, and so on."

"................"

The boy bowed and remained silent at the old man's words.

"By attaining enlightenment and achieving eternal happiness through liberation from everything." The older man added, gazing at the distant mountains.

"And how do we achieve that freedom?" asked the boy.

Instead of answering, Yesac held out his little notebook.

'Jesus; the bread of life, the light of the world, the gate for the sheep, the good shepherd, the resurrection and the life, the way, the truth, the life, the true vine. If you hold to my teaching, you are really my disciples. Then you will know the truth, and the truth will set you free.'

"Ah, yes. So it is the truth that sets us free, and the truth is Jesus Christ," said the boy.

"Jesus is the Bible, the Word, and if we abide in the Word, we will be free," said Yesac.

"Did Siddhartha, who gave up all his riches and his princely position, left empty-handed and walked the ascetic path, attain freedom?" the boy asked.

"Yes. Buddhists use the terms liberation or nirvana rather than freedom," Yesac explained.

"What is the difference between liberation and nirvana?" the boy inquired.

"Nirvana is what is attained through liberation. Liberation is freedom, and nirvana can also be described as emptiness," Yesac answered.

"Can ordinary people experience the emptiness of nirvana?" asked the boy.

"Yes. Selflessness, the state of 'no-self' (無我 무아), is the realization of emptiness (空 공). By being crucified with Jesus, we live a life of selflessness (無我 무아)." Yesac said.

"So you mean that world is cut off from greed, anger, and foolishness and doesn't exist?" the boy asked.

"Yes," said Yesac.

"Then the old man Yesac, who has no greed, who has never seen anger, who has never seen foolishness, has attained freedom? Through the Word, the Truth?" the boy tilted his head, seemingly puzzled by a sense of enlightenment coming and going.

The boy also recalled times when he had experienced freedom and reflected on those memories. He realized that this freedom came from truth and the Word, achievable only through the perfect love of Christ. The boy understood that as we strive to emulate Christ, we too become holy and attain true freedom. The boy's gaze then rested on the old man's small notebook.

'Be holy, because I am holy, and the truth will set you free.'

"You are not yet fifty years old, and you have seen Abraham?" the Jews asked Jesus.

"Truly, truly, I say to you, before Abraham was born, I am." Very truly I tell you, before Abraham was born, I am!" Jesus replied.

The boy asked the old man what he thought about the conversation between the Jew and Jesus.

"The answer is simple if we first know who Jesus is. What matters is a clean mind that approaches the Bible as it is written, neither adding nor subtracting from its own ideas or predictions."

Yesac holds out a small notebook with the facts as they are written in the Bible.

'Jesus is the Lord and my God, God and our Savior Jesus Christ; Christ is true God and eternal life; the Word, who is God, became flesh and dwelt among us; a virgin conceived and bore a son, and they shall call his name Immanuel, which is interpreted, God with us; for unto us a child is born, unto us a mighty God, whose name is Wonderful, who is mighty; he was clothed with a robe dipped in blood, whose name is the Word of God; there is one God, and one mediator between God and men, the man Christ Jesus.'

"So God is Jesus," said the boy.

"Jesus is God," said Yesac.

"Then the one who was before Adam, Noah, and Abraham was God and the Word, Jesus," said the boy.

"In the beginning God created the world by the Word, and the Word was God and Jesus," said Yesac.

"Jesus says that if we keep the truth and words, we will never see death," the boy said, remembering Christ's words.

'Very truly I tell you, whoever obeys my word will never see death.'

"The end of life is death, and those who have been crucified with Jesus Christ are in a state of no-me, having no life of their own, and therefore no death."

"............" The boy was silent at the old man's words.

"If life is not mine, why should the dead exist? The only things that are eternal are truth and the Word, and when one lives as the Word, there is no death," the old man's words seeped into the boy's heart.

"That is the end of enlightenment," the boy said, breaking the silence.

Yesac turned the pages of the Gospel of John with an expressionless face.

*'As long as I am in the world, I am the light of the world...
whether he is a sinner I know not; but one thing I know,
that I was blind, and now I see. I am the good shepherd,
and the good shepherd layeth down his life for the sheep.
The Father loveth me, because I lay down my life
that I might take it up again.
And my sheep hear my voice,
and I know them, and they follow me.
And I give unto them eternal life, and they shall never perish;
and no man can pluck them out of my hand.
For my Father which giveth them is greater than all,
and no man can pluck them out of my hand.
I and the Father are one.'*

*Jesus saith unto them,
'It is written in your law, I have said unto you, that ye are gods.
The Scriptures cannot be destroyed;
for they which have received the word of God are called gods.
How then do ye marvel that I, the Son of God,
whom the Father hath sanctified and sent into the world,
should say, I am the Son of God?'*

Jesus loved Martha, and her brother, and Lazarus.

*Jesus saith unto them, 'I am the resurrection and the life.
He that believeth in me, though he were dead, yet shall he live;
and whosoever liveth and believeth in me shall never die.
Believe ye this?'*

*Jesus shed tears.
And when the stone was rolled away,
Jesus lifted up his eyes, and looked up, and said,
'Father, I thank thee, that thou hast heard me.'
And when he had said these things, he cried with a loud voice,
'Lazarus, come forth.'*

*And behold, the dead man came forth, with his limbs bound,
and his face wrapped in a towel.'*

As the boy looked at Yesac's little notebook, he saw Jesus' big teaching.

'I and the Father are one.'

"From this decisive teaching of Jesus, our humanity should be enlightened," Yesac said.

"......................"

The boy's epiphanies were always accompanied by silence.

"Jesus even said we are gods. He called them 'gods' to whom the word of God came." The old man opened the words written in his small notebook and said,

'If he called them 'gods' to whom the word of God came—and Scripture cannot be set aside—.'

"If Jesus and God and the Word dwell in us, we are called gods too," The old man opened his small notebook and said. It was from Galatians 2.

'I have been crucified with Christ, and it is no longer I who live, but Christ who lives in me.'

"Do you now understand the meaning of the Ten Commandments, to have no other gods before me?" Yesac asked this question, hoping all humanity would attain enlightenment and eternal happiness from this teaching.

"Yes. Jesus called us gods because God already dwells within us. To have gods other than me without realizing it is superstition," The boy answered with freedom and clarity.

"This is what it means to be alone in the heavens and the earth. The secret of all answers lies within me, where God dwells, and it is ignorance and foolishness to look for anything outside of us," said Yesac.

The old man's words resonated in the boy's heart. The boy suddenly recalled the teachings of Buddha, which he had studied with his teacher Yesac: *'In heaven and on earth, I alone am honored; ChunSangChunHaYuAhDokJon* 天上天下唯我獨尊 천상천하유아독존'.

Piercing through everything with one principle? It was the old man Yesac who showed the boy that such a teaching of Buddha is also present in Christ's words in Matthew. The boy was learning that all laws return to one.

The boy's attention was caught by a note in the old man's little notebook. It was Matthew chapter 16.

'For what will it profit a man if he gains the whole world, yet forfeits his soul? What can a man give in exchange for his soul; ChunSangChunHa YuAhDokJon 天上天下唯我獨尊 천상천하유아독존'

"Jesus wept," he said, "and loved Martha and her sister Lazarus, even to the point of tears," the boy said.

"It's a touching scene of Jesus, the Word, coming in flesh like ours, bringing together a very human figure," Yesac said.

"Jesus was so moved and loved that he raised Lazarus from the dead." said the boy.

In the boy's small notebook, he scribbled a Bible verse that gave his teacher Yesac an epiphany that transcends life anddeath.

'The one who believes in me will live, even though they die; and whoever lives by believing in me will never die.'

"There is no life and death in the life of conformity to Jesus, who is the resurrection and the life, the Word and the Truth," said Yesac.

"Yes. The Word and the Truth are eternal," the boy agreed.

Yesac also saw a Bible verse in the boy's little notebook that enlightened him.

'You may know and understand that the Father is in me, and I in the Father,'

'The Father is in me, and I in the Father,' the boy whispered Jesus' words to himself once again.

Yesac and the boy were learning the true mercy and sacrifice of Jesus, who gave his life for the salvation, love, and care of humanity.

The boy turned the pages of the Gospel with an open expression.

'On the next day, when the great multitudes who had come to the festival heard that Jesus was coming to Jerusalem, they took palm branches to meet him, and went out to greet him, crying out, "Hosanna! Hosanna to the King of Israel, who cometh in the name of the Lord." And Jesus saw a colt, and mounted upon it: for it is written, Fear not, O daughter of Zion: behold, thy King cometh upon a colt, the colt of an ass.

Verily, verily, I say unto you, Except a grain of wheat fall into the ground and die, it abideth alone: but if it die, it bringeth forth much fruit. He that loveth his life shall lose it: but he that hateth his life in this world shall keep it unto life eternal. For I am not come to judge the world, but to save the world.'

"Jesus met a young donkey and rode it, just as the Old Testament says He came on a donkey's colt," the boy said with an innocent expression on his face.

"Jesus came as a single grain of wheat and died, bearing much fruit and saving mankind from sin." The old man opened his small notebook and said.

'Unless a kernel of wheat falls to the ground and dies, it remains only a single seed. But if it dies, it produces many seeds.'

"I think I understand now that in the Old Testament, Isaiah was referring to Christ when he saw the glory of Jesus," said the boy.

The boy recalled the words written in Yesac's little notebook.

'PilSaZeukSang PilSangZeukSa 필생즉사 필사즉생 必生則死 必死則生 ; Anyone who loves their life will lose it, while anyone who hates their life in this world will keep it for eternal life.'

"Whoever believes in Jesus believes in the God who sent him." the boy said.

"Whoever sees Christ sees the God who sent him."

The old man said and turned to John's book.

'Before the Passover, Jesus knew that the hour was coming when he would leave the world and go back to his Father, and he loved his people in the world, and he loved them to the end. And the devil had already put it into the heart of Judas Iscariot, Simon's son, to sell him. And when Jesus was at supper, knowing that the Father had given all things into his hands, and that he had come from God, and would return to God, he rose from the place where he was serving supper, and took his outer garment, and took a towel, and girded himself about the waist. Then he took a basin of water, and began to wash his disciples' feet, and to wash them with the towel which he had girded about him.

And he said unto Simon Peter,
"Lord, washest thou my feet?" Jesus answered and said unto him, "What I do thou knowest not now, but afterward shalt know."

"A new commandment I give unto you: that ye love one another; that ye love one another, as I have loved you."

Jesus answered and said unto him,
"Wilt thou lay down thy life for me?
Verily, verily, I say unto thee,
thrice shalt thou deny me before the cock croweth."
"Let not thy heart be troubled: believe in God; believe also in me. And if I go and prepare a place for you, I will come again and receive you unto myself; that where I am, there ye may be also.
Where I go, ye shall know the way."

And Thomas said unto him, "Lord, we know not whither thou goest: how shall we know the way?"
Jesus said unto him, "I am the way, the truth, and the life: no man cometh unto the Father but by me."'

"Jesus is testifying that He did not come into this world to be served or to judge. He even washes the feet of Judas and Peter, who would sell or betray him," said the boy.

"He's witnessing to the new commandment Jesus gave us before he died: love, and what a love it is," Yesac said.

"Yes. No one comes to God except through Jesus, who is the way, the truth, and the life," said the boy.

"The Bible is love." The old man said with love.

The boy carefully wrote down the Lord's new commandment in his little notebook.

'A new command I give you: Love one another. As I have lovedyou, so you must love one another.'

On Saturday and Sunday, when things were still a little more relaxed, Yesac and the boy stretched and turned to the pages of the Bible. 'You are what you eat' It's a healthy statement, of course, but Yesac and the boy were hungry for the Word. Yes, man shall not live by bread alone, but by the Word of God.

'Philip said unto him, Lord, show us the Father, and it shall besufficient for us. Jesus said unto him, Philip, I have been with youso long, and yet thou knowest me not: he that hath seen me hathseen the Father: why sayest thou, Show me the Father? Becausethou believest not that I am in the Father, and the Father in me: for the words that I speak unto you I speak not of myself, but theFather in me, and he doeth the works that I do. Believe me that Iam in the Father, and the Father in me: or if ye cannot, believe me, because of the works that I do.

Verily, verily, I say unto you, He that believeth on me, the works that I do, he shall do also, andgreater works than these; because I will do them, because I speakof the Father; and whatsoever ye shall ask in my name, that willI do, that the Father may be glorified in the Son. If ye shall ask anything in my name, I will do it. If ye love me, ye will keep my commandments. And I will ask the Father, and he will give you another Helper, that he may be with you forever, to be with youeven to the end of the age; even the Spirit of truth.'

"Philip, the disciple of Jesus, presses him to show him God," the boy said.

"When you have seen Jesus, you have seen God," Yesac said.

"The works that Jesus does are said to be the works of God in Jesus," the boy said.

"The things that we do, we do with Jesus in us, so there is nothing we can't do," the old man said.

"Yes. God has given us another Advocate, the Spirit of truth, so that we do not have any anxiety or worry or fear," said the boy.

In Yesac's little notebook, the boy saw the words of a great epiphany that the Master had received while studying in the cave.

'I tell you the truth, whoever believes in me will do the works that I am doing, and they will do even greater things than these, because I am going to the Father.'

"What does the boy learn from these enlightening words?" asked Yesac.

"It's a tremendous teaching that we can do what Jesus did and even greater things," said the boy.

"Another realization?" Yesac asked.

"----------------"

The boy was silent, and Yesac continued.

"In this statement, 'because I am going to the Father', because Jesus is going to God, we can also learn a high degree of humility." the old man said.

"Yes. That's a profound realization because no one else has ever been crucified, paid for the sins of mankind, and gone to God, so no matter how great and great things we do, all the glory goes to Jesus," said the boy.

"The glory of Jesus is the glory of God," the old man said, seemingly moved by the boy's words.

"I believe," the boy replied, his voice loud and strong.

"Above all, what we must do is keep Jesus' commandments," the old man spoke while meditating on the words.

'If you love me, keep my commands.'

"What are Jesus' commandments?" the boy asked.

"KyungChunAeIn," Yesac replied briefly.

KyungChunAeIn 敬天愛人 경천애인; Love the Lord your God with all your heart and with all your soul and with all your mind, and love your neighbor as yourself.

"I see. That's right. To love God with all our heart and soul and to love our neighbor as ourself," said the boy with love.

"You should always meditate on the Word and become the Word yourself," said Yesac.

Yesac and the boy became the Word to themselves and turned the pages of the book.

'The world receiveth me not, because it hath not seen me, neither knoweth me; but ye know me, because I dwell with you, and will be in you. I will not leave you as orphans, but will come to you. A little while, and the world will not see me again; but ye shall see me: because I live, and ye shall live; in that day ye shall know that I am in the Father, and ye in me, and I in you. He that hath my commandments, and keepeth them, he is he that lovethme: and he that loveth me shall be loved of my Father, and I willlove him, and will manifest myself unto him.

Peace I leave with you: my peace I leave with you. Let not your hearts be troubled, neither let them be afraid, for my peace I leave with you; not as the world giveth, give I unto you. Ye have heard that I go away, and come unto you: if ye had loved me, ye would have rejoiced to receive me unto my Father. For my Father is greater than I.'

Yesac and the boy praised and meditated on Jesus' words, which give us peace in our lives so that we may have no anxiety or fear.

'I am the true vine, and my Father is the vinedresser. Abide in me, and I in you. As the branch cannot bear fruit unless it is attached to the vine, so shall you be unless you remain in me. From henceforth ye shall not be called servants: for a servant knoweth not what his lord doeth: but I have called you friends: for I have made known unto you all things that I have heard of my Father: 16 Ye did not choose me, but I chose you, and have chosen you, that ye should go and bear fruit, and that your fruit should abound always, that whatsoever ye shall ask the Father in my name ye may receive it.

These things have I commanded you, that ye should love one another, but that ye might fulfill that which is written in their law, that they hated me without cause:

for when the Comforter is come, whom I will send unto you from the Father, even the Holy Ghost of truth, which proceedeth from the Father, he shall bear witness of me; and ye also bear witness, because ye have been with me from the beginning.'

"God is the farmer, Jesus is the vine, and we are the branches that bear much fruit. Jesus also speaks of the loyalty of a friend," the boy said.

"By keeping Jesus' commandments, we have earned the privilege of being his friend," Yesac added.

The boy wanted to be a real friend of Jesus, so he carefully recorded Christ's words in his little notebook.

'Greater love has no one than this: to lay down one's life for one's friends. You are my friends if you do what I command. I no longer call you servants; I have called you friends.'

The boy handed him a cup of warm green tea in response to his sudden reflection.

'I tell you the truth, it is for your good that I am going away. For if I go not away, the Comforter will not come unto you: but if I go, I will send him unto you: and he shall convict the world of sin, and of righteousness, and of judgment: of sin, because they believe not in me: and of righteousness, because I go unto the Father, and ye see me not again.'

Yesac left the text messages in the KakaoTalk room with six people. Born the youngest and only son among five older sisters, Yesac shared a KakaoTalk room with his sisters. When his father passed away at the age of 90, Yesac had heard a dream where his father told his older sister, who was begging him not to leave, "I have to go for you guys," and left. Although Yesac was always calm and composed in any situation, he showed a solemn demeanor whenever the topic of his parents came up. Seeing such a teacher, the boy could understand why the first commandment for us was to "honor your father and mother" in Moses' Ten Commandments. Filial piety can never be overemphasized, and the only time Yesac showed a solemn appearance was when it came to honoring his parents.

"Jesus went away for our good." The boy remembered the words and said.

'It is for your good that I am going away.'

"The only righteous man who gave his life for the good of mankind," Yesac added.

"Yes. He testified to righteousness by going to God.'

'About righteousness, because I am going to the Father.'

Old man Yesac turned the pages of the Gospel.

'But when he, the Holy Spirit of truth, is come, he will guide you into all truth: for he shall not speak of himself, but what he heareth; and he shall declare unto you things to come   Verily, verily, I say unto you, ye shall weep and lament, and the world shall rejoice; ye shall be sorrowful, but your sorrow shall be turned into joy. When a woman is in childbearing, she is sorrowful, for the time is come; but when she is with child, she remembers not her sorrow again for the joy that is in the world: now are ye sorrowful, but I will see you again, and your heart shall be glad, and no man shall take away your joy; and in that day ye shall ask me nothing.
Verily, verily, I say unto you, Whatsoever ye shall ask the Father, he will give you in my name. Hitherto ye have asked nothing in my name: but ask, and it shall be given you, and your joy shall be full.... These things have I spoken unto you, that in me ye might have peace. In the world ye shall have tribulation, but be of good cheer. Be of good cheer, I have overcome the world.'

The boy was learning from Jesus' teaching that God, the Truth, the Holy Spirit, and Jesus were one.

"The agony of the crucifixion became the joy of the resurrection," said the boy.

"No one can take away the joy of seeing Jesus again. It is in the arms of Jesus that we can have peace in our lives," Yesac said.

"Our friend Jesus has overcome the world, so what is there to be rough or fearful about?" the boy said.

The boy's voice was booming and unyielding.

Yesac and the boy took a breath, straightened their posture, and sat down. Jesus' holy and great prayer was being prepared.

Jesus' prayer

'And when Jesus had said these things, he lifted up his eyes to heaven, and said, Father, the hour is come: glorify thy Son, that thou mayest be glorified, and the Son may glorify thee. For thou hast given him power over all things, that he should give eternal life to all whom thou hast given him. And this is life eternal, to know the only true God, and Jesus Christ, his Son, whom he has sent. The works which thou gavest me to do, I have done, and have glorified thee in the world: glorify me, O Father, with thyself even now, with the glory which I had with thee before the foundation of the world. I have manifested thy name to them which thou gavest me out of the world.

They were thine, and thou gavest them unto me, and they have kept thy word. I have given them the words which thou hast given me, and they have received them, and have believed that I came from thee, and have believed that thou hast sent me. And I pray for them: and my prayer is not for the world, but for them which thou hast given me. They are thine own. All that are mine are thine, and thine are mine: and I am glorified in them. I am no more in the world, but they are in the world, and I go unto the Father: Holy Father, preserve them in thy name, which thou hast given me; that they may be one, even as we are.

And when I was with them, I preserved and kept them in thy name, which thou gavest me; that not one of them should perish, but the children of perdition: which fulfilleth the scripture. And now I go to the Father, and these things have I spoken unto the world, that they may have my joy in them, that my joy may be in them in full. And I have given them my Father's word, and the world hated them: because I am not of the world, neither are they of the world, as I am not of the world.

The old man and the boy were genuinely absorbed in a state of ecstasy by Jesus' great prayer.

I pray not that thou shouldest take them out of the world, but that thou shouldest keep them from falling into evil. For as I am not of the world, so are they not of the world. Sanctify them in thy truth, O Father. Thy word is truth. As thou hast sent me into the world, even so have I sent them into the world; and for their sakes I sanctify myself, that they also may be sanctified through thy truth. My prayer is not for these alone, but also for them that believe on me because of my word; that they may all be one, as thou, Father, art in me, and I in thee, that they may be in us; that the world may believe that thou hast sent me.

The glory which thou hast given me I have given them, that they may be one, even as we are one; that they may be made perfect in one, as thou, Father, art in me, and I in thee, that they may be made perfect in one; that the world may know that thou hast sent me, and hast loved them, as thou hast loved me.

Father, I will that they whom thou hast given me may be with me where I am, that they may behold thy glory, which thou hast given me, because thou hast loved me before the foundation of the world. O righteous Father, though the world hath not known thee, yet have I known thee, and they have known that thou hast sent me. I have made them know thy name, and will make them know it: that the love with which thou hast loved me may be in them, and I in them.'

Yesac and the boy remained silent for a long time. They had meditated on it so much that the book of Jesus' prayer, John 17, was more worn than Matthew's Sermon on the Mount.

In the boy's small notebook, he wrote Jesus' words that taught his teacher Yesac to experience the 'abundance of no possession'.

'All I have is yours, and all you have is mine. And glory has come to me through them, they are yours.'

"Truly holy and great is Jesus, who came into the world and lived not for himself but only for the glory of God and the peace of mankind," the boy said.

"................."

Yesac was silent for a moment.

It was the first and last time the boy had seen tears in Yesac's eyes.

His eyes were especially red in the passage where he prayed for the unity of mankind.

'Holy Father, protect them by the power of your name, the name you gave me, so that they may be one as we are one.'

The old man and the boy remained silent for a long time because of Christ's profound prayer.

'Just as the Father and I are one, may all of humanity know that they are one and protect them by the power of Your name,'

they reflected deeply on Christ's prayer, which leads to enlightenment. This prayer signified that the world would be united through the Word and humanity would become one through love, completing the journey with the novel scriptures.

The truth is that God's kingdom is within us, that all humanity in the universe is one, and that the world, which God loved so much that He gave His only Son, is a living heaven where life breathes and walks with Christ. With this realization, the boy could always rejoice, pray without ceasing, give thanks in all circumstances, and enjoy the kingdom of eternal happiness.

"The mercy and compassion of Jesus Christ, who wants to fill us with His joy, brings tears to my eyes." the boy said with gratitude and love.

When the old man remained silent, the boy continued.

"Just as Jesus and God are always together, our humanity will also become one within the truth and words inside us and love each other." the boy said with a sincere wish.

"Days when we become one and love each other? God has already created our humanity as one in love. The fact that in the beginning, there was only one language is proof of that. However, humans were divided by their pride and foolishness. Remember the Tower of Babel incident? The important thing is to realize that, just like in the beginning, our humanity is already one." The boy was silent. Yesac's thunderous words echoed through the boy's head.

The thought that the languages, once confused by human pride, might become one again with the advent of the cold, genius AI bestowed by the divine in this century flashed through the boy's mind. He smiled slightly.

Instead of yearning for humanity to unite, as Master Yesac discovered on Big Bear Mountain and the realization that 'all answers are already within oneself,' the profound truth is that humanity is already one and is the key to eternal happiness.

This profound thought resonated in the boy's mind.

"Jesus is awakening us to the love and truth of God within us," the boy said, staring at the notes in the old man's small notebook.

'The love you (God) have for me may be in them and that I myself may be in them.'

"It is the truth of God's word that sanctifies us," The old man also looked at his small notebook and said.

'Sanctify them by the truth; your word is truth.'

The boy was astonished that Yesac could recite Jesus' prayer in both Korean and English from memory. The boy had always seen his teacher striving to become the living word and to emulate Jesus.

Meanwhile, Jesus entered a garden near the Kidron Valley, where He often met with His disciples. Judas, who betrayed Jesus, was also there.

Yesac, who had always displayed a composed demeanor, turned the pages of the scripture with trembling hands today. This trembling was born out of love for humanity's peace and eternal happiness. The old man turned the page of the book.

'And the soldiers, and the tetrarch, and the chief ruler, and the servants of the Jews, seized Jesus, and bound him, and led him first to Annas: for Annas was the father-in-law of Caiaphas, the high priest of that year. And Annas delivered him bound to Caiaphas the high priest Jesus answered and said unto him, My kingdom is not of this world: for if my kingdom were of this world, my servants would have fought against it, and would not have delivered me into the hands of the Jews.
Now my kingdom is not of this world. Pilate saith unto him, Art thou then a king? Jesus answered, as thou sayest, I am a king; for this cause was I born, and for this cause came I into the world, to bear witness unto the truth. He that is of the truth heareth my voice. Then Pilate took him, and scourged him.'

"Jesus is telling Pilate, who scourged Him, that He was born for the truth and that He came into this world for the truth and to testify to the truth," said the boy.

"The truth that sets us free is God, the Word, Jesus Christ," Yesac said.

"Pilate didn't find sin in Jesus after all."

The boy fixed his eyes on the Word again.

'And the soldiers wove a crown of thorns, and put it on his head, and clothed him in a purple robe, and came before him, and said, Peace be unto thee, King of the Jews: and they smote him with the palms of their hands. And Pilate went out again, and said, Behold, I bring this man unto you, that ye may know that I find no sin in him.

And Jesus came forth, crowned with thorns, and clothed with a purple robe: and Pilate said unto them, Behold, this is the man: and when the chief priests and the servants saw him, they cried out, saying, Crucify him, crucify him. Pilate saith unto them, Take ye him, and crucify him. For I find no sin in him. The Jews answered and said unto him, We have a law, and by that law he deserveth to die: for he saith that he is the Son of God.'

In the end, the Jews crucify Jesus Christ for calling himself the Son of God.

'And by the cross of Jesus stood his mother, and his aunt, and Mary the wife of Globa, and Mary Magdalene. And when Jesus saw his mother and the disciple whom he loved standing by him, he said unto his mother, Woman, behold, it is thy son: and he said unto the disciple, Behold, thy mother: and from that time the disciple brought him into his house. .....

After this, Jesus, knowing that all things were fulfilled, and that he might answer by the Scriptures, said, I thirst: and there was a jar of wine vinegar full of sour wine. And they took a sponge dipped in sour wine, and tied it to a hyssop plant, and put it into his mouth: and when he had received the sour wine, he said, it is finished; and he bowed his head, and his spirit departed from him.'

"................."

Yesac and the boy remained silent.

'And two angels clothed in white sat at the place where Jesus' body had lain, the one at his head and the other at his feet. And the angels said unto him, Woman, why weepest thou, for I know not where the men have taken my Lord and laid him? And when she had said these things, she turned aside and saw the writings of Jesus, and knew not that it was Jesus.

And it came to pass on the same day, the first evening after the Sabbath, when the disciples had shut the doors where they were

assembled for fear of the Jews, Jesus came and stood in the midst, and said unto them, "Peace be unto you."
And when he had said these things, he showed them his hands and his side. And when his disciples saw him, they rejoiced.
Then said he to Thomas, "Reach hither thy finger, and behold my hands; and reach hither thy hand, and thrust it into my side: and be not faithless, but believing."
And Thomas answered and said unto him, "My Lord and my God."
Jesus saith unto him, "Thomas, because thou hast seen me, thou hast believed: blessed are they that have not seen, and yet have believed."

"Jesus is risen," said the boy.

"To believe without seeing, rather than to see and believe, as Thomas did, is the substance of things hoped for, the evidence of things not seen," Yesac said.

"Love is the evidence of things not seen," the boy continued.

Yesac looked at the boy, a little surprised by his words of realization.

Regardless of Yesac's feelings, the boy turned the pages of the Gospel.

'And there were with them two other disciples, Simon Peter and Thomas, whose name is Didymus, and Nathanael, a Cana of Galilee, and the sons of Zebedee, and two other disciples: and Simon Peter said, I go to fish: and they said, we will go with you: and they went out and got into the boat: and they caught nothing that night: and when it was day, Jesus stood by the sea: and his disciples knew not that it was Jesus. And he said unto them, Men, have ye any fish: and they answered him, no, we have none.'

"Jesus caught 153 fish in the sea of Tiberias." the boy said.

"After betraying Jesus, Peter jumped from the boat." Yesac said.

"Nevertheless, Jesus' love for me knows no bounds as he forgives Peter and takes care of him to the end."

"This is the same Jesus who prayed for forgiveness even for those who crucified him," Yesac said.

"How beautiful and merciful is the image of Jesus roasting the loaves and fishes on a fire of burning coals for his disciples," saidthe boy.

"We should be gracious disciples who serve our neighbors by imitating Jesus Christ, who came into this world to serve," said Yesac.

"Yes," the boy said.

"And now that the four Gospels are finished, what has the boy learned?" asked Yesac.

"It was a gracious journey through the Gospels," said the boy.

"I have seen Jesus Christ, the Prince of Obedience, prophesied in the Gospels of Matthew and Mark," Yesac said.

"I have seen Jesus Christ, the Son of God, fully human, from the Gospels of Luke and John," the boy said.

The hue shone on the faces of old man Yesac and the boy, as it did on the face of Moses as he came down from Mount Sinai carrying the cross. It was a picture of the light of the world with God and Jesus together.

SJCB Dialogue - Gospel of John

"The Gospel of John is a unique gospel that deeply reveals the divinity and love of Jesus, as well as salvation and life within the truth. We must listen closely to the teaching that 'The Word was God.' That Word is the unchanging Scripture, the truth itself, and Jesus Himself." Buddha Siddhartha spoke calmly as he looked at a slightly worn scripture.

"Jesus is not merely a prophet but the embodiment of God's love who came into the world in human flesh. Jesus is the light of the world, the lamp of life and hope to humanity wandering in the darkness. God and Jesus are one—and they are love." Socrates spoke the truth with clear eyes.

"Eternal life is knowing God and Jesus. It is not found in knowledge or achievement, but in a relationship that longs for the Word. The Lamb who holds and guides lost humanity to the end—Jesus is the way, the truth, and the life." Confucius spoke with life.

"The way to be free and bold, breaking free from the oppression and bondage of life, is to realize the truth of the Word that sets us free. The cross is love that overcame death and a promise of life that transcends time and the flesh. We dwell in God, and God dwells in us." Jesus spoke these words with holiness, filled with love for all humanity.

"The Gospels offer a multi-dimensional description of Jesus through his life, teachings, personality, his death, and resurrection. These accounts help us better understand his message, his mission, and the depth of his compassion for the people." The boy spoke with love for humanity.

"The gospels invite the readers to experience the transformation that comes through Jesus' grace and love and also compels us to respond in faith while following the disciples of Jesus." As the old man spoke with grace, Buddha and Jesus opened the book of Acts side by side.

Chapter 2: Acts of the Apostles

Volume 5: Acts

"What is the book of Acts?" Yesac asked after returning from his morning workout.
"The Acts of the Apostles(사도행전 使徒行傳), as the name suggests, is a book that records the activities of the apostles after Jesus ascended into heaven. Written by Luke 1943 years ago, Acts and Luke's Gospel were originally written as one book, making it the largest book in the New Testament, comprising about 28%. The English name of the book is Acts, which means todo, just as the Master, you always emphasized." the boy's response was unstoppable.

"Remember, faith without acts is dead, unless you put it into practice in your life. Peter, Philip, and Paul spent 29 years preaching the gospel to Jews, Samaritans, and Gentiles. It's not just the boy and I. We're all God's apostles, taking the gospel to the ends of the earth," said Yesac.

"Yes. Peter, Philip, and Paul preached the gospel in Jerusalem, Judea, Samaria, and then to the ends of the earth, with all their sufferings," the boy said.

After a quick breakfast of Korean kimbap, Yesac flipped to the book's first page and chronicled the apostles' travels.

'Theophilus, in the first things which I have written, I have written the things which Jesus began to do and to teach, from the beginning of his ministry, when he commanded his chosen apostles with the Holy Ghost, unto the day that he ascended into heaven. And after his sufferings he manifested himself unto them with many convincing evidences, and appeared unto them forty days, and spake unto them the things of the kingdom of God: and when he had assembled them together as an apostle, he charged them, saying, Depart not from Jerusalem, but wait for the things which I have heard of, and which the Father hath promised.

For John baptized with water, but ye shall be baptized with the HolyGhost in a few days. And when they were assembled together, they asked him, saying, Is it not time for the Lord to restore the kingdom of Israel? And he said unto them, The Father hath set the times and the end in his own power: but ye shall receive power when the Holy Ghost is come upon you: and ye shall be witnesses unto me both in Jerusalem, and in all Judea, and in Samaria, and unto the uttermost part of the earth. And when he had said these things, he was taken up out of their sight: and a cloud overshadowed him, that he should not be seen. And when he was taken up, his disciples were gazing intently into heaven: and two men in white stood by them, saying, Men of Galilee, why stand ye standing and gazing into heaven: for this Jesus, which is taken up from among you, shall come in the same manner as he was taken up into heaven.

And the disciples returned unto Jerusalem from the mount which is called the garden of Olives, which is near unto Jerusalem, and a good way to go on the Sabbath day. And they went up into the upper room, and found Peter, and John, and James, and Andrew, and Philip, and Thomas, and Bartholomew, and Matthew, and James the son of Alphaeus, and Simon the son of Zebedee, and Judas the son of James: and there were all the women, and Mary the mother of Jesus, and the brothers of Jesus, all of them of one accord in prayer.'

"Jesus' disciples usually practiced on a boat close to Jerusalem, studying Jesus' words," the boy said.

"In English, it's called the Mount of Olives. Olives are an absolute health food," Yesac said.

"When is Jesus coming again? They say it's the day of the Second Coming," the boy asked.

Instead of answering, Yesac wrote directly into the boy's little notebook.

'It is not for you to know the times or dates the Father has set by his own authority.'

"So does the Master live beyond time and space, or does it mean nothing to old man because God is always in him?" The boy whispered to himself.

"And did you receive power when the Holy Spirit comes on, enough to preach the gospel to the ends of the earth?" the boy asked.

"Each one receives his own portion," Yesac replied.

The week has already gone by like an arrow. Today is another soccer game day, and Yesac, the 63-year-old healthy man, is heading to the soccer field in two hours.
Regardless, the old man Yesac turned the pages of the book.

'And they were all filled with the Holy Ghost, and began to speak in other tongues as the Spirit gave them utterance..."
"I will show wonders in the heavens above and signs on the earth below—blood, fire, and smoke. The sun shall be turned to darkness and the moon to blood before the coming of the great and glorious day of the Lord. And everyone who calls upon the name of the Lord shall be saved.

He was handed over by the predetermined plan and foreknowledge of God; and you, with the help of lawless men, put Him to death by nailing Him to the cross. But God broke the chains of death and raised Him up, for it was impossible for death to hold Him.

He foresaw the resurrection of the Christ, that He would not be abandoned to Hades, nor would His body see decay. Of this, we are all witnesses. David did not ascend into heaven, yet he spoke...
Then Peter said, 'Repent, and let each of you be baptized in the name of Jesus Christ for the forgiveness of your sins, and you will receive the gift of the Holy Ghost.'

All the believers were together and had everything in common. They sold their property and possessions and distributed to anyone who had need. Day by day, they continued to meet together in the temple courts. They broke bread in their homes and ate together with glad and sincere hearts, praising God and enjoying the favor of all the people. And the Lord added to their number daily those who were being saved."

"Do you speak in other tongues when the Holy Spirit comes on you?" the boy asked, disregarding the old man's words that loving one's neighbor is more important than speaking in tongues.

"As much as God gives us," replied Yesac.

"Who will be saved?" the boy inquired.

"Everyone who calls on the name of the Lord," Yesac replied.

"God raised Jesus from the dead, freeing him from the agony of death," the boy said.

"Because it was impossible for death to keep its hold on him," said Yesac.

"David did not ascend to heaven," the boy said.

"There is only one righteous man, Jesus Christ," Yesac said.

"The Holy Spirit is a gift, so how can I receive it?" the boy asked.

"Repent and be baptized, every one of you, in the name of Jesus Christ, for the forgiveness of your sins, and you will receivethe gift of the Holy Spirit," Yesac responded.

Yesac and the boy prayed together, expressing their hope that the Lord would add to the number of saved people every day. Weare all apostles of Jesus to inherit and advance God's world.

"Master, you really enjoy your food?" the boy said as he looked at Yesac, who was eating an apple and an egg before heading to the soccer field.

"Eat with glad and sincere hearts because the Word says to eat with joy and purity of heart," Yesac said as he packed his soccer bag.

The boy turned the pages of Acts of the Apostles.

'And Peter said unto him, Silver and gold I have not, but with what I have I give thee, that thou mayest walk in the name of Jesus Christ of Nazareth: and he took him by the right hand, and lifted him up: and his feet and his ankles received strength, and he leaped up and walked, and went with them into the temple, walking and leaping, and praising God: and all the people when they saw him walking and praising God, thought that he was the man that used to sit at the gate of the temple, begging, and were greatly astonished and marveled at what was done unto him.
And the better man took hold of Peter and John: and all the people were greatly astonished, and ran, and were gathered together to the act, which they called the act of Solomon: and when Peter saw it, he said unto the people, Men of Israel, why marvel at this thing, as if by our power and piety we had made this man walk. For the God of Abraham, and of Isaac, and of Jacob, the God of our fathers, hath glorified his servant, Jesus. as Moses said, The Lord God will raise up for you

a prophet like unto me from among your brethren, and ye shall hear all his words, whatsoever they may be.'

"It's an amazing transformation of Peter, who betrayed and denied Jesus, and now he's not only healing the sick and performing the miracles that Jesus did, but he's also preaching as a witness to Jesus," said the boy.

"That's how great the gift of the Holy Spirit is, to change people," said Yesac.

The boy flipped to the book of Acts.

'Rulers and elders of the people! If we are being called to account today for an act of kindness shown to a man who was lame and is being asked how he was healed, then know this, you and all the people of Israel: It is by the name of Jesus Christ of Nazareth, whom you crucified but whom God raised from the dead, that this man stands before you healed. Jesus is "the stone you builders rejected, which has become the cornerstone." ... Stretch out your hand to heal and perform signs and wonders through the name of your holy servant Jesus. After they prayed, the place where they were meeting was shaken, and they were all filled with the Holy Spirit and boldly spoke the word of God.

All the believers were one in heart and mind. No one claimed that any of their possessions was theirs, but they shared everything they had. With great power, the apostles continued to testify to the resurrection of the Lord Jesus. And God's grace was so powerfully at work in them all that there were no needy persons among them. For from time to time, those who owned land or houses sold them, brought the money from the sales, and put it at the apostles' feet, and it was distributed to anyone who had need. But Peter and the apostles replied, We must obey God rather than human beings!'

Meanwhile, like the suffering of Jesus, trials and tribulations also came upon Peter and John.

'"Brothers and sisters, choose seven men from among you who are known to be full of the Spirit and wisdom. We will hand over this responsibility to them and devote ourselves to prayer and the ministry of the word."

This proposal pleased the whole gathering. They chose Stephen—a man full of faith and of the Holy Spirit—along with Philip, Prochorus,

Nicanor, Timon, Parmenas, and Nicolas from Antioch, a convert to Judaism. These men were presented to the apostles, who prayed and laid their hands on them.

All who were seated in the Sanhedrin fixed their eyes on Stephen and saw that his face shone like the face of an angel.
Then the high priest asked him, "Are these charges true?"

Stephen replied,
"Brothers and fathers, listen to me! The God of glory appeared to our father Abraham while he was still in Mesopotamia, before he lived in Haran. 'Leave your country and your people,' God said, 'and go to the land I will show you.' So he left the land of the Chaldeans and settled in Haran. After the death of his father, God sent him to this land where you now live."

Even in the face of hostility, Stephen stood unwavering in faith, his voice steady with conviction. He boldly proclaimed the word of God.'

"The number of Jesus' disciples increased as they added to the seven those who were praised for being full of faith, the Holy Spirit, and wisdom." the old man said.

"These were Stephen, Philip, Brogorus, Nicanor, Timon, Barmena, Nicolas, and Nigella. Stephen, Philip, Procorus, Nicanor, Timon, Parmenas, Nicolas," read the boy.

"I wish I had the face of an angel like Stephen. Stephen's face was like the face of an angel," the boy said, thinking of Yesac, whose face often shone.

"That's what happens when the Holy Spirit comes upon you. Like Moses." Yesac suddenly called out, startling the boy.

After returning from the soccer game, Yesac's face was bright. Today, the team had won 4:2 against the Americans. He was a compassionate old man, but when it came to the world of competition, he was as cold and decisive as the situation demanded.

Together, the two once again began their lessons with Yesac reading out the words.

'"The covenant of circumcision was given to Abraham. He became the father of Isaac, and circumcised him on the eighth day. Isaac became the father of Jacob, and Jacob the father of the twelve patriarchs.

Because of jealousy, the patriarchs sold Joseph into Egypt—but God was with him. He rescued him from all his afflictions, and granted him favor and wisdom before Pharaoh, king of Egypt, who made him ruler over Egypt and all his household.

Then Joseph sent for his father Jacob and his whole family—seventy-five in all.

Moses was born, beautiful in the sight of God. He was raised for three months in his father's house. But when he was exposed, Pharaoh's daughter took him and brought him up as her own son. Moses was educated in all the wisdom of the Egyptians and became powerful in speech and action.

When he was forty years old, an angel appeared to him in the wilderness of Sinai, in the flame of a burning bush. As he approached to understand the vision, the voice of the Lord called out:

"I am the God of your fathers—the God of Abraham, Isaac, and Jacob."

Moses trembled and dared not look. Then the Lord said to him: "Take off your sandals, for the place where you are standing is holy ground. I have indeed seen the oppression of my people in Egypt. I have heard their groaning, and I have come down to deliver them."'

"It seems like just yesterday we were studying Genesis, and now we're studying Acts. It's refreshing to see Stephen bring back Abraham, Isaac, Jacob, Joseph, and Moses," remarked the boy.

"It's refreshing to hear God's words to Moses, 'Take off your shoes from your feet, for the ground you are standing on is holy ground,'" said Yesac.

"Yes. The Master said that if we are with the Lord Jesus, that place is holy ground, and that's why we are always walking in heaven," the boy agreed, smiling.

Yesac gave the boy a 9 out of 10 because he lives by what they studied together. In today's soccer game, the boy gave Yesac a 9.5 because he completed 100% of his passes and didn't lose the ball once. His teammate Samsong also praised 62-year-old man Yesac's ball control.

Later, Yesac and the boy listened to a sermon by Stephen, a great deacon in the early church after Jesus' ascension.

'This is Moses, the man who led the people out of Egypt and did signs and wonders in the Red Sea and the wilderness for forty years, saying to the children of Israel, 'God will raise for you a prophet like me from among your brethren. This is the same Moses who was with the angel who spoke on Mount Sinai, and with our fathers in the church in the wilderness, who received the living words, and gave them to us.

And our fathers received them and brought them with Joshua when they took possession of the land of the Gentiles, whom God had driven out from before us, until David. And David found favor with God, and asked that he might prepare a house of God for the house of Jacob, and Solomon built him a house; but the Most High dwelleth not in a house made with hands, as the prophet hath said, the heavens are my throne, and the earth is the footstool of my feet: what house will ye build for me, and where shall I rest?

....And Stephen, being filled with the Holy Ghost, lifted up his eyes to heaven, and saw the glory of God, and Jesus standing at the right hand of God, and said, Behold, the heavens are opened, and I see the Son of man standing at the right hand of God: and they shouted with a loud voice, and plugged their ears, and rushed upon him with one accord, and cast him out of the city, and stoned him: and the witnesses took off their clothes, and laid them at the feet of a young man named Saul. And when they had stoned him, he cried out, saying, Lord Jesus, receive my spirit: and falling on his knees, he cried out with a loud voice, saying, Lord, lay not this sin to their charge.'

"Stephen was martyred because he warned the Jews of their idolatry and formal religion and identified Jesus as the only true Savior," explained Yesac.

"The image of Stephen praying, 'Lord, do not hold this sin against them,' even as he was being stoned to death, reminds me of Jesus on the cross," noted the boy.

Moved by Stephen's prayer for his enemies even on his deathbed, Yesac said, "Thank you, Jesus, for making heaven our throne and the earth our footstool. Heaven is our throne, and the earth is our footstool."

"A man!"

Yesac pressed his lips to his cup of green tea and amended.

'In that day there was a great persecution against the church in Jerusalem, and they were scattered abroad throughout all the land of Judea and Samaria, except the apostles; and the godly men wept bitterly for the burial of Stephen. And when Saul had destroyed the church, he went into every house, and took men and women, and delivered them into prison; and they that were scattered went about, and preached the word of the gospel: and Philip went down to a city in Samaria, and preached Christ unto the people: and the multitude heard his words, and saw the signs which he did, and followed him with one accord.

when they believed that Philip preached the kingdom of God, and the name of Jesus Christ, they were baptized, both men and women: and Simon also believed, and was baptized, and followed him with all his heart, and marveled at the signs which he did, and at the mighty works. And when Simon saw that they received the Holy Ghost at the laying on of the apostles' hands, he offered them money, saying, give me also this power: that whosoever I lay my hands upon may receive the Holy Ghost. And the messenger of the Lord said unto Philip, Arise, turn thou southward, and go from Jerusalem unto the road that goeth down to Gaza: for it is a desert road.

'And when he arose and went, he saw an Ethiopian, a eunuch [jú:nsk] of great authority, who had charge of all the treasury of Kandake, the queen of Ethiopia, coming to Jerusalem to worship, and returning, riding in a chariot, and reading the words of Isaiah the prophet. And he commanded That the chariot should stay,
and that Philip and the eunuch should both go down into the water, and that Philip should baptize him, and that they should both come up out of the water; and the Spirit of the Lord should lead Philip. The eunuch went his way and was not seen again. Philip appeared at Azotus, and went through many cities, and preached the gospel, and came to Caesarea.'

Yesac pressed his lips to his cup once more and began to teach the boy about Stephen.

"It was 34 AD when Stephen, one of the seven deacons after the 12 apostles of Jesus Christ, became the first recorded martyr," said Yesac.

"A man of great knowledge of the Scriptures, Stephen was a young man full of faith and the Holy Spirit," the boy said.

"He was a second-generation apostle of Jesus who was known for his grace and power, and he worked many miracles among the people," the old man said.

"Next, Philip traveled through the wilderness and the cities of Samaria, preaching the gospel and traveling to Caesarea," the boy said.

"Like Jesus, who loved all mankind, Philip showed great mercy by converting an Ethiopian eunuch, loving the Gentiles as his own," said Yesac.

"Simon is rebuked by Peter for thinking that the Holy Spirit, a gift of God, can be bought with money. May your money perish with you because you thought you could buy the gift of God with money!" the boy continued.

"The more precious things are not bought with money. Or, to put it another way, the things that money can buy may not be precious." Yesac finished.

"Love, air, faith, dreams, hopes, freedom, happiness, gratitude, etc. These are precious things that money can't buy and can't live without." The boy pointed out.

"Yes. Joy, peace, mercy, gentleness." Yesac whispered the words that neither the boy nor he could see or buy but that guided their lives to happiness for those who have ears to hear.

"And he fell to the ground and heard a voice, saying, Saul, Saul, why persecutest thou me? And he answered and said, Lord, let me go; for I am Jesus whom thou persecuteth... And Saul rose up from the ground and opened his eyes but saw nothing. He was led by the hand of men into Damascus, and he saw no sight for three days and abstained from food. And there was a disciple in Damascus, whose name was Ananias: and the Lord called unto him in a vision, and said unto him, Behold, I am Jesus whom thou persecutest. And the LORD said unto him, Go, for this man is my vessel, whom I have chosen to bear my name before the Gentiles, and before kings, and before the children of Israel: .... Saul ate and was strengthened.

Saul tarried a few days with his disciples (disáipsl) in Damascus and immediately began to preach in every synagogue that Jesus was the Son of God: and all that heard him were astonished, saying, is not this the man that destroyed them that called upon this name in Jerusalem, and that came hither to bind them, and to bring them to the chief priests? Saul grew stronger, proved that Jesus was the Christ, and brought the Jews of Damascus into subjection.

Saul went to Jerusalem to make disciples, but they were afraid. They did not believe in his discipleship: and Barnabas took him, and brought him to the apostles, and told them how he had seen the Lord on the road, and what the Lord had said unto him, and how he had spoken boldly in the name of Jesus in Damascus. And the church in all Judea, Galilee, and Samaria stood fast in peace, and proceeded in the fear of the Lord, and the comfort of the Holy Ghost, and were increased in number."

"Peter was an apostle who had a great influence on the Jews," the boy noted.

"Paul's encounter with Jesus resulted in a remarkable transformation that extended beyond Judaism and Palestine to the entire human race." Yesac agreed and read on.

"With the help of Jesus, Saul made a remarkable transformation, spreading the gospel to mankind with the fear of the Lord and encouraged by the Holy Spirit."

"When anyone receives power from Jesus, there is nothing he can't accomplish," declared the boy.

Yesac nodded with a knowing smile—for he had lived it. It had been six months since he began strength training. By combining cardio and weight training, the 63-year-old's body had not aged but grown younger. Even when he ran, his lung capacity surpassed that of a young boy. The body and mind are one (SimSinIlYeo, 心身一如, 심신일여). The boy began to grasp this truth: that maintaining both mind and body in their best condition was yet another key to attaining eternal happiness. With diligence and a lively spirit, it was never a burden, and the old man's secret to lasting joy lay precisely in that realization.

"How can people long for happiness," the boy wondered, "while neglecting such a simple truth?"
He frowned, troubled, and pondered humanity's restless pursuit of happiness—as he turned the pages of the Acts.

'There was a man in Caesarea, whose name was Cornelius, centurion of the army, called the Italian Regiment; and he was pious, and feared God with all his house, saved many people, and

prayed to God all the time. And all the house of Judea praised him, and he was sent by a holy angel to call thee unto his house to hear him, and said unto him, Ye know that it is lawful for a Jew to have fellowship with a Gentile, and to be near him: but God commanded me, saying, call no man unclean or unclean, and send a man to Joppa, and ask for Simon, whose name is Peter. And he said, He dwelleth in the house of Simon the son of Zebedee, which is by the seashore.... And Peter opened his mouth, and said, I know that God is no respecter of persons, butthat he accepteth him that feareth God, and worketh righteousness among all nations. And God anointed Jesus of Nazareth with the Holy Ghost, and with power: and he went about, doing good works, and healing all that were oppressed ofthe devil: for God was with him.... And all the circumcised believers that came with Peter were astonished because of the outpouring of the Holy Ghost upon the Gentiles: for they spake with tongues, and heard God glorified.'

Yesac stopped here for a few moments to impart some lessons on to the boy.

"Cornelius was a righteous and God-fearing man who saved many people and was always praying, just like Tabitha, the female disciple of Joppa. Cornelius broke out of the formal legalism of Judaism as a bird breaks out of its egg, and practiced the great mercy and love of Christ, which transcends nations, races, and cultures to encompass all humanity," the old man said.

The boy looked at his teacher thoughtfully.

"The teachings from the Analects that you shared with me last time brought me great enlightenment," the boy said, recalling the contents recorded in the old man's small notebook.

'GunJa(君子군자) KeungYiBuJaeng GunYiBuDang (君子 矜而不爭 群而不黨 군자긍이부쟁 군이부당); The righteous person feels compassion for others without engaging in disputes, associates with others but does not create factions.'

Yesac nodded, before continuing on with his explanations.

"That was Christ's teaching to enlighten Jews who were bound by law and blood ties and discriminated against Gentiles," the old man said.

"Peter and Cornelius practiced these words of Jesus and became the cornerstone of the first Gentile church, the Church of Antioch," the boy said.

"SaHaeJiNae GaeHyungJeYa 사해지내 개형제야 四海之內, 皆兄弟也), all brothers within the fou seas are brothers and sisters, and all human beings in the whole world are brothers and sisters. The spirit of repentance and salvation is God's gift to all our neighbors, including the Gentiles." The old man's words were always as free as flowing water, never hindered.

"God, who does not show favoritism, has taught me that I should not call anyone impure or unclean God has shown me that I should not call anyone impure or unclean." The boy thought of Rahab, the prostitute of Jericho who helped Joshua and became part of the lineage of Jesus, and he said.

"By judging people by their appearance, the suffering and conflict that block happiness begin," Yesac said, recalling Luke 6:37 and 1 Corinthians 12. The old man, not adding or subtracting from the word, observed his neighbors just as they were, and by knowing that we are different parts of Christ's body, he could always maintain a peaceful and happy heart.

The 100-degree Texas weather was long gone, and a crisp fall breeze was blowing in. Yesac and the boy enjoyed the crisp fall weather and ate ramen and kimbap for lunch at the office as they continued the lesson, learning now about Barnabas.

The boy, with a free expression, turned the pages of the Acts.

'Now Barnabas was a good man, full of the Holy Spirit and faith, and a great multitude was added to the Lord. And Barnabas went to Tarsus to seek Saul and found him, and brought him to Antioch, and they were together in the church a year and taught the great multitude: and it was in Antioch that the disciples were called Christians.

Then King Herod lifted his hand against some of the church, and slew James the brother of John with the sword: and when he saw that the Jews rejoiced at this, he sought to take Peter also: and it being the festival of the unleavened bread, he took him, and put him in prison, and committed him to the charge of four soldiers, who were four in number, to guard him, and to bring him out before the people after the Passover. Now Peter was in prison, and the church prayed earnestly to God for him, And suddenly the messenger of the Lord stood by him, and there shone in the prison a brightness, and struck him on the side, and woke him up, saying, arise quickly, and the chains were loosed from his hands. And the angel said unto him, put on a girdle, and take up the gods: but Peter did as he was told: and the angel said unto him, put on thy outer garment, and follow me: and Peter came out and followed him: for he knew not whether the angel's words were true, or whether he saw a vision.'

The boy sighed, looking wistful.

"I want to be a good man, full of the Holy Spirit and faith, like Barnabas, so that I can bring many people to God. Barnabas was a good man, full of the Holy Spirit and faith, and a great number of people were brought to the Lord."

"When you live by the words of Jesus, that's great evangelism," said Yesac, encouragingly.

The boy turned to Luke's book of Acts and read out its words.

'Then Peter came to his senses, and said, I know now indeed that the Lord hath sent his angel to deliver me out of the hand of Herod, and out of all the expectation of the Jews: And Peter beckoned unto them, and told them what the Lord had done to bring him out of the prison: and he bade James and the brethren tell these things and departed, and went to another place.
And
Herod chose a day, and sat upon the throne, clothed in his royal robes, and spake to the people in an eloquent manner: and the people cried aloud, saying, this is the voice of God, and not of man: but because Herod would not give glory to God, the messenger of the Lord smote him, and the worms were eaten up, and he died: and the word of God was multiplied. And Barnabas and Saul returned from Jerusalem, taking with them John, whose name is Mark, from the work of the mission.'

Suddenly a thought came to the boy "King Herod, who did not recognize the voice of a god and killed James, was eaten by worms."

The old man nodded, "This was the punishment for the sin of those who persecuted the apostles, even though they had ears to hear."

"Peter, who recognized the voice of God, experienced the miracle of being released from prison, the valley of the shadow of death." As the boy spoke, he flipped through the pages of the book that chronicled the apostles' lives.

'Now there were teachers in the church at Antioch: Barnabas, Simeon called Niger, Lucius of Cyrene, Manaen (a close companion of Herod the tetrarch), and Saul.

As they were worshiping the Lord and fasting, the Holy Spirit said, "Set apart Barnabas and Saul for the work to which I have called them."
So they fasted and prayed, laid their hands on them, and sent them off.

Paul and his companions set sail from Paphos and arrived at Perga in Pamphylia. John, however, left them and returned to Jerusalem. From Perga, they continued on to Pisidian Antioch. On the Sabbath, they entered the synagogue and sat down.
Then Paul stood up, motioned with his hand, and said:
"Men of Israel, and you who fear God, listen to me!
Therefore, brothers, I proclaim to you the forgiveness of sins through Jesus Christ. Through Him, everyone who believes is justified from everything you could not be justified from under the law of Moses."'

"Barnabas and Nigel, Lugio and Manaen, Saul, and Paul served the church in Antioch," said the boy contemplatively.

Yesac nodded. "We'll have to listen to Paul's great sermon about how we can't be justified by the law but by faith in Jesus Christ."

"Yes. Conforming to Jesus, who is the way, the truth, and the life, is the way to be justified," agreed the boy.

"Those who have found divinity and humanity in the person of Christ are the people of Antioch, Paul's main stage." The old man noted.

'And many devout people—both Jews and converts to Judaism—began to follow Paul and Barnabas. The two apostles spoke to them, urging them to continue in the grace of God.

On the following Sabbath, nearly the entire city gathered to hear the word of God. But when the Jews saw the crowds, they were filled with envy and began to oppose and slander what Paul was saying.

Still, Paul and Barnabas spoke boldly:

"It was necessary that the word of God be spoken to you first. But since you reject it and judge yourselves unworthy of eternal life, we now turn to the Gentiles.

For this is what the Lord has commanded us:
'I have made you a light to the Gentiles, that you may bring salvation to the ends of the earth.'"

When the Gentiles heard this, they rejoiced and glorified the word of the Lord. And all who were appointed for eternal life believed.

The word of the Lord spread throughout the whole region. But the Jews stirred up devout women of high standing and the leading men of the city. They incited persecution against Paul and Barnabas and expelled them from their region.

So the apostles shook the dust off their feet and went on to Iconium. But the disciples were filled with joy and the Holy Spirit.'

The boy flipped through the pages.

"The gospel journey of Paul, Barnabas, and Mark, witnessing to Jesus as the fulfillment of the Davidic covenant and the forgiveness of sins through him, continues from Indio to Rome."

Yesac nodded. "Yes. Christ's will be being fulfilled by making Paul and Barnabas a light for the Gentiles, bringing salvation to the ends of the earth."

"How gracious it is to see the Gentiles rejoicing in the knowledge that they will receive eternal life," chirped the boy.

"How beautiful the disciples were filled with joy and with the Holy Spirit," agreed Yesac.

Yesac and the boy were also filled with love and the Holy Spirit, and their faces were radiant.

For lunch, they went to Whataburger. Not many people had come in yet, so they decided to once again open the book once and continue the lesson.

'And when Paul heard him speaking, he took notice of him, and when he saw that he had faith worthy of salvation, he cried out with a loud voice, saying, stand up on all fours; and the man leaped and walked. And when the multitude saw what Paul had done, they cried out in the Lycaonian tongue, saying, Gods have

come down among us in the form of men. Barnabas is called Zeus, and Paul is called Hermes, because he is a speaker among them, and said unto them, why do ye these things, for we are men of the same sex as ye, only human. For we preach unto you the gospel, that ye should turn from these vain things, and return unto the living God, who hath made heaven and earth, and the sea, and all that is in them.

And exhorting the disciples to harden their hearts, and to abide in this faith, and to know that we must go through many tribulations to enter the kingdom of God, they chose elders from every church and fasted and prayed, and committed them to the Lord for their faith. And Pamphylia, preached the word in Perga, and went down to Attalia, and from thence by ship to Antioch, where they had formerly implored the grace of God for the work which the two apostles had accomplished.'

"Paul and Barnabas, who was called the son of encouragement, traveled through Ignatian, Lystra, and Derbe in Asia Minor and returned to Antioch," Yesac explained.

The boy smiled. "I like Paul's sermons where he teaches people who want to deify themselves by calling themselves Zeus or Hermes for healing the sick and working miracles, that the Holy Spirit and Jesus are the masters of evangelism."

In the boy's small notebook, he wrote down Paul's sermon.

'We must go through many hardships to enter the kingdom of God.'

"We must always dwell on God's word and be enlightened by it so that we can always walk with Jesus in heaven," said Yesac.

'The apostles, the elders, and the whole church agreed to choose men from among them and send them to Antioch with Paul and Barnabas. Among those chosen were Judas and Silas—leaders among the believers, also known as Barsabbas.

They were sent along with our beloved Barnabas and Paul, who had risked their lives for the name of our Lord Jesus Christ.
Paul then traveled to Derbe and Lystra. There, he met a disciple named Timothy, whose mother was a Jewish believer and whose father was a Greek.

At one point, Paul was deeply troubled and turned to a man tormented

> *by a demon. He said,*
> *"In the name of Jesus Christ, I command you—come out of him!"*
> *And the demon left the man immediately.*
> *Later, the man who had been freed asked earnestly,*
> *"Men and teachers, what must I do to be saved?"'*

"Paul met Timothy, a good disciple, in Lystra, and meeting Timothy was to Paul what giving wings to a tiger was to a tiger," explained Yesac.

In the boy's little notebook, Jesus' big teaching for humanity was written.

> *'He did not discriminate between us and them, for he purified their hearts by faith.'*

From Peter's testimony that God did not discriminate between Gentiles and Jews, but purified their hearts by faith, the boy was gradually learning how to love all humanity without discrimination.

> *'Believe in the Lord Jesus, and you will be saved—you and your household.'*

Why did the boy, who trusted and believed 100% in the words of the Bible, place three question marks? It was because he recalled an old conversation with the old man, Yesac.

In Korean Bible translations, the fact that both salvationand saveare translated as 'GuWon 久遠 구원' could pose serious problems for poor souls," said Yesac. Although usually untroubled, his expression was unusually serious.

"........................" The boy, not understanding, remained silent.

"The word salvation, meaning 'to be saved,' appears about 160 times in the Bible, and save, meaning 'to be preserved or protected,' appears about 200 times. The fact that Korean Bible translations render both of these words as salvation 360 times isa source of theological or religious confusion for imperfect humans. Even now, we must correct this to help all neighbors grow healthy and upright in their religious lives."

"1987 was a particularly bleak year for South Korea, marked by many tragedies. Following the Odaeyang incident, incidents exploiting salvation as bait have continued without end, which only proves that the errors in Bible translation have been fatal," the boy said, recalling the words recorded in Yesac's little notebook.

'More important than individual salvation is to love God with all you have and to regard others as better than yourself, loving them as your own body. In doing so, salvation naturally comes as a gift from God, and within walking with Christ, salvation is already there.'

"When will true enlightenment come to modern people who have already surpassed the benefits of advanced civilization like AI?" the boy said while staring off into the distant mountains.

Just by studying and realizing the mistranslated Bible verses with the old man, the boy could protect himself from being misled and could live freely. After all, enlightenment is the secret pathway to freedom.

The boy, who was gaining enlightenment, expressed gratitude as Yesac turned the pages of the Acts of the Apostles with a compassionate expression.

'And we came to Amphipolis and Apollonia, and came to Thessalonica: and there was a synagogue of the Jews there, which explained the will, and proved that Christ must suffer and rise again from the dead, and said, this is the Christ, whom I preach unto you. And the Berean Jews, being more gentlemen than they which were in Thessalonica, received the word with eagerness, and searched the Scriptures daily to see whether this was so.

Having made of one blood all the families of mankind to dwell on all the face of the earth, and having appointed times and years for their dwelling, and bounded the boundaries of their habitation, that man might grope after God, and find him: but he is not far off from each one of us. For in the days of ignorance, God was not slack: but now he commandeth all men everywhere to repent. After these things, Paul departed from Athens, and came to Corinth.

'Silas and Timothy came down from Macedonia, and Paul was caught up in the word of God, and testified unto the Jews that Jesus is the Christ, and in the night the Lord spake unto Paul in a vision, saying, Fear not, be not silent, but speak. For I am with thee, and no man shall prevail against thee to do thee any harm: for in this city are many of my people.'

"Paul finally begins his grueling evangelism in Corinth, the center of idolatry and material civilization," Yesac noted with satisfaction.

"Paul had couples that God sent to him, like Timothy and Silas and Aquila and Priscilla," noted the boy.

Yesac nodded. "Yes. And Paul had powerful words of comfort and strength from God."

In the boy's little notebook, God's words to Paul were recorded.

'Do not be afraid; keep on speaking, do not be silent. For I am with you, and no one is going to attack and harm you. Praise be to God, who made all the families of mankind of one blood and made them dwell on all the face of the earth. From one man, he made all the nations that they should inhabit the whole earth, and he marked out their appointed times in history and the boundaries of their lands.'

"A man!"

As the boy read the words, the old man said, 'A men.'

It was lunchtime, and the Whataburger restaurant was beginning to fill up with customers. Yesac and the boy closed the book of Acts to make room. Even though they couldn't order food, they were grateful that the restaurant didn't kick them out. They left the restaurant and headed to the car.

'And it came to pass, when Apollos was at Corinth, that Paul went up into the upper country, and came to Ephesus, and met certain of the disciples, who said unto him, did ye receive the Holy Ghost when ye believed? And Paul said unto them, what baptism then were ye baptized with? And Paul said unto them, John baptized with the baptism of repentance, saying unto them, believe on him that cometh after me, which is Jesus: and they heard, and were baptized in the name of the Lord Jesus: and Paul laid his hands upon them: and the Holy Ghost came upon them: and they spake with other tongues, and prophesied: and there were about twelve of them.

'And Paul went into the synagogue three months, boldly preaching and exhorting them concerning the kingdom of God: but some were hardened in heart, and would not obey, but slandered this doctrine before the multitude: and Paul left them, and set apart disciples, and preached daily in the lecture hall of

Tyrannus: and so, he did for two years: and all that dwelt in Asia heard him, both Jews and Greeks. And God enabled him to do wonderful works by the hands of Paul, even as they took a handkerchief or apron from his body, and laid it on a sick man, and the sickness departed from him, and the devil went out of him: for the word of the Lord had power. And prevailed.'

"If Jerusalem was the center of evangelism to the Jews, Antioch in Syria was the center of evangelism to the Gentiles." The boy noted.

Yesac nodded, instructing the boy further. "Paul gained Silas, Timothy, and Luke to spur his evangelism, but he was beaten and imprisoned."

"The living Word of God worked through Paul in prison to bring the jailer and his family to salvation." the boy said.

"Paul and Silas demonstrated that they practiced what they preached, just like Jesus," Emphasizing action and practice, Yesac said.

"It was the spirit of Christ in action that they did not harbor hatred or resentment toward those who beat them and imprisoned them." Recalling Jesus praying for the forgiveness of those who crucified Him, the boy said.

A crisp fall breeze blew across the faces of Yesac and the boy as they left the restaurant. Their moods were refreshed, and so were their expressions. Once they reached the office, they continued the lessons.

'And Paul sent a man from Miletus to Ephesus and called for the elders of the church, and said unto them, Ye know how I have always behaved myself among you, from the first day that I came into Asia unto this time: with all humility and tears, and under temptation through the plots of the Jews, serving the Lord, and whatever was profitable. Whatsoever things were profitable, which I have not shunned to preach unto you, both publicly, and in every house, teaching, and testifying unto Jews and Greeks, repentance toward God, and faith in our Lord Jesus Christ: and now I am bound in the spirit, and am going to Jerusalem, not knowing what things I shall meet there.

But the Holy Spirit testifies unto me in every city, that bonds and tribulations await me: but I count not my life of little value, that I may finish my course, and the commission which I have received of the Lord Jesus, to be a witness unto the gospel of the grace of God.'

"Leaving Ephesus, Paul's main stage, he heads for Jerusalem, where bonds and hardships await him." the boy said.

"Paul's attitude of willingness to die to finish the race and complete the task of testifying to the good news of God's grace should make us ponder." the old man mused.

"The fact that Paul served the Lord with great humility and with tears and amid severe testing by Jewish plots in Ephesus is truly a great achievement that our descendants should receive as a legacy," the boy said.

"That he bore witness to the fact that we must turn to God in repentance and have faith in our Lord Jesus is also a spirit of Christ that we must carry on." said Yesac.

The next day, Yesac and the boy switched places for the day and met at McDonald's. They didn't have a home, but their hearts were always full. That didn't matter to them; the only important thing was the Word.

'Therefore, remember that I admonished each one of you with tears for three years, day and night, without ceasing. And now I commend you to the Lord, and to the word of his grace, which can strengthen you and to make you an inheritance among all them that are sanctified. For I have not coveted any man's silver, or gold, or raiment, but have suffered with my own hands, as ye know, that I and my companions might set you an example in all things; that ye should labor thus, and help the weak, and remember that it is more blessed to give than to receive, as the Lord Jesus Himself said.'

"This is Paul's last teaching to the world," said the boy, astonished and read it out.

"We are to remember that for three years, I never ceased to admonish each one of you night and day with tears," said Yesac.

"'It is the word that can build us up and sanctify us' brings tears to my eyes," the boy said.

"It is more blessed to give than to receive, and must help the weak, are the golden rules of life that we should keep in mind as we go through life." said Yesac.

"Paul was a wonderful apostle of Christ. He worked at the Duranno Vow to provide for himself, wrote, and pursued his ambition to reach Rome, the center of the world at the time." the boy said.

"Isn't that the path Master is on now?" the boy asked.

Yesac remained silent, expressionless at the boy's words.

Injuries can be devastating for athletes. The hamstring in Yesac's right thigh, the one he injured playing soccer, looked pretty serious. Still, Yesac was grateful and looked forward to a few weeks of rest.

It occurred to him that McDonald's is a great place for fellowship. He would likely have to bring the boy here one day.

> 'And they that were with me saw the light,
> but heard not the voice of Him that spake unto me.
> And that night the Lord stood by Paul, and said unto him,
> "Be of good courage: for as thou hast borne witness of my works at Jerusalem, so must thou bear witness also at Rome."
> Then, as the days went on, the Jews took a covenant together, saying,
> "We will neither eat nor drink till we have slain Paul."
> And there were about forty of them who made such a vow.
> "For I also have hope in God," said Paul,
> "that there shall be a resurrection of the just and the unjust
> — a hope we all wait for. For this cause,
> I strive always to keep a clear conscience toward God and men."'

"How compassionate and holy were the disciples of St. Paul, 'on the seashore, we knelt to pray' that they might not go away," asked the boy.

"Paul's determination to fulfill Jesus' words about mortality, that he was not only willing to be bound but even to die in Jerusalem for the name of the Lord Jesus," said the old man.

The boy looked at his teacher curiously. "Mortality?"

Instead of answering, Yesac unfolded Jesus' words about mortality from his small notebook. It was the same teaching recorded in Matthew 10:39, Mark 8:35, Luke 17:33, and John 12:25.

"It's one of the few rare teachings recorded in all four gospels." He spoke.

Now, the boy's curiosity was piqued. "Why would the same words about transcription be recorded in all four gospels?"

"To enlighten those who are told once, twice, or thrice, but do not understand, and those who have ears to hear but do not hear," Yesac instructed.

The boy transcribed Yesac's teaching on transcription into his little notebook. For his enlightenment.

'PilSaZeukSang PilSangZeukSa (필생즉사 필사즉생 必生則死 必死則生); whoever tries to keep their life will lose it, and whoever loses their life will preserve it; for whoever finds his life will lose it, and whoever loses his life will save it.'

Mortal is mortal, noted the boy.

"If you realize the Word, you will see the light and understand the voice of him who was speaking to Jesus." The old man pointed out.

The boy was silent, and it was the silence of realization that led to eternal life.

"He who speaks is God." The boy whispered to himself. Finally coming to the realization.

"Jesus is giving Paul the boldness to witness in Rome as he witnessed for Christ in Jerusalem." the boy said.

"Courage, fearless, is a virtue that every one of Christ's apostles should possess," Yesac said.

"Paul seems holy to me because he strives always to keep his conscience clear before God and man." the boy said.

"The boy looks holy too." the old man said.

The boy was silent at Yesac's words, and after a while, he whispered to himself.

"I strive always to keep my conscience clear before God and man!"

'O king, it was about noon, and I saw in the road, and behold, a light brighter than the sun shining round about me and my companions, as the heavens....to open their eyes, and to turn them from darkness unto light, and from the power of Satan unto God, for the forgiveness of sins, and inheritance among the

multitude that are sanctified by faith in me. For I know that Christ must suffer and that he must rise again the first from the dead and be declared a light unto Israel and to the Gentiles. Therefore, gentlemen, be of good cheer; I believe God that it shall be as he hath said unto me.

Now there was a certain man named Publius, the highest man on the island, who had an estate near him; and he received us and lodged us hospitably three days: and his father lay sick with a fever and dysentery: and Paul went in, and prayed, and laid his hands on him, and healed him: and other sickmen of the island came and were healed, and hospitably received us, and put our things on board the ship when we departed. And we appointed a day, and came many to his abode: and Paul preached from morning till evening, testifying the kingdom of God, and taking the law of Moses, and the words of the prophets, and the things of Jesus. And he said unto this people, "Ye have heard, and yet ye understand not; and seen, and yet ye perceive not.'

"I did not know that there was a light brighter than the sun under heaven," said the boy after he had finished reading.

"It is the light of the eternal Word, brighter than the sun, that brings us out of the darkness of unbelief into the light," Yesac pointed out.

The boy's little notebook contained Paul's words, brighter than the sun.

'So, keep up your courage, men, for I have faith in God that it will happen just as he told me.'

"The text mentions a man named Publius."

The boy looked at his teacher in curiosity.

"Yes. He's the highest man on the island, and he owns land." the boy answered.

"We should note that the highest man or richest man is always associated with land. Jesu'' ancestors, Abraham, Isaac, Jacob, Joseph, Job, David, Solomon, Daniel, and others, were fabulously wealthy, and you'll notice that it was land, or real estate, that God gave them as an inheritance." the old man Yesac said.

"Yes. Even today in the United States, Jews who are extremely wealthy are known for owning real estate and passing it on to their descendants without selling it. The owner of the land is called the landlord, and the Lord is God." The boy pointed out.

Suddenly, he realized that the real estate studies he had learned from Yesac would help him a lot in the future.

If I knew the Word and real estate, life would be easy.

Still, he preferred Paul's words to Boblio's land. The boy flipped to the last page of the book of Acts. Paul's words triumph over matter.

He began to read the words.

'You will be ever hearing but never understanding; you will be ever seeing but never perceiving.'

The boy was entering a world of hearing, realizing, seeing, and knowing—a world of freedom where all was transcendent.
It was the world of his teacher Yesac, who was always accompanied by the words of the Lord Jesus.
Happy without a home, content without possessions, Master Yesac's life was always relaxed, full of abundance, and overflowing with gratitude.

"Think of this Act as a continuation of the Gospel of Luke. It speaks of the early church and the spread of Christianity. It also bridges the gap between Jesus' life and Paul's epistles," the old man said, reflecting on Jesus and Paul.

"It shows how the apostles and believers spread Jesus' message to many nations. It also recounts Paul's journeys, his trials, and his imprisonments." the boy, now speaking as an apostle, gently opened the book of Romans—Paul's first letter.

SJCB Dialogue - The Book of Acts

"The transformation of humanity begins with the presence and power of the Holy Spirit. It is the power that transcends human limitations — the true beginning of all things. The Holy Spirit dwells within all humanity; truth and the Word are the Holy Spirit." Buddha spoke, recalling the Trinity — God, Jesus, and the Holy Spirit — and quoted the Gospel of John: *'In the beginning was the Word, and the Word was with God, and the Word was God... And the Word became flesh (Jesus) and dwelt among us.'*

"The gospel must be proclaimed to all humanity, transcending nations, races, cultures, and religions. Through the story of Cornelius, it was declared that even Gentiles received the same Holy Spirit. Though we are all different, we share the same destiny — a longing for eternal happiness." Socrates spoke, filled with the emotion of truth.

"Anyone who longs for the Word and walks the path of awakening can encounter God. Peter, John, Mark, Barnabas, Paul... even their failures and weaknesses became part of their mission. The Word has the power to set people free — it breaks chains and opens prison doors." Confucius spoke with the spirit of liberty.

"True enlightenment is revealed in the boldness that transcends death. Though Paul was a Roman citizen, he cried out the gospel to Rome. The Book of Acts is not merely a historical record — it is God's message of love, freedom, boldness, and unity for all humanity." Jesus gently opened the pages of Romans, speaking with the voice of love.

"The Acts of Apostles show how the Holy Spirit empowered the early church and how the church overcame hardships and strife, spreading the gospel to the world." The boy spoke through the Holy Spirit.

"The conversion of the Gentiles gave Christianity a global status, which further transformed the lives of entire communities. Not only does it inspire us, but it also challenges us to carry Jesus' mission forth." The old man spoke through revelation.

Chapter 3: The Epistles

(Romans ~ Jude)

Volume 6: Romans

"Name the book of Romans," Yesac instructed.

"This is Paul's letter to the Romans that concludes the book of Acts. A Roman citizen, Paul studied theology under Gamaliel in Jerusalem," answered the boy.

Paul the Apostle wrote from Corinth, the main stage of his evangelism.

The boy continued, "Paul was a big man who preached the gospel to the saints in Rome and resolved the conflict between Jews and Gentiles."

"Yes. Paul taught the Jews that all are under sin and that no one can be called righteous apart from Jesus Christ, and the Gentiles who claimed more righteousness for themselves by keeping the law."

Yesac flipped to the first chapter of Romans and began to read out loud.

'Paul, a servant of Jesus Christ, called to be an apostle, set apart for the gospel of God, which he promised beforehand in the Scriptures by the prophets concerning his Son. Of this Son, who was born of the seed of David according to the flesh, and of the Spirit of holiness according to the resurrection from the dead, and was acknowledged to be the Son of God according to power, even Jesus Christ our Lord Therefore, as much as I am able, I desire to preach the gospel also to you who are in Rome.

For I am not ashamed of the gospel, for it is the power of God for salvation to everyone who believes; to the Jew first, and also to the Greek(Gentile). For a Jew inwardly is a Jew, and circumcision is in the heart, and in the spirit, and not in the letter: and the praise is not from man, but from God.'

Saturday was still a busy day for Yesac, although it was usually a quieter day. Luckily, he was grateful that the laundromat and fitness center were close by to save time. Yesac could work out while he waited for his laundry.

'Being justified without cost by the grace of God through the redemption that is in Christ Jesus, whom God has set forth as a propitiation through his blood, a sacrifice for sins by faith, so that he might show his righteousness, not counting the sins that were committed before, while he was long-suffering, but in this present time, that he might be just and the justifier of him that believeth in Jesus.

Wherefore there is no room for boasting; not by the law, nor by works, but only by the law of faith: therefore, we acknowledge that a man is justified by faith, and not by the works of the law. For God is the God of the Jews only, and not of the Gentiles: yea, verily, the God of the Gentiles also. For there is one God, that the circumcised may be justified by faith, or the uncircumcised by faith: wherefore we do not abolish the law by faith, neither can we: but we establish the law.'

"Paul was wary of the faith of Jews who boasted of their privileges, physical circumcision, and Jewish heritage while not living by the law or the truth." The boy noted down.

"God is not only the God of the Jews but of all of us, including the Gentiles," chided Yesac.

"Rather than being bound by the law and a sense of privilege, Paul taught the mercy, love, and compassion of God," the boy said as he turned the page.

'For what then shall it be said of our father Abraham in the flesh, that he was justified by works, that he might have something to boast of, but not before God?' ... Jesus was delivered for our offenses and was raised for our justification.
Therefore, since we have been justified by faith, let us have peace with God through our Lord Jesus Christ our Savior; by whom also we have access into this grace in which we stand by faith, and rejoice in hope of the glory of God.
Not only this, but we also rejoice in our tribulations, knowing that tribulation produces patience, patience produces a podium, and a podium produces hope. God commendeth his love toward us, in that, while we were yet sinners, Christ died for us.

*And so death passed upon all men,
because sin entered into the world through one man,
and death through sin; and so, death passed upon all men,
for that all sinned.
'For sin was in the world before the law,
but when there was no law, sin was not considered sin.
But death reigned from Adam unto Moses,
even upon them that had not sinned as unto the offense of Adam;
for Adam was a figure of him that was to come.
But the gift was not as unto the offense; for as by the trespass
of the one man died the death of many, much more so the grace of God,
or the gift that came by the grace of the one man,
Jesus Christ, abounded for many.'*

The boy began to pray. "Praise be to Jesus, who forgave us our sins by his crucifixion and justified us by his resurrection."

"The peace of mankind comes from faith, hope, and love. We rejoice in our trials because tribulation, chastening, and perseverance produce hope," said the old man Yesac.

"Through one man, Adam, the human race fell into sin and death, but through the grace of Jesus Christ, we all have salvation and eternal life as a gift," the old man continued speaking while the boy remained silent after his prayer.

"Yes. Adam, a pattern of the one to come, Jesus Christ," the boy broke the silence and said.

"The only thing we have to boast about before God is the cross of Christ," Yesac said and opened Paul's letter.

'For we were buried with him through baptism into his death, that we might walk in newness of life, even as he also raised Christ from the dead by the glory of the Father; for if we have been joined together in imitation of his death, we shall also be joined together in imitation of his resurrection.

For we know that our old man is crucified with him, that the body of sin might be destroyed, that we should no more be slaves to sin: for he that is dead is made alive unto righteousness from sin; and if we have died with Christ, we believe that we shall also live with him: for we know that Christ, having been raised from the dead, shall not die, neither shall death have any more claim upon him.' He read out.

"Paul's letter is a great reminder to us that we have been buried with Christ and raised to new life with Christ," said the boy.

"We, the human race, who have been set free from sin, but rather justified by Jesus Christ, are true children and brothers of God," Yesac said.

"It is a blessing to know that we died with Christ and will live again with him. Being not under the law but under grace, we have been freed from sin and made servants to God, whose reap leadsto holiness, which is the gift of God: eternal life." The old man spoke with compassion and freedom.

"For the wages of sin is death, but the Lord Christ is eternal life," the boy said.

The boy's face always shone with grace as he understood that eternal life is not after death but a new life of life that begins with his walk with Jesus. So, he began to read.

'There is therefore now no condemnation to those who are in Christ Jesus; for the law of the Spirit of life in Christ Jesus has made you free from the law of sin and death. For what the law could not do through the weakness of its own flesh, God did, sending his own Son in the likeness of sinful flesh, to condemn sin in the flesh, that the demands of the law might be fulfilled in us, who walk not after the flesh, but after the Spirit. For to them that are after the flesh the things of the flesh are minded, but to them that are after the Spirit the things of the Spirit: for to them that are after the flesh are death, but to them that are after the Spirit are life and peace.

'If the Spirit of him that raised Jesus from the dead dwelleth in you, he that raised Christ Jesus from the dead shall also quicken your mortal bodies if his Spirit dwelleth in you. Therefore, brethren, let us not walk in the flesh, that we should die to the flesh: for if ye live in the flesh, ye shall surely die: but if ye put to death the deeds of the body, ye shall live: for as many as are led by the Spirit of God, even so are they the sons of God: for ye have not received the spirit of a slave again to fear, but the spirit of adoption, whereby ye cry, Abba, Father. The Spirit himself beareth witness with our spirit that we are the children of God: and if children, then heirs also, heirs of God, and heirs with Christ: if we are heirs of God, then shall we also suffer with him, that we may be glorified with him: for I reckon that the sufferings of this present time are not worthy to be compared

with the glory that shall be revealed to us.'

The boy continued to read and meditate on Paul's great letters of the Holy Spirit.

"Christ Jesus, the law of the Spirit who gives life." The boy meditated again and again.

"That's the law that set us free from the law of sin and death," Yesac said.

"Yes. God has made the demands of the law fulfilled for those of us who walk not after the flesh but after the Spirit." The boy discerned between spirit and flesh and said.

"Jesus came into the world to serve, not to abolish the law, but to fulfill it," Yesac spoke with gratitude for the boy's deepening enlightenment as the days went by.

What God did by sending his own Son in the likeness of sinful flesh was that if by the Spirit you put to death the misdeeds of the body, you will live, and that meant the fulfillment of the law, that the law might be fully met.

The boy's little notebook contained the words of Paul's letter that raised his teacher, Yesac from the dead.

'I consider that our present sufferings are not worth comparing with the glory that will be revealed in us.'

As he battled a Job-like illness, hovering between life and death, Yesac held on to Paul's letter, enduring it with gratitude and determination and believing it without question. If you do strength training consistently, your muscles will develop and become stronger. If you practice positivity, gratitude, and faith long enough, they become strong like muscles. Such beliefs and convictions have the power and ability to survive death. That's why Jesus said that the righteous survive death. Amid his illness, homelessness, and loneliness, Yesac focused on the glory to come rather than his present suffering. Yesac's tears were a mixture of pain, gratitude, and faith. This is what the boy saw in his teacher.

The boy read Paul's letter in Yesac's notebook,

'If the Spirit of him who raised Jesus from the dead is living in you, he who raised Christ from the dead will also give life to your mortal bodies because of his Spirit who lives in you.'

It was a busy Saturday evening in Carrollton, Dallas, a neighborhood with a strong Korean culture. The parking lot in front of Yesac's office, located next to H Mart, was crowded as always, with cars looking for a place to park. It was also a time of hunger for the boy.

The old man, without hesitation, opened Paul's letter to the Christian community in Rome.

'If we hope for what we do not see, we wait patiently for it; so also, the Spirit helps our weaknesses; for we know not what we ought, but the Spirit Himself maketh intercession for us with groanings which cannot be uttered. For he that searcheth the hearts knoweth the mind of the Spirit: for the Spirit maketh intercession for the saints according to the will of God. And we know that all things work together for good to those who love God, who are called according to his purpose. What then shall we say to these things, if God be for us, who can be against us?

'He that spared not his own Son, but delivered him up for us all, how shall he not also with him freely give us all things? Who shall deliver the elect of God: for it is God that justifieth, and not man that condemneth; who died, and rose again, but Christ Jesus, who is at the right hand of God, and maketh intercession for us: who shall separate us from the love of Christ, neither tribulation, nor distress, nor persecution, nor famine, nor red sea, nor peril, nor sword?

For as it is written, we are slain for thy sake all the day long, and are counted as sheep for the slaughter: but in all things we conquer through him that loveth us: for I am persuaded, that neither death, nor life, nor angels, nor principalities, nor powers, nor things present, nor things to come, nor height, nor depth, nor any other creature, shall be able to separate us from the love of God, which is in Christ, Jesus our Lord.'

"Humans possess a weak nature due to sin. To be strong, we must distance ourselves from sin."

The boy's face, always pure and shining, reflected this light, a sight that inspired reverence and respect, just like the light and salt of the world.

"The law bound us because of Adam's sin, but Jesus fulfilled all the requirements of the law, granting us freedom." Yesac was inwardly surprised by the boy's statement that sin makes humans weak.

"Paul, John, and James were the apostles who demonstrated by their actions that 'it is not knowing that makes one right, but doing that makes one right.'" the boy said.

"That's what Jesus really taught." The old man's words were brief, but they sounded strong and refreshing.

It's sunset in a Korean-American neighborhood in Dallas, and the boy heads to H Mart to pick up some dinner.

After finishing a simple dinner, the old man turned the pages of Romans.

'If thou shalt confess with thy mouth that Jesus is Lord, and shalt believe in thine heart that God hath raised him from the dead, thou shalt be saved: for with the heart man believeth unto righteousness, and with the mouth, confession is made unto salvation. There is no distinction between Jew and Greek, neither is there any difference: for the same Lord is Lord of all, and rich unto all that call upon him.

For whosoever shall call upon the name of the Lord shall be saved. There is no remorse in the gift and calling of God. The depth of the riches of the wisdom and knowledge of God: his judgments shall not be measured, neither shall his ways be found. Who hath known the heart of the Lord, and who hath been his counselor, and who hath given unto the Lord first, that he may receive his due: for all things proceed from the Lord, and unto the Lord return: to him be glory to the ages of ages? Amen.'

"How great is God's love for all mankind, transcending nation, ethnicity, culture, and language, for there is no difference between Jew and Gentile." The boy spoke with a heart full of sincerity.

"Let us live in love with one another, imitating the great love and grace of God, who transcends religion and sees in each other the same, not differences." The old man said with an open heart.

"We praise God for calling us and giving us gifts without regret. God's gifts and his call are irrevocable." The boy spoke with a prayerful heart.

"It is God who gives us all things and takes them away, so we should strive to live as the Word, showing compassion to one another rather than material things. From him and through him and for him are all things." The old man spoke with a merciful expression.

The way to righteousness and salvation is to believe with the heart and confess with the mouth. Paul's letter, which began with Romans, continues for thirteen books until Philemon.

> 'I urge you therefore, brethren, by all the mercies of God, that you present your bodies a living sacrifice, holy, acceptable to God, which is your spiritual service, which is your reasonable service. And do not be conformed to this world, but be transformed by the renewing of your minds, that you may discern what is that good, and acceptable, and perfect, will of God. I say to each one of you, by the grace given to me, do not think any more than you ought to think but think wisely, according to the measure of faith that God has distributed to each one of you. For as we have many members in one body, and all the members do not have the same office, so we, being many, and all partakers of one body in Christ, are joined together.
>
> For every one of us has received a different gift according to the grace given to us: if he prophesies, according to the measure of faith; if he serves, according to the measure of service; if he teaches, according to the measure of teaching; if he has authority, according to the measure of authority; if he relieves, with sincerity; if he governs, with diligence; if he has compassion, with cheerfulness; if he hasmercy, with joy; for in love there is no deceit: hate evil, and abound in good.'

"Paul is writing us a letter of grace because of all the mercy of God," said the boy.

"The mercy of God is the fifth fruit of the Spirit," The old manremembered and said of the nine fruits of the Holy Spirit. Love, Joy, Peace, Patience, Kindness, Goodness, Faithfulness, Gentleness, Self-control.

"How sweet is St. Paul's letter to the world's cacophony and reincarnation, where there is nothing new under the sun, to search the heart to discern what is the good, pleasing, andperfect will of God," the boy exclaimed.

In the boy's little notebook, a gracious passage from Romans was carefully written in English.

> 'Do not conform to the pattern of this world, but be transformed by the renewal of your mind. Then you can test and approve what God's will is his good, pleasing, and perfect will.'

"Let's end wasteful wrong thinking and live in acceptance, love, and forgiveness of one another according to the amount of faith God has given each person," the old man said.

"By the faith God has distributed to each of you according to the measure of faith God has given each of us." The boy whispered to himself.

"In Christ we, though many, form one body, and each member belongs to all the others. We must live in broad love, with the consciousness of human community, that we are not two, but one in the end, just because we speak a different language or color or think differently."

Yesac's eloquence came as a loud bang of realization that hit the boy in the back of the head.

"We have different gifts, according to the grace given to each of us." The boy whispered again, this time in English, to himself.

"Love must be sincere. Hate what is evil; cling to what is good." Yesac also whispered to himself in English.

"Praising God who encourages good and punishes evil (KwonSunJingAk勸善懲惡권선징악), I am grateful for the teaching, 'if it is to show mercy, do it cheerfully.'" The boy said with a kind expression of gratitude.

"Do not do anything you will regret, do not regret what you have already done, and do good deeds so that even your right hand does not know." The old man's words were as free as the floating clouds.

"Yes." The boy nodded fiercely.

Back on Sunday, Yesac was packing his bag to go to a soccer game.

"You have a hamstring under your butt. Please take it slow and be careful today." The boy said, concerned for the old man. Even though it was just a practice game, the boy couldn't help but be amazed by the old man scoring as many as seven goals in 90 minutes against the opposing team. Yesac loved soccer and was really good at it. The 63-year-old had surpassed an amateur level in stamina, technique, and shooting power.

"I will." Yesac laughed.

They departed the office and left for the soccer field.

The next day, the old man, who had finished his workout and shower early in the morning, turned the pages of the Book of Romans.

> 'Love your brothers, be kind to one another, honor one another, be diligent, not slothful, serve the Lord with fervor. Rejoice in hope, be patient in tribulation, be constant in prayer, supply the necessities of the saints, hospitality to the hands of the saints. Bless those who persecute you, and do not curse them. Rejoice with those who rejoice, and weep with those whoweep. Be of one mind with one another, and do not set your hearts on high, but rather on the lowly, and do not be wise in your own eyes.
>
> Repay no man evil for evil, but seek to do good before all men. And if it be possible, as far as it is possible, ye shallhave peace with all men. My beloved, ye sinners, render no thanks unto your enemies, but leave it to wrath: for it is written, Vengeance is mine, I will repay, saith the Lord. If thine enemy give, feed him; if he thirst, give him drink; and thou shalt heap coals of fire upon his head. Do not be overcome by evil, but overcome evil with good.'

"As Paul says, if we are diligent and not slothful, we have no time to be depressed," the old man Yesac said.

"Yes. A rolling stone gathers no moss, the busy bee has no time for sorrow." The boy said, recalling the Latin and English proverbs he had studied with the old man.

"It's easy to bless those you love, but it's hard to bless those who persecute you," the boy said.

"The path through the narrow gate is always difficult. Not everything can be good as one lives, but showing mercy to those you dislike is a great realization of overcoming evil with good," Yesac said calmly.

The boy wondered what it was about Master Yesac that made him so patient and grateful in the midst of any tribulation. He wondered if he had developed muscles from the affirmations he had practiced in the wilderness. A fleeting thought flashed through the boy's mind. He thought about the importance of associating with people of low position, being humble, and living in harmony with one another, as Paul wrote in his letters.

"Do not be overcome by evil, but overcome evil with good, for God is the repayer of enemies. Not be overcome by evil, but overcome evil with good?" The boy whispered to himself and wrote down the words of Paul's letter in his little notebook.

"Do not be overcome by evil, but overcome evil with good. It is the goodness of God that overcomes evil." Yesac's voice was low and quiet.

"Overcome evil with good, not succumbing to it?" The boy whispered to himself and copied the content of Paul's letter into his small notebook:

'Do not be overcome by evil, but overcome evil with good.'

"It is God's goodness that allows us to overcome evil (wickedness, sin)." Yesac, the old man said as he gazed at the distant mountains.

'You owe no one anything except a debt of love. For he that loveth another hath fulfilled the law: Thou shalt not commit adultery, thou shalt not murder, thou shalt not steal, thou shalt not covet, and whatsoever other commandment there be besides this, Thou shalt love thy neighbor as thyself, thou hast heard it said, Love doeth no evil unto thy neighbor: therefore love is the fulfilling of the law. The night is deep, and the day is at hand; therefore let us cast off the works of darkness, and let us put on the armor of light.

Walk soberly, as in the daytime; abstain from drunkenness and revelry, from lewdness and lasciviousness, from strife and envying; clothe yourselves with the Lord Jesus Christ, and fleshly things, not promoting the flesh to lusts. Receive him that is weak in the faith, and do not criticize his doubts. For one man hath faith enough to eat all things, and the weak man eateth vegetables: he that eateth, let him not despise him that eateth not: and he that eateth not, let him not judge him that eateth. For God has received me.'

"What a wonderful life it is to live as Paul wrote, owing nothing to anyone." The boy spoke refreshingly.

"There is no reason to live a cowardly life when you have a precious and upright life," The old man said like the horn of a rhinoceros.

"What a tremendous teaching it is to say that the law is fulfilled by loving others. It closely aligns with your expression of the entire Bible as 'KyungChunAeIn,'" said the boy, delighted.

'KyungChunAeIn(敬天愛人 경천애인): Love God with everything, love your neighbors as yourself. - Matthew 22'

"The Ten Commandments are love, and Paul's letter to love your neighbor as yourself is very enlightening," the old man said with love.

"It even goes so far as to say that love is the fulfillment of the law," the boy also said with love.

"Because love is God, the Holy Spirit, and Jesus," Yesac said.

The tire was screeching. There was a big nail in it. He went to the Discount Tire Store, which had a free hot beverage station and a free flat tire. He started his day with gratitude. It occurred to him that if a business can meet the needs of its customers and be compassionate, that is the key to business success.

Yesac turned the page of Paul's Letter to the Romans.

'For as long as we live, we live for the Lord, and as long as we die, we die for the Lord; therefore, whether we live or die, we are the Lord's. For this cause Christ died and rose again, that he might be Lord of both the dead and the living. Whereby he that serveth Christ is well pleasing unto God, and commendable unto men: wherefore let us strive for the things of peace, and for the edifying of one another in virtue: For he that eateth and drinketh in doubt is condemned: for it is an ointment of unbelief: and everything that is not of faith is sin.'

In the boy's little notebook were the sweet words of Paul's letter.

'If we live, we live for the Lord; and if we die, we die for the Lord. So, whether we live or die, we belong to the Lord.'

"There's a singer I love, Pat Benatar, who sings a song called 'We live for love'. It's a very good song. Yes, we live for love, we live by love. Love is the truth, the Word, and God." Yesac said.

"Yes. We live for the truth and the word, and we die for the truth and the word, for we all belong to God, who is truth and love." the boy said.

"We eat, drink, and are merry in the world, but the kingdom of God is of righteousness, peace, and joy in the Holy Spirit." the old man said.

"The way we live for the Lord is to strive for peace with one another and to build each other up in virtue," the boy said.

"Yes, striving for peace and building each other up is the way to live for the Lord," Yesac said.

The team drew 2-2 with the Americans in a soccer match, but Yesac's injury worsened. He decides to focus on his recovery.

"I think it's a fact of life that people go through life and get innocently hurt in relationships," the boy said.

"That's life. Wounds caused by thoughtless words breed hatred, and hatred belongs to sin, but the remedy for all woundsis found in the Word, and the secret of forgiveness is in the love of Jesus Christ, who asks us to forgive those who crucify him, for they know not what they do." Yesac said calmly, and the boy noted thoughtfully.

"Yes. If we learn the great forgiveness of Jesus Christ, there is nothing in this world that we cannot forgive; rather, the wounds we receive are objects of grace and gratitude that lead us to enlightenment." The boy's face overflowed with love, mercy, and grace as if he had come to a great realization about how to live his life. It occurred to him that wounds are also grace.

Yesac turned the page of the book.

'Let each one of us will to please his neighbor, to do good, and to build up virtue. May the God of hope fill you with all joy and peace in believing, that you may abound in hope by the power of the Holy Spirit in believing. Your obedience is heard by all men; therefore I rejoice in you, that you may be wise in good and wise in evil. Now it hath been made manifest, according to the commandment of the eternal God, according to the revelation of his mystery, which he hath made known by the writings of the prophets, that all nations should believe and be obedient; to the wise God, who is able to strengthen you with this gospel, be glory through Jesus Christ to the ages of ages. Amen.'

"We should all strive to please our neighbors for their good, to build them up, as St. Paul wrote," Yesac said.

"And may the God of hope fill us with all joy and peace in believing, so that we may overflow with hope by the power of the Holy Spirit." the boy said.

"The letters of Paul, which are secret revelations from God, will be able to strengthen us with the gospel," the boy said.

Of the 27 books of the New Testament, 13 are Paul's letters. After finishing Paul's letter to the Romans, the boy opened a new letter, Paul's letter to the Corinthians.

SJCB Dialogue – Romans

"No one can be perfectly righteous, thus we need freedom from the very idea of righteousness. Life, like golf, is not a perfect game. The greatness of life lies in its imperfection being embraced by perfection. Without leaning too far to either side, we are to live freely, not as possessors, but as existence itself. Like birds flying in the sky, like water flowing freely." Said Siddhartha Gautama, as he became the stream.

"The sacrifice of Jesus is the key to salvation for all of humanity, and grace is a gift that cannot be earned. Salvation is not something we attain through effort, but something given by God as we walk in love with others and journey with Jesus, the Word made flesh." Said Socrates, who once showed that truth must be discovered by oneself.

"God's love is eternal. The power that lets us survive in any circumstance is precisely the power of love. That is why we have hope even in suffering." Said Confucius, who defined Yn(인 仁 benevolence) as Ae(애 愛 love).

"The Book of Romans is God's invitation to all humanity. Rather than mere intellectual knowledge, we must respond through faith expressed in acts of love toward others." Said Jesus with deep love for humanity, and Siddhartha turned the page of 1 Corinthians.

Volume 7: 1 Corinthians

"Where is Corinth?" Yesac asked.

"Corinth is a city-state in ancient Greece, located seventy-eight kilometers southwest of Athens, and is famous for being the site of the Apostle Paul's activities," answered the boy.

"Paul's ministry included planting churches in Rome, Corinth, and Thessalonica," he continued.

Corinth was the commercial center of southern Greece, but it was a morally corrupt city. The boy opened the first chapter of Paul's letter.

'Paul and Sosthenes, called according to the will of God to be apostles of Christ Jesus, and our brother Sosthenes, to the church of God at Corinth, to all who are sanctified in Christ Jesus and called to be saints, and to all who call on the name of our Lord and Savior Jesus Christ in every place, Grace and peace to you from God our Father and the Lord Jesus Christ. For ye are in Christ Jesus, who is of God, and Jesus is of God and became unto us wisdom, and righteousness, and sanctification, and redemption: For as it is written, He that boasteth, let him boast in the Lord. For I have determined that nothing should be known among you except Jesus Christ and him crucified and that my speech and my preaching should not be in the counsel of wisdom, but in the manifestation and power of the Holy Spirit, that your faith might not rest in the wisdom of men, but in the power of God.'

"We praise Jesus, who has become our wisdom, righteousness, sanctification, and redemption," the boy said as if in praise.

"For we have nothing to boast in but the cross, so that we may boast in the Lord alone. Let the one who boasts boast in the Lord." Old man Yesac said with a humble heart.

The boy also, with a humble heart, turned the pages of Paul's letter to the Corinthians.

'For we are God's fellow laborers, and ye are God's field, and ye are God's house. Know ye not that ye are the temple of God, and that the Spirit of God dwelleth in you? Whosoever defileth the temple of God, God shall destroy him. For the temple

of God is holy, and so are ye. Let no man deceive himself. If any of you think to be wise in this world, let him be foolish, and he shall become wise, and you shall be wise. For it is written, The wisdom of this world is foolishness with God, and it is written, The wisdom of the wise shall bring them to their own devices, and the Lord knoweth the thoughts of the wise as vain. Let no man therefore boast of himself. For all things are yours. For all things are yours, whether Paul, or Apollos, or Cephas, or the world, or life, or death, or things present, or things to come: for ye are Christ's, and Christ is God's.'

"It is said that the Holy Spirit searches all things, even the deep things of God. How do we receive the Holy Spirit?" asked the boy.

"We have the mind of Christ, so we will each receive the gifts of the Spirit according to our portion and deeds. We will each be rewarded according to our own labor." Yesac said.

"It is a great awakening to know that we have the mind of Christ. We are all God's field, God's building." The boy said with a look of realization.

"If we know that we are God's temple and that God's Spirit dwells in our midst, therein lies the reason why we should keep ourselves clean. Since God's temple is sacred, we should endeavor to keep ourselves holy." The old man spoke with a holy expression.

"Paul says that by becoming foolish, you become wise. We should become fools so that we may become wise," the boy said with an innocent expression.

"Worldly wisdom, which has nothing new under the sun, catches the wise in their craftiness but is foolishness to God," cautioned Yesac.

"Yes. Man is an object of love, not of boasting or reliance," the boy said, remembering Yesac's teaching.

'People ought to regard us as servants of Christ and stewards of the mysteries of God... Therefore, only judge something before the appointed time; wait until the Lord comes. He will reveal what is hidden in darkness and expose the heart's motives. At that time, each will receive praise from God. For who makes you different from anyone else? What do you have that you did not receive? And if you did receive it, why do you boast that you did not?... The kingdom of God is not a matter of talk but of power. What do you prefer? Shall I come to you with a rod of discipline,

or shall I come in love and with a gentle spirit?... But you were washed, sanctified, and justified in the name of the Lord Jesus Christ and by the Spirit of our God...'

The boy drank the remaining water and continued to meditate on the Word.

'Do you not know that your bodies are members of Christ himself?... But whoever is united with the Lord is one with him in spirit... Do you not know that your bodies are temples of the Holy Spirit, who is in you, whom you have received from God? You are not your own; you were bought at a price.

Therefore, honor God with your bodies... I say to the unmarried and the widows: It is good for them to stay unmarried, as I do. But if they cannot control themselves, they should marry, for it is better to marry than to burn with passion... Circumcision is nothing, and uncircumcision is nothing. Keeping God's commands is what counts... Those who use the things of the world should not become engrossed in them, for this world in its present form is passing away.'

"Let us strive to live as saints with the fragrance of Christ so that we, too, may be reborn as servants of Christ and as those entrusted with the mysteries God has revealed." the old man said.

"How grateful I am for St. Paul's letter, 'Judge nothing before the appointed time; wait until the Lord comes.'" The boy said with a free heart that judged neither anyone nor anything.

"We should just try to walk in love and gentleness, which are the fruit of the Spirit," Yesac said.

"Yes. Because the kingdom of God is not in words, but in power." the boy said.

Yesac looked at the words written in the boy's little notebook.

"I pray to be washed, sanctified, and justified in the name of the Lord Jesus Christ and by the Holy Spirit of our God.'

In the boy's pursuit of eternal words and truths, despite his poverty, regardless of how much or little he had, or how much he could use of what he possessed, as he remained detached from the fleeting material things and deeds of a world that was passing away, Yesac perceived a glimmer of holiness.

> *'As also the Lord hath commanded that they which preach the gospel should live by the gospel: I have nothing to boast of, though I preach the gospel: but woe unto me, if I preach not the gospel: for though I am free to all men, yet have I made myself a slave unto all, that I might win the more.*
>
> *For to the Jews I became as a Jew, that I might win the Jews; to those who were under the law, though I was not under the law, I became as one who was under the law, that I might win those who were under the law; to those who were without the law, though I was not without law to God, but rather as one who was under the law of Christ, or as one who was without the law, that I might win those who were without the law. And to the weak I became as one of the weak, that I might win the weak; and to many, I took on many forms, that I might save some; and I do all things for the gospel's sake, that I might be a partaker of the gospel.'*

"Paul's teaching on humility, that to think I know something is to admit that I don't know what I know, makes me ponder," said the boy.

"Knowledge without love makes one arrogant, but compassionate love builds virtue in us," Yesac said.
"Paul, who was free from all men but made himself a servant to everyone, is a true apostle of Christ," the boy said.

"Recognizing that this is the secret of victory, Paul is a man of God who wills to die (PilSa必死필사) and remains alive (ZeukSang 則生 즉생)." the old man said.

"Sometimes a Jew and a lawyer, sometimes a non-Jew and a proportional lawyer, free from all men, Paul is truly an unstoppable apostle who can face anything for the sake of the gospel," the old man mused.

That night, the boy had dinner with Kimbap, which his coworker brought over. He ate it quickly as if he were hungry.

> *'For I would not that ye should not know, brethren, that our fathers were all under the cloud, and passed through the midst of the sea, and belonged unto Moses, and were all baptized in the cloud and in the sea, and ate the same sacred food, and drank the same sacred drink, from the same sacred rock, which is after them, which is Christ. For the conscience which I have spoken of is not yours, but another's: for my liberty shall be judged by*

another's conscience.

Whether therefore ye eat, or drink, or whatsoever ye do, do all to the glory of God: and be ye not as Jews, or as Greeks, or as strangers to the church of God: but please all men in all things, as I did, not seeking your advantage, but the advantage of the many, that they may be saved.'

"Paul's letters are alive and well, and the gospel that Moses, who passed under the clouds and through the midst of the sea and was baptized, and our ancestors, who all ate and drank the same sacred food, that the Rock is Christ, is coming to us in the Holy Spirit." the boy said.

The boy's little notebook contained Paul's letters, written by the Holy Spirit. He had meditated on it over and over again.

'They all ate the same spiritual food and drank the same spiritual drink; for they drank from the spiritual rock that accompanied them, and that rock was Christ.'

It also records the words of life that saved Master Yesac from death. It was, of course, Paul's letter from Ephesus to Corinth.

'No temptation has overtaken you except what is common to mankind. And God is faithful; he will not let you be tempted beyond what you can bear. But when you are tempted, he will also provide a way out so that you can endure it.'

It was the golden rule of life that there is no trial that a man cannot bear, and all the teachings of Christ, muscled by the thought of a firm conviction of the word and truth of Christ, had become habitual in the life of the master Yesac. There was, of course, an openness of realization and freedom from being judged by anyone; it was a world of love.

"How can I live my life so that whatever I do, whether I eat or drink or whatever I do, I do it all to the glory of God?" asked the boy.

"To live not seeking one's own good, but the good of one's neighbor," his teacher answered.

The boy fell silent, showing that this was not easy.

"How can I be an openly religious person, with no barriers anywhere?" the boy asked again.

Instead of answering, Yesac showed him his little notebook

with a quote from Paul's letter.

'Do not cause anyone to stumble, whether Jews, Greeks, or the church of God—even as I try to please everyone in every way. For I am not seeking my own good but the good of many, so thatthey may be saved.'

"A life lived seeking to please everyone in everything and not seeking my own benefit, but the benefit of many," the boy whispered with a sincere and earnest expression.

The old man turned the page of Paul's letters.

'For I want you to know that the head of every man is Christ, and the head of the woman is the man, and the head of Christ is God. For the man is the image and glory of God and does not deserve to be called the head, and the woman is the glory of the man. For neither was man-made of woman, but woman of man; neither was man made for woman, but woman for man.

But in the Lord is not the woman without the man, neither is the man without the woman: for as the woman was made of the man, sowas the man made of the woman: but all things are of God. Therefore whosoever eateth the bread of the Lord, or drinketh the cup of the Lord, unworthily, is guilty of the body and blood ofthe Lord: for he eateth this bread, and drinketh this cup, after that he hath examined himself: but whosoever eateth and drinketh the bread of the Lord, without having defecated the body of the Lord, eateth and drinketh his own sin.'

"All the many gifts and manifestations, which are distributed to each one, are of the same person," the boy said.

"The giver is God, the Holy Spirit, and Jesus," Yesac said.

"Yes, all of us human beings are brothers and sisters with one Father," the boy said.

On a calm Tuesday morning, magpies strolled peacefully in the McDonald's parking lot.

'For by one Spirit were we all baptized into one body, whether we be Jews or Greeks, whether we be slaves or free, and were all made to drink of one Spirit: and there is not one member of the body, but many: and if the foot says, I am not a hand, and am not attached unto the body: and if the hand say, I am not an eye and am not attached unto the body: and if the ear says, I am not an ear and am not attached unto the body.

Saith, I am not an eye, and am not attached unto the body: but by reason of this, it is not attached unto the body: for if the whole body were an eye, where would it see, and if the whole body hears, where would it smell: but now God hath put the members into the body, each one as he pleased: and if it were but one member, where would the body be? Now the members are many, but the body is one.

The eye shall not say, I am useless, nor the hand, I am useless; nor the head, I am useless; nor the foot, I am useless; but the weaker members of the body, which seem to be of the same substance, are all useful. If one member suffers, all the members suffer with it; and if one member be glorified, all the members rejoice with it; for ye are the body of Christ, and every part of it.'

"The weaker members of the body, like the eyes and the brain, are often the most useful." Yesac pointed out.

"Yes. Whatever we did to one of the least of these, we did to Jesus Christ," the boy responded.

"We are all members of the body of Christ, and our differences are proof of our coexistence, not of our differences, and it is the order of the universe and the law of God that if one member suffers, all members suffer with it," Yesac continued.

"Yes, to suffer together, to rejoice together, to love together, that's our way of life," the boy agreed.

"That's right. The path of life for us is to suffer together, rejoice together, and love each other."

"Corinth, reminiscent of the city of pleasure, Las Vegas, attracted attention as a global commercial city," said the old man.

"Corinth was where merchants and sailors from across the Mediterranean, connected to the Atlantic, gathered for gambling, prostitution, and new challenges," the boy continued.

"The more idolatry and sin there were, the more Paul's gospel mission to change the world shone brightly," the old man said with strength.

With a happy, beaming smile, the boy turned to 1 Corinthians 13, a love letter.

'If I speak with the tongues of men and the words of angels, but have not love, I am as tinkling copper and a clanging cymbal; if I have the power to prophesy, and know all secrets and all knowledge; if I have all faith to move mountains, but have not love, I am nothing; if I deliver with all that I have, and give my body to be burned, but have not love, it profits me nothing.

Love is longsuffering, love is gentle, love is not envious, love is not a speculator, love is not boastful, love is not proud, love is not rude, love is not insolent, love seeks its good, love is not angry, thinketh no evil, rejoiceth not in unrighteousness, rejoiceth with the truth, beareth all things, believeth all things, hopeth all things, endureth all things: love abideth for ever, but prophecies shall cease, tongues shall cease, knowledge shall cease. For we know in part and prophesy in part: and when that which is perfect cometh, that which is in part shall be abolished.

For when I was a child, I was like a child in speech, and like a child in understanding, and like a child in mind; but when I became a man, I cast away the things of a child. For now, we see in a mirror, as in a dim way, but then we shall see face to face; now I know in part, but then I shall know fully, as thou knowest me; now faith, hope, love: these abideth ever, these three: but the greatest of these is love.'

The boy thought that Paul's letter of love was indeed noble and great.

"It teaches us that all the abilities and riches in life are of no use if we don't have love," the boy said.

"Especially when it comes to speaking the Scriptures, let's make sure we're speaking in love." Yesac agreed.

"How great is the power of love, which bears all things and endures all things," said the boy with delight.

"Everything has a beginning and an end, but love is endless and eternal," Yesac said wisely.

"Yes. Love is God," responded the boy.

"Faith and hope are great, but greater than these is love." The

boy was finished almost reciting 1 Corinthians 13 in English.

'What then shall I do? I will pray with my spirit, but I will also pray with my mind; I will sing with my spirit, but I will also sing with my mind... But I would rather speak five intelligible words to instruct others in the church than ten thousand words in a tongue... So what shall we do, brothers? When you come

together, everyone has a hymn, a word of instruction, a revelation, a tongue, or an interpretation. All of these must be done to strengthen the church... But everything should be done in a fitting and orderly way.'

Paul, an apostle of Christ who wrote 13 letters, nearly half of the 27 books of the New Testament, prayed, praised, and preached the gospel with his spirit and heart.

"Paul says it is better to speak little with an enlightened mind for the instruction of others than to speak much in tongues," said the boy.

"Tongues belong to the individual, and to teach enlightened things is selfless and may benefit many brethren," countered Yesac.

"Paul also says that whatever you do, do everything to build up virtue."

Instead of answering, Yesac scribbled something in Chinese characters on the boy's small notebook.

'DukBulGoPilYuRin(덕불고 필유린德不孤 必有隣); virtuouspeople are not solitary, they always have neighbors'
  - Confucius in The Analects of Confucius.

Paul's teaching to do everything for the sake of building virtue penetrated the boy's heart. He looked at the words written in Yesac's little notebook.

'Everything should be done in a fitting and orderly way. JungYong (moderation 中庸 중용) and JulJe (temperance 節制 절제)'

The boy remembered that moderation is not leaning to the left or right and that the final fruit of the Spirit is temperance. Paul's letter to do everything in moderation and order was also a teaching on moderation and self-control.

The old man turned the pages of the book of Corinthians.

'I make known unto you, brethren, the gospel which I preached unto you, which ye received, and in which ye stand. By this, ye shall be saved if ye hold fast the word which I preached unto you, and have not believed in vain. I delivered unto you first of all that which I received, that Christ died for our sins, and that he was buried, and that he rose again the third day according to

the scriptures; and that he appeared to Cephas, and afterward to the twelve disciples, and afterward to the five hundred brethren at once, some of whom are now in the womb, and some are asleep;

and afterward to James, and afterward to all the apostles, and last of all to me, which was born of a woman, and was not full grown. For I am the least of the apostles, and unworthy to be called an apostle, because I have persecuted the church of God; but my becoming is by the grace of God: and his grace which was bestowed upon me was not in vain, so that I labored more than all the apostles: but not I, but the grace of God which was with me: therefore I preached, and ye believed.'

The true happiness of being homeless is to have a place to shower. It is important to keep your body, the temple where God dwells, in tip-top shape. Mind, body, and spirit are one, and when the body is sick, the mind is sick, and when the mind is sick, the Holy Spirit is sick, so Yesac always feels grateful and happy when he starts his day with a workout at the fitness center at dawn anda shower.

Exercise and showering also increase a person's happiness quotient. Looking at Yesac's life, which is nothing but gratitude and positivity, the boy's heart is also happy and grateful. That's how his day started today.

"After Jesus rose from the dead, he appeared to Cephas, the twelve disciples, and the five hundred brothers at once," the boy said.

"Then he appeared to James, then to all the apostles, and last of all to Paul, the least of these," Yesac instructed.

"Why did Paul call himself the least of the apostles, the one who was not even worthy to be called an apostle?" asked the boy.

"Because he was an abnormally born, retarded man, and a Jew who was a leading persecutor of those who believed in Jesus," answered the boy.

After hearing the voice of Jesus, the Apostle Paul was converted and became one of Christ's greatest apostles, leadinga religious reformation.

The boy recalled the biblical figures recorded in old man Yesac's small notebook: Moses, David, Esther, Ruth, Rahab, Joseph, Paul, and Jesus. They were all chosen by God from among the least and most humble people. The God who loves the small also chose the exceedingly small nation of Israel. Old man Yesac, born in a remote mountain village without electricity, once confessed to living with such an unyielding will because of his small yet precious hope that God might use someone as small as himself. The journey we are all on with this 'Novel Scripture' is proof of that. It is because God has taken hold of old man Yesac's pen. We are all small individuals with great hope.

"Paul's faithfulness and humility in attributing all his gospel labors to the grace of God seems sublime," Yesac said, finishing the lesson.

A call from a coworker at the office. Brother Brian, who had just closed a real estate deal, was taking his coworkers to lunch. Yesac was overwhelmed and grateful to be taken care of. "Me, the least of them," Yesac whispered to himself as he walked out of McDonald's.

On a clear and cool afternoon, the boy turned the pages of Paul's letter to the Corinthians.

'But now Christ is risen from the dead, the first fruits of those who have fallen asleep. For as death came by man, so also the resurrection of the dead by man. For as in Adam all die, even so in Christ shall all be made alive.

Brethren, I declare unto you the boast which I have in Christ Jesus our Lord, that I die daily. Be not deceived: be sober, and do righteousness, and sin no more. For the glory of the sun is different, and the glory of the moon is different, and the glory of the stars is different, and the glory of the stars is different.

The sting of death is sin, and the power of sin is the law. Thanks be to God, who giveth us the victory through our Lord Jesus Christ: Therefore, my beloved brethren, be ye steadfast, unmoveable, always abounding in the work of the Lord, abounding in the faith, knowing that your labor is not in vain in the Lord. Be ye therefore sober, steadfast in the faith, manly, strong. Do all things in love.'

"For as we are dead in Adam, so in Christ, we, all of humanity, will be brought to life," the boy said.

"To gain life, we must die daily, like Paul's only boast," Yesac said as he pointed to a verse in Corinthians with his finger.

'I face death every day, just as surely as I boast about you in Christ Jesus our Lord.'

"Yes. We are already crucified and dead with Jesus Christ, so what is there to be afraid of?" declared the boy.

Yesac looked into the boy's eyes, a little surprised by his words.

"It's all there, and there's nothing new under the sun, so let's be zealous in the things of life, zealous for the Word, which is the truth." the old man continued.

"Yes. Stay awake, do not be deceived, turn away from sin, do righteousness, and live," the boy said.

"As the sun, stars, and moon have different glories to God, so do we all have different gifts, but we all have one Father, God, and the best life is to live in Christ, loving one another," Yesac said.

"Thanks be to God, who gives us the victory through our Lord Jesus Christ. How can we be steadfast and unshakable in our lives, as St. Paul exhorts?" said and asked the boy.

"We need to do all things in love and always be striving for the truth and the Word of the Lord," Yesac answered.

"In 1 Corinthians 16:13, it says to be strong like men, but there is no word for manly in the English Bible. 'Be on your guard; stand firm in the faith; be courageous; be strong'." The boy questioned the errors in the Korean Bible translation as he spoke.

"In ancient societies, there was a hierarchy of men and women, but in the love of Christ, all are equal. Maybe there is an error in the translation. Some versions of the Bible may have the word men in verse 13, but men are not only used in the plural of men but can also mean people of any gender." The old man said, like a floating cloud.

"Do everything in love," the boy whispered to himself.

"That's right. If you do everything in love, you accomplish everything," old man Yesac advised.

Today, they walked back and forth between McDonald's and Whataburger. The boy felt sorry for himself on the days they didn't buy food, but they were grateful for the restaurants and the world that didn't kick them out.

SJCB Dialogue - 1 Corinthians

"All gifts and acts of faith without love for others are meaningless. Knowledge and power may be great, but love is the greatest of all. Faith is not merely a beginning, but a journey of perseverance and practice. Every believer is a part of Christ's body, and each part— though different—is precious." Buddha Siddhartha spoke with compassion for all humanity.

"Differences are not reasons for conflict, but reasons for coexistence and unity. All gifts come from one source—the Holy Spirit, who is the truth and the Word. It is not the difference in ability that matters, but the unity in origin. This is the reason for humility." The philosopher Socrates spoke as if from the stars.

"The resurrection of Jesus, who overcame the fear of death, is humanity's greatest hope. In Christ, all are given new life. Just as all die in Adam, so all are made alive in Christ. The Gospel is restoration— a promise of rebirth for all humankind."
Old man Yesac's small notebook whispered quietly.

"The teaching to seek not one's own benefit, but the benefit of others, is a truly great lesson. Though it may seem difficult, if you truly embrace this mindset, it is easier than you think— and within it, you will find eternal happiness. Indeed, the heart that considers others above oneself walks the narrow and wise path to enlightenment." Confucius said and smiled with happiness.

"As Saint Paul said, no matter how truthful your words may be, if they are without love, they are mere noise and pollution. Truth begins in love and is perfected in love. Even suffering and weakness can be overcome through the love of God. When imperfect beings are united in love, a wondrous history begins. Because God is love." Jesus spoke with a heart full of love for all humanity.

Volume 8: 2 Corinthians

"Where was Corinth located now?" asked the boy, curiously.

"It's in what is now Greece, and it's surrounded on three sides by the sea, which looks a bit like our Korean map," answered Yesac before looking at a map.

"It was near Athens, Greece." Yesac pointed out.

"Corinth was a geographical hub between the Mediterranean Sea and the Aegean Sea, and it was known for being a city of decadence with a lot of commerce." the old man said.

"It was a place where Paul suffered especially hard as he spread the gospel in Europe." The boy said and then turned the first page of 2 Corinthians.

'Paul, an apostle of Christ Jesus by the will of God, and Timothy our brother, to the church of God which is at Corinth, and to all the saints which are in all Achaia, Grace, and peace to you from God our Father and the Lord Jesus Christ.

Blessed be the God and Father of our Lord Jesus Christ, the Father of compassion and the God of all comfort, who comforts us in all our tribulation, so that we may be able to comfort them that arein any trouble with the comfort which we ourselves have received from God; for as Christ's sufferings overflow with us, soour comfort also overflows with Christ.

For if we suffer, we sufferfor your comfort and salvation; if we are comforted, we are comforted for your comfort; that this comfort may work in you, that ye may be able to bear the same afflictions which we also suffer; knowing that our hope for you is steadfast, that just as yeare partakers of our afflictions, so shall ye be also of our comfort.

For we do not want you, brethren, to be ignorant of the tribulation which we suffered in Asia, in which we were so severely afflicted beyond strength, that even the hope of life was cut off, and we thought that we had received a death sentence in our hearts; that we might not trust in ourselves, but in God, who raises the dead; who hath delivered us from so great a death, and will deliver us again, and we hope in him that he will also deliver us afterward.

Help ye also by intercession for us. Forwe have received gifts by the prayers of many, that many also may give thanks for us. And this is our boast, that we walk in holiness and sincerity of God in the world, especially toward you,not according to the wisdom of the flesh, but according to the grace of God, which is the testimony of our conscience.'

It was not a short letter, but the boy read it in one sitting without pause. Like a sweet chocolate, he ate it simply. You are what you eat; the boy's face always shone with happiness and joy as he fed on the Word.

"How sweet is the comfort of Christ, as we share abundantly in the sufferings of Christ," he said while smiling from ear to ear.

"The trials of life that we encounter in our lives are for the comfort and salvation of Jesus Christ." Yesac nodded.

"God's steadfast hope for us is more than able to conquer all our troubles," said the boy.

"We should remember the tribulations that St. Paul and the apostles suffered in Asia, which were so severe that we despaired of life itself, so far beyond our ability to endure," Yesac instructed.

"Yes. That's what you are writing about," said the boy enthusiastically.

It was a novelized Bible. The boy's words were bold, but his expression was peaceful and free, a face that also smelled of the gospel and Christ. Like an enlightened man.

The old man turned the page of the second book of Corinthians.

'Thanks be to God, who always gives us the victory in Christ, and gives us the odor of the knowledge of Christ in every place; for we are the fragrance of Christ to God, to them that are being saved, and to them that are perishing; to this man the odor of death unto death, and to that man the odor of life unto life.

Whocan bear this, that we do not muddle the word of God, as men of discourse do, but speak in the presence of God and in Christ, as we received it from God in purity: For ye are the epistle of Christ,which is manifested through us: not written with ink, but with theSpirit of the living God; not on tablets of stone, but on tablets ofhuman hearts.

And since we have this confidence in God throughChrist, we shall not be satisfied with ourselves, thinking that whatsoever things are of us, they are of God; but our satisfaction is from God alone, who hath made us partakers of the new covenant: not in spirit, neither in letter, but in spirit: for the letter killeth, but the spirit quickeneth.

For the Lord is the Spirit: and where the Spirit of the Lord is, there is liberty. For we all, with unveiled face, beholding as in a mirror, beholding with unveiled face the glory of the Lord, we are changed into the same image, from glory to glory, even as by the Spirit of the Lord.'

"Paul preaches the gospel as a comforter, a laborer, and a suffering apostle," the boy noted.

"Like Paul, we are to be to God the pleasing aroma of Christ to our neighbors, and that means being a word unto ourselves and living by our actions, which are worth a thousand words. In the love of Christ." Yesac advised.

"Yes. We are the letter from Christ, written on the tablets of human hearts by the Spirit of the living God." The boy agreed with his teacher.

"Freedom from all things comes from enlightenment, and the Lord is the Spirit, and where the Spirit of the Lord is, there is freedom," explained Yesac.

The boy liked the teacher who did not peddle the word of God, who did not add to it or subtract from it, but spoke it with the sincerity and simplicity of the word God had given him. Especially, the old man experienced a mystical world but refrained from speaking mystical words.

'Do not give what is holy to the dogs; do not throw your pearls before swine.'

"Am I not even worthy as a dog or a pig, that Yesac does not share such mystical experiences with me?" The boy frowned slightly as he recalled Jesus' Sermon on the Mount.

'Wherefore, as we have received this office, and have received compassion, we do not lose heart, but lay aside the hidden work of shame, and walk not in deceitfulness, neither do we confound the word of God, but only manifest the truth, giving an account of ourselves to every man's conscience before God.

For if our gospel be hidden, it is hidden unto them that are perishing; in whom the god of this world hath blinded the minds of them that believe not, lest the light of the gospel of the glory of Christ should shine unto them, who is the image of God. For we preach not ourselves, but Christ Jesus as Lord, and for his sake we are your servants.

For the same God, who hath said, Let light shine out of darkness, hath shined in our hearts to give the light of the knowledge of the glory of God in the face of Jesus Christ. For we have this treasure in earthen vessels, that we might know that the exceeding greatness of the power is of God, and not of us.

For though we are besieged on every side, yet we are not crushed; though we are in trouble, yet we are not despondent; though we are persecuted, yet we are not forsaken; though we are upside down, yet we are not destroyed; but we carry about in the body the dying of Jesus, that the life of Jesus might also be manifested in our bodies.'

"As light shines out of darkness, so Paul's gospel is shining in dark Corinth," said the boy.

"As God created man in his image, so Christ is the image of God. Paul, too. You, too," said Yesac.

"God has shone in our hearts to give us the light of the knowledge of the glory of God displayed in the face of Jesus Christ." As the boy said, he turned to Paul's letter to the Corinthians.

'All this is for your benefit, so that the grace that is reaching more and more people may cause thanksgiving to overflow to the glory of God. Therefore, we do not lose heart. Though outwardly, we are wasting away, inwardly, we are being renewed daily.

For our light and momentary troubles are achieving for us an eternal glory that far outweighs them all. So we fix our eyes not on what is seen but on what is unseen since what is seen is temporary, but what is unseen is eternal... For we live by faith, not by sight... He died for all, and those who live should no longer live for themselves but for him, who died for them and was raised again.

Therefore, if anyone is in Christ, the new creation has come: The old has gone, the new is here!... All this is from God, who reconciled us to himself through Christ and gave us the ministry of reconciliation... God made him who had no sin to be sin for us so that in him we might become the righteousness of God.'

"Whatever we do, all grace and love we do for the glory of God," the boy declared.

"Inwardly, we are being renewed day by day. Paul speaks of the sublimity of the eternal Word and truth, which is invisible, rather than the things seen, which are temporary." the old man Yesac said.

"Eternal is unseen," the boy whispered, "and the holy life that walks in its path." The boy whispered to himself once again.

"We should be thankful to endure temporary trials, for eternal glory comes from enduring suffering." the old man said.

"Yes. Troubles are light and momentary, the trials we face in this life." Yesac agreed.

"The anguish of momentary suffering comes from a foolish heart. One must realize that there are answers and secrets hidden within suffering," the boy said with a mature expression. Spiritually.

"Yes. We do not act based on what is seen (not on what is seen), but by believing in what is unseen, we reach the freedom of truth. Truth and freedom lie within suffering." Yesac spoke as if he were someone living beyond the constraints of time and space.

"A person of enlightenment lives not just by what is seen, but with the faith in what is unseen (live by faith, not only by sight)." Even as he spoke holy words, the boy's expression was innocent, like a child gazing upon heaven.

"We do not live for ourselves, but for Jesus Christ, who died and was raised again in our place." The old man and the boy were conversing as if they were walking through the true sunset of enlightenment.

"That is the life of holy words that are unseen." They were freely traversing between the visible world of matter and the invisible world of the Word. Like the Apostle Paul.

"Thus, we all live as new creations in Christ, living a new life."

The boy and Yesac, grateful for having received the ministry of reconciliation from God, turned the pages of Paul's letter to the Corinthians.

'We exhort you, as workers together with God, not to receive the grace of God in vain. For as it is written, he that hath reaped much hath not abundance, neither hath he that hath reaped little abundance: That we may be careful to do good, not only before the Lord but also before men: Every man according as he hath determined in his heart; not with stinginess, nor with compulsion: for God loveth a cheerful giver.

Humble yourselves in the presence of God, bold in the absence of God, I, Paul, now exhort you in the gentleness and forbearance of Christ, andexhort you for the weapons of our warfare are not carnal but mighty to the pulling down of strongholds in the presence of Godso that he who boasts may boast in the Lord.'

"In order not to receive God's grace in vain, we must love our neighbors with the humility and gentleness of Christ," Yesac instructed.

"Yes, every good work faces obstacles, but we must overcome them with perseverance to accomplish good," the boy nodded in agreement.

Yesac continued, highlighting the profound teaching of being good not only in the eyes of God but also in the eyes of others. He reiterated that this is a key aspect of living a virtuous life and progressing on our spiritual journey.

"We should love our neighbors as we love God, not just as we love people, always remembering the words of Jesus, 'Whatever you do for the least of these, you do for me.' Because God is love." As he said, the old man's face radiated with the light of grace.

"The concept of InNaeChun (人乃天 인내천 People is God) in DongHak also aligns with the teachings of Christ," the boy said, reflecting on the idea that all truths converge into one, as expressed in ManBupGwill (萬法歸一 만법귀일).

"In the end, those who have much will have nothing left, and those who have little will not lack. Such is life, so we must not lose sight of eternal happiness by being blinded by the vanity of what is visible," the old man said with detachment.

"Yes. Eternal happiness is loving your neighbor with the truth of God's word," the boy said, his expression filled with the promise of eternal happiness.

They were waiting at a traffic light when they heard the loud siren of a police car. In an instant, the fugitive's car hit theirs. From the stopped car, three young men got out and started running away. Yesac acted as if nothing had happened. On the contrary, the boy looked at Yesac with a puzzled expression.

"Is this a person with no heart, someone completely indifferent? How can the old man Yesac remain so calm?" The boy whispered in his heart.

'Are we of Christ,' they said, 'and speak out of their minds, and so, am I? For I have been in many labors, and in prison morethan once, and have been beaten many times, and have almost died many times, and have been beaten by the Jews five times with forty strokes, and three times with rods, and once with stones, and three times shipwrecked, and have spent twenty-four hours in the depths.

And many times, in journeys have I beenin peril of rivers, and in peril of robbers, and in peril of my own countrymen, and in peril of strangers, and in peril of streams, andin peril of the wilderness, and in peril of the sea, and in peril of false brethren; and many times, have I been sleepless, and manytimes have I been hungry, and many times have I been thirsty, and many times have I been cold, and many times have I been naked. Notwithstanding these things, but these things press upon me day by day: for which I am anxious for all the church.'

"Paul's greatest trial was second only to the pain of crucifixion." Yesac reminded the boy.

"In prison, he was beaten with stones and sticks, suffered 195 blows, wandered around in a trance, and spent 24 hours in the sea, half dead and half alive," he continued.

"To be so hungry, cold, naked, and in danger from bandits, Jews, and Gentiles, and yet concerned for all the church to the end, Paul's love for humanity is truly touching," the boy said sorrowfully.

The H Mart shopping mall in Dallas was hosting a Korean festival. The boys and Yesac had a great time enjoying the many events and coming together as people of many races. The Korean spirit and culture were being celebrated around the world. Together with all humanity!

Later, they continued their lesson on Paul's letter.

'The Lord gave me a thorn in my flesh, a messenger of Satan, to smite me, that I might not be overconfident, because of the greatness of the revelations I had received; and I prayed to the Lord three times that it might depart from me: and he said unto me, my grace is sufficient for thee. For he said unto me, my grace is sufficient for thee, for my power is made perfect in weakness. Therefore, I will glory in my infirmities with great joy, that my grace may rest upon me, for the power of Christ is sufficient for thee: therefore, I glory in infirmities, in reproaches, in distresses, in persecutions, in afflictions, for the sake of Christ: for when I am weak, then am I strong.'

"Paul accepted the thorn in his flesh as God's will to keep him from becoming conceited, and through it, he revealed himself as an even stronger apostle," the boy said, recalling the image of his teacher, Yesac, who once groaned in pain due to illness.

"God's power is made perfect in weakness," Yesac said, grateful for being one of the least.

"Rejoicing in suffering and allowing Christ's power to rest on him, Paul is a great apostle of Jesus," the boy said, expressing gratitude for his connection with Yesac, who guided him on enlightenment and eternal happiness.

"The hope that all of us weak people have is that by enduring hatred, poverty, trials, and conflicts for Christ, and rejoicing through them, we achieve perfection," Yesac said, with a sense of gratitude for the past painful sufferings.

Today, Yesac, who has decided to focus on healing from his soccer injury, was graciously given acupuncture by an elder who provides medical care at the church. He was also given a daily lunch. All were beautiful brothers and sisters in Christ. As he left the clinic, Yesac thanked God for the beautiful world He had given him.

'Until this time you think that we are making excuses for you, we say to God in Christ. Beloved, all this is done for your virtue's sake, for if Christ was crucified in weakness, but lived by the power of God, we also, though we are weak in him, shall live withhim in the power of God toward you. Examine yourselves, whether ye be in the faith, and confirm yourselves.

Know ye notyourselves that Jesus Christ is in you, except ye be of God, whomye have forsaken. Finally, I say unto you, brethren, be of good cheer. Be of good cheer, be of good comfort, be of one accord, be of one mind; and the God of love and peace be with you. Greetone another with the kiss of holiness. The grace of the Lord Jesus Christ, and the love of God, and the fellowship of the Holy Ghost, be with you all.'

Like Paul's letter, which states that all things work for the building up of virtue, the boy wrote and wrote and wrote, engraving on his heart's tablet the words he had shared with Yesac that would never be forgotten.

'DukBulGoPilYuRin(덕불고 필유린 德不孤 必有隣), a virtuous person is never alone but always has a neighbor. In the life of the Word, there was always virtue, and that virtue was the love of Christ.'

"A virtuous person lives by the power of God's love, peace, and faith," The old man spoke without hesitation.

"Yes. Because Jesus Christ is in us." The boy agreed.

"The work of all humanity is to rejoice and encourage one another, to be of one mind, to live in peace and love," Yesac responded.

"Such is the blessed life of love and the fellowship of the HolySpirit," he continued.

On a quiet morning in the crisp fall weather, fresh from a workout and a shower, Yesac, looking peaceful and happy, flipped through Corinthians to Galatians.

SJCB Dialogue - 2 Corinthians

"Life is filled with joy, anger, sorrow, and pleasure (HuiNoAeRak 희노애락 喜怒哀樂). Yet all things are born from the heart, and those who are enlightened choose a life of joy and delight (HuiRak 희락 喜樂) rather than anger and sorrow (NoAe 노애 怒哀). They understand that suffering is a gateway to grace. In truth, when one looks back on life, they come to see that trials and hardships refine and renew the human spirit." This, the Buddha said, speaking of rebirth.

"Faith is a journey toward the unseen. What is seen is temporary, but the truth that is unseen is eternal. Paul rejoiced in suffering, persecution, poverty, and insult because the power of Christ was revealed in such trials." So said Socrates, who once asked humanity,

"How should we live?"

"If one is to boast, let it be in their weakness and pain— for only through them does the grace of the Cross shine. The proper response to that grace is to live joyfully, doing good to the neighbors we love. This is a life that builds virtue, and in that life, the great love of God resides." So spoke Confucius, with reverence for the Divine.

"True joy does not come from outside. It springs up from the well within, drawn by faith. For God dwells within us. Paul did not impose joy, but helped others to find it. That is what true love is."
Jesus spoke these words through Paul's letter.

Volume 9: Galatians

"Where is Galatia?" the old man asked the boy.

"Galatia is a region located in central Anatolia, where the Celts once lived. It corresponds to the area near modern-day Ankara in Turkey. Paul wrote letters to the churches there to warn them not to distort the gospel of Christ with the law," the boy replied, looking at the large map on the wall.

"Galatia was an important region connected to other cities like Philippi, Ephesus, and Colossae. However, it was quite distant from Jerusalem and Antioch. The letters Paul sent to the Galatians were crucial in helping the early churches in that region preserve the true gospel," the old man said with a compassionate smile, finding the boy's understanding admirable. Yesac smiled benevolently at the boy.

"Paul saw the doctrine of circumcision and the law as a condition of salvation as a serious distortion of the gospel." The boy, thinking of the open-minded Apostle Paul, spoke.

"It is God's grace and love that sets us free, but without enlightenment, the law keeps us in bondage." The old man said with an open heart.

The boy opened the first chapter of Galatians with a look of freedom on his face. In fact, he preferred the Word to bread.

'Paul, an apostle, to all the brethren that are with me, and to the churches of Galatia, which are not of men, neither was it of men, but of Jesus Christ, and of God the Father, who raised him from the dead: Grace to you, and peace, from God our Father, and the Lord Jesus Christ, to all the churches of Galatia, which arewith us. For I make known unto you, brethren, that the gospel which I preached unto you is not after the will of man: for I received it not of man, neither was I taught it, but it was by the revelation of Jesus Christ, knowing that a man shall not be justified by the works of the law, but by faith in Jesus Christ: for we also believe in Christ Jesus, that we might be justified by faith in Christ, and not by the works of the law.

For by the deeds of thelaw, there shall no flesh be justified, I am crucified with Christ: nevertheless, it is no longer I who live, but Christ liveth in me: andthe life which I now live in the flesh I live by faith in the Son of God, who loved me and gave himself for me. For I will not abolishthe grace of God: for if it be by the law that one is justified, thenChrist died in vain.'

"Paul says that the gospel he preaches is not something he learned, but only by the revelation of Jesus Christ. That's a far cry from my idea of learning," the boy said thoughtfully.

"When the Holy Spirit comes and we learn the Word in love, that is also a revelation. Let's not compare, but let's go with what God gives us." Yesac cautioned.

The boy was silent.

"Revelation isn't something scary, it's a gift from God through His Holy Spirit of love," he finally said.

"Yes, it is not the law that sets us free, but faith in Christ and love for our neighbors."

"The fulfillment of the law was accomplished through Jesus' love and the cross."

"Yes. Christ's love for mankind fulfilled the law." Yesac agreedonce again.

The boy's small notebook contained a letter from Paul that his teacher, Yesac, said gave him an epiphany while he was in a cave on Big Bear Mountain.

'I have been crucified with Christ and I no longer live, but Christ lives in me. The life I now live in the body, I live by faith in the Son of God, who loved me and gave himself for me.'

Yesac handwrote something in the boy's little notebook.

'MuAhYuJu(無我唯主 무아유주): There is no I, only Jesus'

"Siddhartha said, 'I am the only one,' so is he the only master? Yes, Jesus is in me, and those who have ears to hear will understand." The boy whispered to himself while meditating alone.

'For it is evident that no man shall be justified by the works of the law before God: for it is written, the just shall live by faith: that the blessing of Abraham might be made known to the Gentiles in Christ Jesus, and that we might receive the promise of the Holy Ghost by faith: so that the law might be a tutor to bring us to Christ, that we might be justified by faith: for after faith came, we were not under tutors. For ye are all sons of God

through faith in Christ Jesus; for as many of you as were baptized into Christ have been clothed with Christ; for there is neither Jew nor Greek, there is neither scion nor bond nor free, there is neither male nor female, for ye are all one in Christ Jesus; and if ye be Christ's, then are ye Abraham's seed, and heirs according to the promise.'

"Paul likens the law to a schoolmaster, a guardian of children's studies," the boy said thoughtfully.

"The law brought us to Christ to be justified by faith," Yesac said.

"We are all one in Christ Jesus, whether Jew or Greek, whether European or Asian, whether North or South American, whether ethnic, racial, or cultural." The boy spoke with a generous heart.

"Yes. We have the same Father, and we look to Jesus, Mohammed, Buddha, and Brahma for guidance. We all coexist in our differences; we just need to respect and love each other as is." The old man Yesac said with a heart full of love for allhumanity.

Time for a brisk walk at the fitness center is the only time to Google the news. "Today is October 8, 2023," said the boy who searched the news.

"There are more than 5,000 casualties in the war between Israel and Palestine today." The boy spoke with a sad expression. At that moment, he simultaneously recalled Abraham, Sarah, Hagar, Ishmael, and Isaac, contemplating the beginning of the conflict between Arabs and Israelites.

"After 4,000 years, Isaac and Ishmael are still fighting underground," Yesac said, his usual first response to any news.

"Yes," he said, "all the answers are in the Word." The boy remembered a verse from Yesac's little notebook. In the hope of enlightenment.

'There is nothing new under the sun, what has been will be again, what has been done will be done again; Generations come and generations go, but the earth remains forever.'

This time, the Palestinians (Islamic/Mohammedan) in the Gaza Strip, located in the coastal area on the Egyptian border, rather than the West Bank of the Jordan River, have attacked Israel under the name Operation Al Aqsa Storm Flood, and Israel has been fighting a war under the name Operation IronSword.

"The same sons of Abraham are fighting," the boy said.

"Sons of Sarah and Hagar." Yesac nodded.

This was ongoing knowledge. Yesac and the boy were familiarizing themselves with the old to learn the new. After watching the news.

The boy turned the page of Paul's letter to the Galatians.

'For Christ has set us free to be free; therefore, stand firm and take no more a yoke of servitude. Behold, I, Paul, say unto you, that if ye be circumcised, Christ shall be of no profit unto you. For I testify again unto every man that is circumcised, that he is bound to do the whole law. 16 I say unto you, Walk ye after the Spirit. And ye shall not fulfill the lust of the flesh. For the lust of the flesh lusteth against the Spirit, and the Spirit against the flesh: and these two are contrary to each other, that ye should not do the things which ye desire: for if ye be led by the Spirit, ye shall not be under the law.
For the works of the flesh are manifest, which are these: fornication, uncleanness, lasciviousness, idolatry, envying, strife, envying, anger, revellings, dissensions, heresies, speculations, drunkenness, revellings, and such like.
Again I warn you, that they which do these things shall not inherit the kingdom of God: but the fruit of the Spirit is love, joy, peace, longsuffering, mercy, goodness, faithfulness, gentleness, temperance: against such there is no law forbidding: for the people of Christ Jesus have crucified with the flesh the passions and desires of the mind; and if we live by the Spirit, we shall also walk by the Spirit: not being agitated one against another, jostling one against another, seeking vain glory.'

"Paul is presenting Christ as the one who is obligated to fulfillthe whole law." The boy said with an expression seeking understanding.

"Christ is the Holy Spirit, so if you are led by the Spirit, you arenot under the law." The old man said with freedom.

"Yes. We are set free from everything by the love and grace of Christ, not by the law."

"The law and the flesh are bondage, but freedom is life," Yesac said.

"We need to walk by the Spirit, which is contrary to the desires of the flesh," the boy said.

"By thinking with love, speaking with mercy, and acting with compassion, we can walk in the sunset of heaven even as we live." The old man said, and the boy meditated once more.

'Since we live by the Spirit, let us keep in step with the Spirit.'

The boy carefully recorded in his little notebook the words of truth that Yesac always lived by in his heart.

'The fruit of the Spirit is love, joy, peace, forbearance, kindness, goodness, faithfulness, gentleness, and self-control.'

'SaHuiHwaO JaYangChungOnJul, GGFF JKL PS.'

The boy whispered to himself as he thought of ways to remember the nine fruits of the Spirit.

"As Christians, we should go about our lives and bring the fragrance of these nine fruits of the Spirit to our neighbors." Yesac thought of the nine fruits of the Spirit, sweeter and more delicious than honey, and said.

Yesac worked at the office, unaware that today was Columbus Day, a holiday. For lunch, he ate ramen noodles with quinoa. It was a hearty lunch, he thought.

The boy turned the page of Paul's letter.

'Brethren, if any man is found to have trespassed, you who are godly, in a meek spirit, correct him, and examine yourselves, lest you also be tempted. Bear ye one another's burdens, and so fulfill the law of Christ. If any man thinketh that he is nothing and that he hath become much, he deceiveth himself: let every man examine his own work, so that he may boast, and not of another: for every man shall bear his own burden, and not deceive himself.

For God is no respecter of persons, for whatsoever a man soweth, that shall he also reap. But I have nothing to boast of, save the cross of our Lord Jesus Christ: for by him the world is crucified unto me, and I unto the world: Brethren, the grace of our Lord Jesus Christ be in your hearts. Amen.'

Paul is teaching the principle of TaSanJiSuk GaYiGongOk(他山之石 可以攻玉 타산지석 가이공옥), which means 'using the rough stone of another mountain to polish a precious gem.'

This wisdom originates from the Shi Jing(시경 詩經), also known as the Book of Songs, one of the revered works among the Four Books and Five Classics (사서오경 四書五經) in Chinese Classics.

"Restore those who have transgressed and watch yourselves is the TaSanJiSuk," Yesac said.

"Yes. Even a stone from another mountain (他山 타산) can grind (지석之石) my own jade." the boy said.

"As St. Paul wrote to the Galatians, we should carry each other's burdens and strive to fulfill the law of Christ. Carry each other's burdens, and in this way, you will fulfill the law of Christ."

the old man said.

"Paul teaches the virtue of humility using mysterious expressions."

In the boy's small notebook, he had written a letter from St. Paul about the virtue of humility.

> *'Each one should test their own actions, then they can take pride in themselves alone, without comparing themselves to someone else.'*

"That's the secret of standing alone on the rock, reflecting the truth of Christ." The old man said with the same resoluteness as before, like the horn of a rhinoceros.

"Yes. Life is about going it alone and boldly, like the horns of a moose, as one author put it." The boy, recalling the novel 'Go Alone Like a Rhinoceros Horn' by author Gong Ji-young in Korea, remarked.

"A man reaps what he sows is also a great teaching in the letter. A man reaps what he sows. The man I am today is the result of yesterday, and the man will be tomorrow, which is the result of the man today, and there is no mystery in life," Yesac said with a cool-headed tone.

"Paul moves on to Ephesus, a town to the left of Galatia." The boy said, flipping through the pages of Ephesians.

SJCB Dialogue - Galatians

"The gospel of truth is not a human creation, but a 'revelation' that comes from heaven. It is the truth. Faith is greater than the law. Through being crucified with Christ, Paul confesses that he has died, and now Jesus lives within him. We must awaken to the life of no-self (無我), where 'I' no longer live, but Christ on the cross lives within me." Siddhartha Gautama spoke through the wisdom of 'no-self (muah무아 無我)'."

"All of humanity becomes children of God through faith, transcending nation, race, language, and religion. This is a proclamation of transcultural unity that overcomes discrimination and conflict. The true root of oneness lies in Christ Jesus on the cross." Socrates spoke as he read Galatians 3:28, a verse recorded in Confucius' little notebook.

'There is neither Jew nor Greek, slave nor free, male nor female, for you are all one in Christ Jesus.'

"Spiritual maturity is not shown by words or knowledge, but by the fruit of one's life. True freedom comes from love that goes beyond the law. We are freed not by law, but by the love and grace given by Christ."Confucius said this while looking over Galatians 5:22–23, written in Siddhartha's small notebook.

'The fruit of the Spirit is love, joy, peace, patience, kindness, goodness, faithfulness, gentleness, and self-control.'

"'You reap what you sow (종두득두 種豆得豆)' and the law of cause and effect (인과응보 因果應報) — this simple truth penetrates the entire moral and spiritual structure of life. The one who sows ultimately writes the letter of his own life. One's thoughts, words, and actions — they are one's very life." Jesus spoke while reading a passage from Socrates' notebook, and as he did, the Buddha turned to the tenth book of the New Testament, Ephesians.

'A man reaps what he sows.' – Galatians 6

Volume 10: Ephesians

"What is the book of Ephesians?" Yesac asked.

"I know that Ephesians is a letter to the people of Ephesus (Turkey), written by Paul while he was in prison in Rome in 62 AD." The boy responded.

"Ephesus was located in what is now Turkey, between the Black Sea and the Mediterranean Sea, and also in the center of Europe and Asia. Although it is closer to Europe." The old man said, thinking of Turkey, a country that has historically maintained a close and friendly relationship with South Korea.

"There's Romans, which was written to the Romans, and Ephesians, which was written from a Roman prison, and Rome comes up a lot." The boy said with curiosity.

"All roads lead to Rome, as the saying goes, and Ancient Rome was a huge empire that occupied the entire area around what is now the Mediterranean and Black Seas, stretching from the border of present-day Syria to Spain, the landlocked tip of Europe." The old man spoke while looking at the ancient map.

"Rome was the center of the world, right?" The boy pointed out.

"The proverb 'All roads lead to Rome' comes from the fact that Roman engineers built 85,000 kilometers of roads," Yesac explained.

The boy opens Paul's letter to the Ephesians and begins to read.

'Blessed be the God and Father of our Lord Jesus Christ, who hath blessed us in Christ with every spiritual blessing in the heavenly places, having chosen us in Christ before the foundation of the world, that we should be holy and without blame before him in love, according to the good pleasure of his will, that we should be sons by Jesus Christ, according to the grace of his Spirit, which he freely gave us in the beloved, to the praise of the glory of his grace.

In whom we have redemption through his blood, the forgiveness of sins, according to the riches of his grace in Christ Jesus, in whom he hath made known unto us the mystery of his will, according to his good pleasure, which he hath purposed in Christ for the dispensation of his good pleasure, that in him all things should be united, both in heaven and on earth, in one body, in Christ; according to the purpose of him who worketh all things after the counsel of his own mind, that we should be the workmanship of his purpose, to the praise of his glory, which he hath before ordained in Christ Jesus.'

The boy paused his meditation for a moment and drank some cold water.

'In whom also ye have heard the word of truth, the gospel of your salvation, in whom also ye have believed, and have been sealed with the Holy Ghost of promise: May the God of our Lord Jesus Christ, the Father of glory, give unto you the spirit of wisdom and revelation, to give the eyes of your heart to know what is the hope of his calling, what are the riches of the glory of his inheritance in the saints, and what is the exceeding greatness of his power to us who believe according to the working of his mighty power.'

"Praise be to God, who in love gives us love and mercy, that we should be holy and without blame before him." The boy spoke as if praising.

"That is God's pleasure and will for mankind. God has lavishedon us with all wisdom and understanding so that life itself is full and abundant." The old man spoke like the wind, with joy and gratitude, without any hindrance.

"He has enlightened the eyes of our hearts so that all things in heaven and on earth may be one in Christ." The boy spoke with brightness.

"The eyes of your heart. Yes, the eyes of your heart, so that you may see the invisible Word and be enlightened." The old man spoke with enlightenment.

The boy left the office for an appointment with a real estate client. He remembered Yesac's words—that no matter what you're doing, attacking it head-on with honesty is the way to get good results. 'Leaders are clear. Leaders are clear, clear, clear.' Isn't that also what the Sermon on the Mount teaches about being pure in heart?

The old man turned the page of Ephesians, the fifth letter of Paul.

'For the same God who wrought in Christ, who raised him from the dead, and seated him at his own right hand in the heavenly places, far above all principality, and power, and might, and dominion, and every name that is named, not only in this world, but also in that which is to come; and put all things in subjection under his feet, and gave him to be head over all things to the church, which is his body, the fullness of him who fills all in all.

For God, who is rich in mercy, because of his great love with which he loved us, made us alive together with Christ, even when we were dead in trespasses (for by grace are ye saved) in order that in the ages to come he might show the exceeding riches of his grace in his mercy toward us in Christ Jesus.'

Yesac took a sip of licorice tea with a yellow color.

'For by grace are ye saved through faith; and that not of yourselves: it is the gift of God. Not of works, lest any man should boast: For ye are now made nigh in Christ Jesus by the blood of Christ, wherein ye that were far off are made nigh: for he is our peace, who is both our reconciliation, having broken down the middle wall of partition and hath reconciled both in one body to God by the cross. And having abolished in himself the enmity by the cross the enmity, that you should be built together in Christ Jesus for a habitation of God in the Spirit.'

"For it is by grace you have been saved, through faith and that not of yourselves, it is the gift of God, not as a result of works, so that we may not boast." The boy spoke freely as if he had gained freedom.

"God, who is our peace, has destroyed the enmity and the wall of hostility between people by the cross to reconcile us in one." The old man said with a grateful heart as he turned the pages of the book.

'I am made a partaker according to the gift of God's grace, which was given to me according to his power for this gospel. For to me, who am the least of all the saints, this grace was given, that I might preach to the Gentiles the unsearchable riches of Christ, and to make known what are the things of the mystery, which have been hid in God from all eternity, who created all things.

That now through the church he might make known to the principalities and powers in the heavenly places the manifold

> *wisdom of God, according to the purpose of his will, which he purposed in Christ Jesus our Lord from eternity past.'*

The usually hot August weather in Dallas, Texas, was unexpectedly cool today. With a bright and serene expression, the boy turned the pages of Ephesians.

> *'Wherein we have boldness and confidence to approach God with confidence through faith in him: wherefore I beseech you, be not dismayed at my various tribulations for your sakes. For it is your glory...*
>
> *That Christ may dwell in your hearts through faith, and that you, being rooted and grounded and established in love, may be able to comprehend with all the saints what is the breadth and length and height and depth, and to know the love of Christ that passeth knowledge, that ye may be filled with all the fullness of God.'*

"The gift of God is not just a gift, but a gift of mercy, grace, and love," the boy said.

"Paul's stance of lowliness, saying, 'I am less than the least of all the Lord's people,' teaches us that we are exalted by being lowly. By the grace of God, Paul was able to preach to the Gentiles the unsearchable riches of Christ, to make known the manifold wisdom of God." The old man said with a heart of humility and wisdom.

"The manifold wisdom of God enables us not to be discouraged but to overcome all trials," the boy said.

"Being rooted and established in love is the secret to living a full life, realizing what the breadth and length and height and depth are." The old man was poor, but he spoke with a heart full of abundance.

Yesac was working out at the gym like any other dawn when a young white friend approached him.

"You look eager," the friend said.

"Yes, I am. I'm not pushing myself too hard because of my age." Yesac admitted.

"How old are you?" the friend asked.

"Sixty-two," came Yesac's response.

His response elicited a laugh from the friend, "Wow. You motivate me."

Not long ago, a Black friend also asked the same question, suggesting that Yesac's physique might be quite remarkable.

"You are better," Yesac said, laughing off his friend's compliment.

Reminded that motivation is the aroma of Christ, Yesac got out of the shower and left the fitness center. Shining light on his face like Moses coming down from Mount Sinai with the Ten Commandments.

The old man turned the page of Paul's letter.

'I therefore, the prisoner of the Lord, exhort you, that ye walk worthy of the vocation wherewith ye were called, with all lowliness and meekness, with longsuffering, forbearing one another in love, with all lowliness of mind, keeping the unity of the Spirit in the bond of peace: For there is one body and one Spirit, even as ye were called in one hope of your calling: There is one Lord, one faith, one baptism, one God and Father of all, which is the same God and Father of all. Who is over all, and through all, and in all, and through all, and in all?

To each one of us has he given grace according to the measure of the gift of Christ, as the truth is in Jesus, as ye have indeed heard and have been taught by him: that ye put off the old man, which is being corrupted according to the deceitful lusts of temptation, and that ye put on the new man, which is being renewed in the spirit of your mind, and is being created after God in righteousness and holiness of truth; and that ye put away falsehood, and speak one thing true to his neighbor.

'For we are members of one another. Sin no more, neither let your anger go to the sun, nor let your wrath go unchecked, but let no unwholesome thing proceed out of your mouth, but only such good speaking as is useful for building up virtue, that it may grace the hearers; and do not grieve the Holy Spirit of God. For in him, ye are kept unto the day of redemption: laying aside all malice, and anger, and clamor, and wrath, and reviling, with all malice; being patient with one another, tenderhearted, forgiving one another, even as God for Christ's sake hath forgiven you.'

"If we, all mankind, are united in the unity of the Spirit through the bond of peace, forgiving and loving one another in love with perfect humility, gentleness, and patience, that will be the kingdom of heaven." The boy said with an expression of eternal happiness.

"We have quite a few enlightened neighbors who are already living that way."

As the old man thought about how walking withChrist made it feel as though the Kingdom of God had already come to us, the idea that all humanity within the universe had already realized the truth that we are all one passed through hismind, completing the journey with the novelized scriptures.

"Just as there is one God and Father of all, who is over all and through all and in all, and in the Lord, and in baptism, and in faith, and in the Holy Spirit, so all humanity is one."

A homeless man shouted three years ago,

'With a single pen, I will unify the worldand unite humanity.'

The thought that this proclamation is now becoming a reality passed through the boy's mind.

"To each one of us grace has been given, just as God has graciously given the gift of Christ to all humanity, so we coexist inlove with one another, recognizing our differences."

'He will do the works that I do and even greater works than these.' This profound teaching of Christ made the old man believe nothing was impossible. More importantly, the secret to achieving the impossible lay in believing in Christ because Christ had gone to the Father. Ultimately, faith in Christ and the cross was the secret to making all things possible. Thus, it became possible for 'the world to be unified by the Word and humanity to be united by love.'

'SaBanGongBae(사반공배 事半功倍), half the effort, double the result!'

If one understands the secret of how God created the world in six days by His Word, is there anything impossible in human affairs? The old man and the boy embarked on a journey with such 'novelized scriptures' for happiness and peace in humanity. That journey, before long, hadreached the point of Paul's letters to the Corinthians.

"Paul's letter, 'The truth is in Jesus,' is so enlightening."

"I should know the truth by knowing Jesus Christ in me rather than trying to find something outside of me."

The boy's little notebook was filled with words sweeter than honey, written with the marks of countless meditations. It was Paul's First Epistle to the Ephesians in what is now Turkey.

'You were taught, with regard to your former way of life, to put off your old self, which is being corrupted by its deceitful desires; to be made new in the attitude of your minds; and to put on the new self, created to be like God in true righteousness and holiness. Therefore, each of you must put off falsehood and speak truthfully to your neighbor, for we are all members of one body.'

"Master, I don't know much about difficult things, but I want to be a person who speaks what is true with my neighbor. Words come from my mind and heart, expressing who I am, and words are the greatest weapon and tool of mankind, capable of hurting or comforting." The boy said with a heart that sought goodness and embraced love for his neighbors.

Yesac silently extended his small notebook.

'Good words are like honeycombs—sweet to the heart and a balm to the bones. Words are a seed and mirror of actions. A wound inflicted by a sword can heal, but a wound caused by words can last a lifetime. To speak is knowledge, but to listen is wisdom. You are better than the beast with words, but if you do not speak rightly, the beast is better than you. The words from the mouth of a wise person are like deep waters, and the fountains of wisdom are like springs of water.

A word spoken at the right moment is like a golden apple in a silver tray, engraved with aromas. By the words of your mouth, you may entangle yourself, and by the words of your mouth, you may also be freed. Words are the reflection of the heart. Like a sword that pierces, so too can words; but the tongue of the wise is a balm.'

"Speaking good words in love to your neighbor is being renewed in the spirit of your mind, to be created in holiness of righteousness and truth after God." The old man was explaining to the boy in simple terms what seemed difficult to him.

"Yes. Good words are the fragrance of Christ that we impart to our neighbors." The boy was gradually becoming a free man.

"Do not let the sun go down while you are still angry, but speak good words to your neighbor, for this is the building up of virtue." Yesac said.

"Be kind and compassionate to one another, tenderhearted, forgiving one another, as God forgave us, for this is the kingdom of heaven." The old man looked at the boy with the same heart that God has when He looks at humanity, filled with Christ's love.

After a long time, his daughter sent a KakaoTalk message asking to have a meal together. It was Yesac's 63rd birthday. He had taught his daughter golf since she was five years old, and she had even competed in the LPGA U.S. Women's Open 2022. Yesac's expression, always solitary, was no different from usual.

After finishing dinner with his daughter and returning home, Yesac turned the pages of Paul's letters.

'Be ye therefore imitators of God, as dearly beloved children, and walk in love, as Christ also hath loved you. For he gave himself up for us, an offering and sacrifice of a fragrant savor, a living sacrifice to God. Fornication, all uncleanness, and covetousness, let none of these things be called by any name among you. For the fruit of the light is in all goodness, and righteousness, and truthfulness.

Redeem the days, for the days are evil; be ye therefore not fools, but understand what is the will of the Lord. Speaking to one another in psalms and hymns and sacred songs, singing and making melody in your heart to the Lord, giving thanks always to God the Father for everything in the name of our Lord Jesus Christ, with all submission in the fear of God.'

Darkness and light, the boy had indeed experienced a world of darkness and light. Before he knew the Bible, he was a child of darkness, but after he read it and became enlightened, he saw the world of eternal light. Also, goodness, righteousness, and truth were the fruits of the light that the boy picked daily; the fruit of the light consists in all goodness, righteousness, and truth.

"What does 'redeem the years, for the days are evil' mean?" Confused by the difference in meaning between the English Bible and its interpretation of Korean, the boy asked.

The old man and the boy had long realized that errors in Bible translation could become a severe obstacle to enlightenment. The phrase 'Redeem the time, for the days, are evil' is not an accurate translation in Korean and leads people to be cautious or take a passive stance. The boy was learning that there are both good and evil times, and the wisdom to discern between them lies within the Word. The correct translation, 'Make the most of every opportunity,' encourages people to adopt an active and resilient approach, as taught in Proverbs, with the concept of falling seven times and rising again.

"There must have been a slight error in the Korean translation. 'To spare' is to save, and 'to make' is to create. The correct interpretation is to make the most of every opportunity, which is expressed as IlChonKwangEumBulGaKyung(一寸光陰 不可輕, 일촌광음불가경), meaning 'Not even an inch of time should be taken lightly.'" the old man said.

The boy saw a phrase in Yesac's notebook that caught his eye. It was a poem by Zhu Xi, a scholar from the Southern Song dynasty (Hangzhou) in China, about the value of time, expressed in the saying, *'An inch of time is worth an inch of gold.'*

'SoNyunYiRoHakNanSung (소년이로학난성(少年易老學難成)
; Boys are easy to grow old, learning is hard to achieve.'

'IlChonKwangEumBulGaKyung (一寸光陰 不可輕
일촌광음불가경); An inch of time is too precious to be taken lightly.'

'MiGakJiDangChunChoMong(미각지당춘초몽(未覺池塘春草夢);
The spring grass has not yet awakened from its dream.'

'KyeJunOhYupYiChuSung(계전오엽 이추성(階前梧葉 已秋聲) ;
The paulownia leaves in front of the island stone are already making autumn sounds.'

"In the end, Paul's letter is about making the best of every moment, not letting a single moment go to waste," said the boy in realization.

"That's what people who accomplish great things do." Yesac nodded.

"Yes, you used your spare time to work as a professional boxer, professional golfer, real estate and finance expert, writer, and YouTuber, all while raising your two daughters to become professional golfers with nothing but hard work," the boy said.

Yesac, who did not like to talk about himself, ignored the boy's words and quickly turned to the last page of Ephesians.

'Children, obey your parents in the Lord, for this is right. Honor thy father and mother, for this is the first commandment, which hath promise: that it may be well with thee, and that thou mayest live long on the earth. And fathers, do not provoke thy children to old age, but bring them up in the nurture and admonition of the Lord.

With all prayer and supplication, by prayer and supplication with thanksgiving let your requests be made known in the Spirit; and in this, by watching and praying with all prayer and supplication, with thanksgiving, let your requests be made for all the saints; and for me, that he may giveme words, that I may open my mouth, and make known with boldness the mystery of the gospel to all them that love our LordJesus Christ steadfastly.'

"It has taught me a great deal that the first commandment with promise is honor to parents," the boy said.

"The first four of the Ten Commandments given to Moses are the commandments of reverence for God, and the other six are the commandments of love for our neighbor, and the first commandment to love our neighbor is to be filial to our parents." the old man said.

"Ah, yes. So you are free from everything, but only when you think of your parents, you look a little more compassionate and wistful," the boy said.

"................"

Yesac was silent as he gazed at the distant mountains.

"Filial piety is the golden rule of life, emphasized by all religions, both ancient and modern," he finally said.

The boy's eyes fell again on Yesac's small notebook. It was a precious piece of writing about filial piety.

'The tree wishes to be still, but the wind does not stop blowing; the child wishes to be filial, but the mother does not wait. There are three thousand sins in this world, but disobedience to one's parents is the greatest of them all. If you are not filial to your parents, you will regret it when you die; serve your parents as you would a child. Those who love their parents do not hate others, and those who honor their parents do not look down on others. From the time you rise in the morning until the time you go to sleep at night, the heavens will surely recognize you, even if people do not.

If I am filial to my father, my children are filial to me. If I am not filial to my father, how can my children be filial to me? Do unto your parents exactly as you would have them do unto you. Honor your aging mother with respect. For she labored for you in her youth, wearing out her sinews and bones. Of all the things in the world, nothing is more precious than my body. But this body was given to me by my parents. Honoring one's father and mother is a supreme law of nature. Do not associate with anyone who does not honor his parents, for he has left the first steps of humanity.'

Yesac and the boy began to sing the song

'The Grace of Parents'

'When they bore you, they forgot all the pain, and

day and night they toiled with all their might.
They lay you down on the softest spot,

changing your bedding tirelessly,

wearing out their hands and feet.
What in the world could be wider than the sky?

Yet, no sacrifice is greater than that of a parent.
When you were young, they held you in their arms,

carried you on their back, and covered you warmly.
As you grew up, they leaned on the doorframe,

waiting with a heart full of hope.
For every tear and every hurt,

their furrowed brow bore the weight of their child's every thought.
What on earth could be higher than the ground?

Yet, no devotion is greater than that of a parent.
In the hearts of people lie countless desires,

but in the heart of a parent, there is only one.
Selflessly, they give their life for their children,

carving out their flesh and bones to offer with all they have. What in this world could be more sacred?

Yet, no love is greater than that of a parent.'

"The letter from Paul, which states that the secret to wealth and longevity also lies in filial piety, delivers an amazing message. Paul also writes that the best way to educate children is through the teachings and admonitions of Christ found in the Bible." The boy said this while looking at the words written in the old man's small notebook.

'Honoring your father and mother may go well with you, and you may enjoy a long life on the earth.'

"Parents and children alike should strive to live a life that becomes the truth by practicing the Word. Still, children should honor their parents simply because they are their parents."
Yesac finished speaking and handed over a small notebook. It was from the sixth chapter of the Analects, JaRo(자로편子路篇).

'KiShinJung BulRyungYiHang
其身正 不令而行 기신정 불령이행
KiShinBuJung SuRyungBuJong
其身不正 雖令不從 기신부정 수령수종
: If one's conduct is upright, orders will be followed without being given; if one's conduct is not upright, even if orders are given, they will not be obeyed.'

The boy thought it was indeed a wonderful lesson. Indeed, faith without deeds is dead.

SJCB Dialogue - Ephesians

"Before the foundation of the world, God chose us in love to be holy and blameless in His sight. Salvation by grace is not through our own merit but is a gift from God—an unconditional love that no one can boast of. In return, we too must freely extend that same love to our neighbors, without reason." The Buddha spoke of compassion, that is, love.

"There is one Lord, one faith, one baptism, and one God—thus all of humanity is one. Transcending time and space, we must preserve this unity in truth and the bond of peace, loving one another. We must cast off falsehood and speak truthfully, using words that build others up and bring grace to those who hear." Socrates broke the ancient silence to speak.

"'Make the most of every opportunity, for the days are evil'—Paul's letter must be understood with an awakened heart. Time is a blend of good and evil. Not all time is evil; rather, Paul's 'time' refers to moments where God intervenes with divine opportunities. This letter was written from prison in Rome. At that time, the Roman Empire deified its emperor, and Christianity was seen as a treasonous cult. Idolatry, persecution, imprisonment, moral decay, materialism, sexual corruption, the worship of wealth, and self-centered values were rampant in Ephesus, Corinth, and Rome. Indeed, it was an 'evil time.' Yet Paul was pointing not to fear, but to seize such times as divine opportunities." Said the old man Yesac.

"Therefore, believers should not habitually declare, 'The times are evil.' Especially when they say, 'We are in the last days' so lightly, though only God knows the time. Such careless speech can diminish God's glory. Moreover, the Korean Bible has passed through five language layers in translation, leading to errors. These errors have at times led to blind faith, resulting in senseless tragedies and even the loss of lives. Even now, in an age ruled by AI, such misunderstandings cause religious conflicts due to human ignorance. Simply put, it's all too common to see people attending churches or temples yet practicing superstitious faith. Everyone must live their own life according to their given portion. All we can do is respond with love and mercy, and pray for them." Confucius walked as if strolling through heaven.

"For example, in Paul's English letter, the phrase 'Redeem the time' does not exist. The expression 'Redeem the time' leads people to live defensively and cautiously, rather than with love and boldness. What Paul really said was 'make the most of every opportunity'—a highly active and forward-moving mindset. It would have been better rendered with the idiom 'IlChonKwangEumBulGaKyung (一寸光陰不可輕),' meaning 'Not even an inch of time should be taken lightly.'" The old man Yesac continued.

"We must live as bearers of light, as those who hope for restoration, as people who awaken through the Word and use technology righteously. Let us not waste opportunities, but love more and live the present moment as light. Let us walk as children of light—in goodness, righteousness, and truth. Let us cast off the darkness and shine the light of truth. Children must honor their parents and discover that this is the key to long life and blessing." Jesus spoke as light, closing the Book of Ephesians, while the Buddha opened the Book of Philippians.

Volume 11: Philippians

"Tell me about the book of Philippians," Yesac said.

"Paul's evangelistic journey through four imprisonments in Philippi, Jerusalem, Caesarea, and Rome was a great journey indeed, and he writes this epistle to the Philippians because they were the center of communication between Asia and Rome." The boy answered.

The journey with the old man through the novelizedscriptures led to the boy's knowledge growing daily. However, what was even more important than knowledge of the scripturewas the boy's faith in Christ and his actions that demonstrated that faith—loving his neighbors and hoping for the happiness and peace of humanity. Indeed, the boy's demeanor was one of holiness.

"But I'm a little confused between modern Asia and the Asia where Paul was active." The boy said, thinking of South Korea inAsia, a small but strong country where Yesac was born.

"The Asia during Paul's time doesn't refer to the entire modern-day continent of Asia, but to the Roman province of Asia. The province of Asia refers to the western region of present-day Turkey, particularly the area adjacent to the Aegean Sea." Modern-day Turkey is situated between Asia and Europe.

"Even amid such difficult times, Paul found joy in Christ unconditionally. If you look at Paul's example, you'll realize the amazing truth that even joy becomes a habit, a muscle developed by repetitive thoughts. You, too, can become a disciple of Christ like Paul," the old man said with a voice full of conviction.

The boy began to understand why nearly half of the 27 books of the New Testament, precisely 13 books, were recorded as letters from Paul. Paul was indeed a perfect apostle of Christ.

"It has been said that thoughts create actions, actions create habits, habits create character, and character creates destiny. The Apostle Paul is a testament to that."

The boy flipped to the first chapter of Paul's letter to the Philippians and began to read.

> '*I pray for you always with joy and prayer for your flock because of your fellowship in the gospel from the first day until now. Being confident of this very thing, that He who began a good work in you will perform it until the day of Christ Jesus. This is how I think for your flock, that ye are in my mind, and that ye are all partakers of grace with me, in my bonds, and in the vindication and confirmation of the gospel. God is my witness, I pray you, how I long for your flock with the heart of Jesus Christ; and I pray you, I pray you, that your love may increase in knowledge and in all intelligence.*
>
> *That your love may abound more and more in knowledge and in all intelligence, that ye maybe able to discern that which is exceedingly good, and that ye may be sincere, without blame, unto the day of Christ, full of the fruits of righteousness in Jesus Christ, to the glory and praise of God.*'

Today was laundry day. The old man and the boy combined their morning exercise with doing the laundry. Coincidentally, the laundromat was located right next to the fitness center.

The boy gently turned the page of Paul's epistle.

> *For I want you to know, brethren, that my sufferings have been for the furtherance of the gospel. For thus my bonds have been manifested in Christ to all the demonstrators, and to all others; and many of the brethren, because of my bonds, trust in the Lord, and therefore speak the word of God the more boldly, without fear. Then I will rejoice and be glad, for whatsoever is preached, whether in appearance or in truth, or by whatsoever means, is Christ. I am not ashamed in anything, according to my earnest expectation and hope, but now, as before, with all boldness, that Christ may be honored in my body, whether by life or by death: for to me to live is Christ, and to die is gain.*'

"Paul is eloquent about how much he loves his neighbor with the affection of Christ Jesus, even as God can testify," the boy said, filled with the desire to be like Christ and Paul.

"Paul's letter, seeking that the fruits of righteousness may abound through Jesus Christ, bringing glory and praise to God, is truly moving." Thinking about Jesus Christ, the fruit of righteousness, the glory of God, and Paul's letters, Yesac said.

In the boy's small notebook, the content of Paul's letter, transcending life and death for Christ, was written.

'Whether by life or by death, for to me, to live is Christ, and to die is gain.'

People often talk about emptying the mind. Is selflessness the path to liberation? Paul's letters provide the answer.

The boy's real estate office was a little quieter now that the bustling crowd had left. He sat back in his chair, leaned his head back, and closed his eyes for a moment.

Yesac turned the page of Paul's letter to the Philippians.

'Do nothing out of selfish ambition or vain conceit, but instead in humility, each considering the other better than himself, each considering his own affairs and each considering the affairs of others, so that my joy may be full. Let this mind be in you, which was also in Christ Jesus, who, though he was in the form of God, did not consider it a thing to be equal with God, but emptied himself, taking the form of a servant, being made in the likeness of men, and being found in fashion as a man, he humbled himself, and became obedient unto death, even death on a cross. Wherefore God hath highly exalted him, and given him the name which is above every name, that at the name of Jesus, every knee should bow, of things in heaven, and things in earth, and things under the earth, and that every tongue should confess that Jesus Christ is Lord, to the glory of God the Father.

The old man took a breath while the boy continued reading Paul's letter.

'Therefore, my beloved, work out your own salvation with fear and trembling, not only as ye are in my presence, but now more especially as ye are absent. For it is God that worketh in you, both to will and to do of his good pleasure: Do all things without murmuring and disputing; that ye may present yourselves blameless and innocent, children of God without blemish in the midst of a crooked and rebellious generation, shining as lights among them in the world, bringing forth the word of life, so that I may have something to boast of in the day of Christ, that my run was not in vain, nor my labor in vain. And if I shall give myself as a governor over the sacrifice and service of your faith, I will rejoice and be glad for my flock; in like manner, ye also rejoice and be glad for me.'

"Master, like Paul said, it's not easy to value others above ourselves," the boy said, slightly frowning.

"That's because you're trying to do it with your own human heart."

"Is that so?"

"Yes. You need to have the mindset of Christ Jesus, who, being in very nature God, humbled Himself and became obedient to death—even death on a cross. When you do that, God works in you to consider others better than yourself."

"Yes. Then we will exist as children of God without fault, shining like stars in the world, without grumbling or arguing."

"Indeed, once you've truly valued others above yourself and loved your neighbor as yourself, you'll understand why such teachings were given."

"............."

"Truly valuing others above yourself and loving your neighbor as yourself brings joy and happiness that can't be compared to anything else. That's why such a great teaching was given—to let you experience that eternal joy and happiness. Once you've experienced such a world, it becomes a habit always to consider others better than yourself and love them as your own body. That's what the Kingdom of Heaven with Christ is all about."

Yesac's words flowed like love, and the profound realization that came from them led the boy into more resounding silence.

Meanwhile, Epaphroditus and Timothy were brothers, soldiers, and messengers who helped Paul, almost died for the work of Christ, and did not look back on their own lives.

'For though I was circumcised on the eighth day, a son of Israel, of the tribe of Benjamin, a Hebrew of the Hebrews, a Pharisee in the law, a persecutor of the church in zeal, and blameless in the righteousness of the law, yet whatsoever things were gain to me, I counted as loss for the sake of Christ, and all things counted for loss, for the excellency of the knowledge of Christ Jesus my Lord. For my sake, I have suffered the loss of all things, and count them but dung, that I may gain Christ, and be found in him; and that the righteousness which I have is not of the law, but is through faith in Christ, and is from God by faith.

That I may make known Christ, and the power of his resurrection, and my partaking of his sufferings, that I might be conformed unto his death, that I might attain unto the resurrection from the dead: not that I have already attained, nor that I am fully perfected. But I press toward the mark for the apprehending of that for which I have been apprehended of Christ Jesus.

Brethren, I do not yet count myself to have apprehended, but I do reach forth unto one thing, forgetting those things which are behind, and reaching forth unto those things which are before, I press toward the mark for the prize of the high calling of God in Christ Jesus. For our citizenship is in heaven, where we wait for the Savior from whence we come, the Lord Jesus Christ; who shall transform our lowly body to be conformed to the image of his glorious body, by the working of him that is able to subdue all things unto himself.'

"All of humanity, as citizens of heaven, eagerly await the Savior, the Lord Jesus Christ." The boy meditated on Paul's letter and said.

Yesac flipped to the last page of Philippians without saying.

Philippians 4 was Paul's great letter that had been so enlightening to Yeshua while he was in the wilderness.

'Therefore, my beloved and cherished brethren, beloved, who are my joy and crown, stand in the Lord. Rejoice in the Lord always; I say again, rejoice. Let your generosity be known to all men: for the Lord draweth nigh. Be anxious for nothing, but in everything by prayer and supplication, with thanksgiving, let your requests be made known unto God; and the peace of God, which passeth all understanding, shall guard your hearts and minds through Christ Jesus.

I say not that I am in need, but that I am content in all circumstances: for I know how to be in want, and yet to be in abundance; I have learned to abound in all things, both in hunger and in abundance, both in want and in need. For I can do all things through him that strengtheneth me: and I can do all things in all things. And abound in riches: and my God shall supply all your need according to his riches in glory by Christ Jesus.'

"It's beautiful to see Paul living out the love of Christ, calling his neighbor his joy and crown." The boy said, smiling.

"Like Paul's letter, we are not to be anxious about anything but stand firm in the Lord." Yesac nodded.

The boy recalled the biblical passage about Yesac's epiphany while he was homeless in the wilderness of Corona. It was a noble letter from Paul that the boy and Yesac always meditate on in their hearts.

'I am not saying this because I am in need, for I have learned to be content whatever the circumstances. I know what it is to be in need, and I know what it is to have plenty. I have learned the secret of being content in any and every situation, whether well fed or hungry, whether living in plenty or in want.'

Can't tell how many times Yesac has meditated on, written about, and tried to live out this passage of Scripture while watching the birds flying in the sky, looking at the wildflowers blooming in the fields, and being with his Jindo dog and puppies. Through these moments, Yesac practiced and learned all the secrets of being content in any situation, whether in need or abundance, while wandering in the wilderness without a home.

"Yes, we live in a world of everything and abundance. God provides for every need at the right time and place according to His abundance, but it is the greed of our hearts, the foolishness of our unawareness, that eats away at our happiness, that keeps us unsatisfied and always lacking."

Yesac, hiding his surprise at the boy's mature words, closed the book of Philippians and opened the book of Colossians.

SJCB Dialogue – Philippians

"Joy is not determined by circumstances but flows from being centered in Christ. When you awaken to this truth, as Paul did, you rejoice even in prison. Whether I live or die, it is for the glory of Christ. 'For to me, to live is Christ and to die is gain.' This is the essence of anatta(non-self) and transcendence—overcoming death through the life of Christ."
Buddha Siddhartha spoke of transcendence and anatta(selflessness).

"The greatest teaching of Christ is to love others with humility and gentleness, not with strife or vanity. Whatever you did for the least of these, you did for God. Do not be anxious about anything, but in every situation, by prayer and thanksgiving, present your requests to God. God's kingdom is free from worry and anxiety—these are creations of unenlightened human minds." Socrates spoke with the voice of a philosopher who embraces truth.

"Whatever you fill your heart with must be true, pure, and worthy of praise. Focus on what is good and beautiful, because thoughts are the seeds of your life. True freedom is a heart that is not swayed by hunger or abundance, by lowliness or prosperity. This is what Paul called 'the secret of being content in any and every situation.'"
Confucius spoke of the secret to living life well.

"Our citizenship is in heaven. And heaven is God, who is love. Loving your neighbor as yourself is salvation, and that is the kingdom of heaven." Jesus spoke as the answer to life itself.

Volume 12: Colossians

"What is the book of Colossians?" Yesac asked.

"Colossians is another prison epistle that Paul wrote to the believers in Colossae, who had fallen into legalism and mysticism. Colossae is an ancient city in present-day Turkey's southwest region." The thought that even though humanity might live in a four-dimensional world, not everyone may reach enlightenment briefly passed through the boy's mind.

"The truths which are so simple as to be plain and obvious that they are the very teaching of God, the unenlightened deceive people by mystery and strangeness, or by attachingthemselves to laws and abstinence." Yesac, the old man, said with an expression that truth is not complicated but rather simple and clear.

The boy was learning that only by remaining diligent and vigilant in the Word, keeping himself clean and strong, could he be free from deception.

The old man, looking at the boy with the love of Christ, turned the page of Paul's letter.

'Paul, an apostle of Christ Jesus by the will of God, and Timothy our brother, to the saints at Colossae, faithful brethren in Christ, Grace be to you and peace from God our Father, who will grant you all power to do all things according to the strength of His glory, with all endurance and longsuffering with joy. For he is the image of the invisible God, the firstborn of all creation: all things were created by him, whether things visible or invisible, whether thrones, or dominions, or principalities, or powers: all things were created by him and for him: and he was before all things, and in him, all things were created: having made peace through the blood of his cross, by which he was pleased to reconcile to himself all things, things in the earth, and things in the heavens.

And having reconciled you, who were alienated andenemies in your hearts by your former evil deeds, by the death of his body, he hath now reconciled you unto himself, that he might present you before him holy and blameless and without reproach; if ye abide in the faith, and stand fast on the foundation, and are not moved from the hope of the gospel which ye have heard; which gospel is preached to every creature, and I, Paul, am a partaker of it.'

"Our lives have received the gifts of endurance and long-suffering that enable us to overcome all trials and hardships," the boy said, recalling the fourth fruit of the Holy Spirit.

"That fruit of endurance is borne by following the glory of Christ, who is the image of the invisible God," the old man said freely.

"The visible and invisible things in heaven and on earth, all creation, were made for humanity by the Word of God, not by material," the boy said, gazing into the void.

"Our humanity can enjoy peace and live in harmony, loving one another, thanks to the blood of Christ on the cross. Though we were once alienated and enemies in our minds because of our evil behavior, we can become holy, blameless, and above reproach as neighbors. The path to that is by practicing the sacrificial love of Christ, who saved humanity," the old man said, his words flowing smoothly like water.

"Yes. We must always remain in the truth and not waver in the hope of the Word," the boy responded.

Yesac had an appointment with his daughter, so he went to Whataburger. He arrived about an hour early and was reading. Today, he planned not just to sit and study but also to have lunch, which made him feel slightly less guilty about the restaurant.

His daughter, whom he hadn't seen before, opened up about conflicts with people.

"Around 400 AD, approximately 1,960 years ago, Augustine, amonk of Christ, said, 'Hate the sin, not the sinner.' Through thesewords, we learn the great forgiveness of Christ, which allows us to heal the wounds of hatred arising from our relationships withothers," Yesac said.

"Yes. Just understanding that teaching could heal all wounds of hatred," his daughter said, thinking of those who had recently hurt her.

The teaching to overcome evil with good and to forgive those who crucified Jesus was a secret that Augustine, a disciple of Christ, expressed in the words, 'Hate the sin, not the sinner.'

Returning to the office, the old man turned the pages of Paul's letters.

'That they might know what are the riches of the glory of this mystery among the Gentiles. Which mystery is Christ in you, the hope of glory? And as we preach him, exhorting every man, and teaching every man in all wisdom, that we may build up every man perfect in Christ: for which cause I also labor with all my might, according to the working of him that worketh in me with power that in the same way, ye may be comforted in the spirit of your minds, and be united in love, and may pass unto all the riches of the peaceable understanding, to the knowledge ofChrist, which is the mystery of God; in whom are hid all the treasures of wisdom and knowledge. For this is after the heritage of men, and after the elementary learning of the world, and not after Christ.'

"May you be established as perfect in Christ," the boy said.

"That desire is fulfilled when you realize Christ, the mystery of God," the old man said.

"Yes. For there are hidden all the treasures of wisdom and knowledge," the boy admitted.

"You must always be on your guard in the Word, lest you be deceived by hollow and deceptive philosophies, such as those that follow elemental spirituality."

Like the proverbial cow in an empty house, the boy earned $4,500. As a real estate agent, he was paid for closing the sale of the house, and now he could live not only by the Word but also by bread. As he ate his garlic bread, he turned to the book of Colossians and began to read.

'Therefore, if ye have been raised with Christ, seek the things above, for there Christ is seated at the right hand of God. Let the peace of Christ rule in your hearts; for to this end were ye called in one body; and be ye thankful; and let the word of Christ dwell in you richly, teaching and admonishing in all wisdom; singing psalms and hymns and spiritual songs with thanksgiving in your hearts; and whatsoever ye do, whether in word or deed, do all in the name of the Lord Jesus, giving thanks to God the Father through him.'

"The height of idolatry was not only prevalent in Old Testament times, but it is ongoing in the modern age of civilization." The boy looked at the note written in the old man's small notebook and said.

'Put to death, therefore, whatever belongs to your earthly nature: sexual immorality, impurity, lust, evil desires, and greed, which is idolatry.'

"Such is the crippling life of disharmony, of forgetting the Word and being overly focused on material things. Paul is clear that greed for material things is idolatry." Yesac pointed out.

"But the fruits of Christ, that is, the fruits of the Holy Spirit, are compassion, mercy, humility, gentleness, longsuffering, forgiving one another, loving one another, tenderheartedness, meekness, longsuffering. Fruits of Christ, that is, the fruits of the Holy Spirit," he continued.

"Since we are one body for the sake of peace, let us sing psalms and hymns and sacred songs, praising God with thanksgiving in our hearts," the boy declared.

When he finished, the boy began picking at the fruit of the Spirit, which tasted even better than the garlic bread he had eaten earlier.

'Children, obey your parents in everything. For this is well pleasing in the Lord. Fathers, do not provoke your children to anger, lest they lose heart. Servants, obey your natural masters in all things, not with blind eyes, as men do, but with a sincere heart in the fear of the Lord; and whatever you do, do it with all your heart as unto the Lord, and not as unto men. For ye serve the Lord Christ, knowing that ye shall receive the reward of the inheritance from the Lord.

He that doeth unrighteousness shall receive unrighteousness in return: for the Lord is no respecter of persons with outward appearance. Pray always with all earnestness and watchfulness in prayer, with thanksgiving toward men, that ye may redeem the time. Let your speech always be seasoned with salt, with grace; and let every man giveto every man an account.'

"Paul's letter reminds me of the teaching of you, Master, said, 'People are not the object of faith but the object of love.'" The boy took notes in his small notebook and said.

'Whatever you do, work at it with all your heart, as working f or the Lord, not for human.'

"............................"

Yesac was silent at the boy's words, and the boy's gaze rested on Yesac's little note.

'Let your conversation always be full of grace, seasoned with salt. Make the most of every opportunity. Anyone who does wrong will be repaid for their wrongs.'

Yesac went to a church outreach center to have his soccer injury treated, and he was grateful for the grace of Elder Oh's acupuncture.

SJCB Dialogue – Colossians

"Colossians is Paul's essential letter written against mysticism, legalism, false philosophy, and asceticism. He boldly proclaims that Christ is everything and the center of all. Truth is not complicated. Christ alone is the center. There is no need to fall into mysticism or bizarre philosophies." Buddha spoke with resolute awakening.

"Christ is the image of the invisible God. We must no longer depend on images, idols, or outward religious forms. The fullness of God dwells in Christ. Through the blood of the cross, God reconciled all humanity. Therefore, we must love one another." Socrates spoke with the voice of a philosopher shining with enlightenment.

"Through Christ's blood, we are reconciled to God, to our neighbors, and to ourselves—in love, forgiveness, and peace. Life often presents us with difficult people. But the love of Christ, who prayed for those who nailed Him to the cross, teaches us to forgive even seventy times seven. 'Not seven times, but seventy-seven times.' (Matthew 18:22)" Confucius spoke, gazing upon the verse noted in Buddha's small notebook.

"Hate the sin, but not the person—this is the great faith that puts Christ's love into action. True forgiveness and healing come not from religion, but from seeing each other as holy and blameless. Faith is not merely a religious experience; it is the perfection of character achieved through living out the Word. Not academic theory, but the treasure of wisdom and knowledge hidden in Christ. We must awaken this treasure within all humanity." Socrates broke the silence with truth.

"Greed for material things is idolatry born of foolishness. Excessive desire topples the temple of the heart. Clothe yourselves with the Word and the fruit of the Spirit—compassion, kindness, humility, gentleness, and patience. And above all these, love is the perfect bond of unity." Confucius spoke with a heart of non-possession (muso-yu).

"True labor and worship come not from seeking the approval of others, but from serving sincerely and gratefully as if unto the Lord. Colossians teaches not a decorated religion, but a Christ-centered life. Truth is not complex—it is a simple and strong path of love, forgiveness, and seeking what is above." Jesus spoke the simple truth and closed the book of Colossians. Then, Socrates opened the book of 1 Thessalonians.

Volume 13: 1 Thessalonians

"Where is Thessalonica?" Yesac asked.

"Thessalonica was the most densely populated and thrivingcity in the ancient Greek kingdom of Macedonia. Its location meant that it was on the main road connecting Rome to Asia andhad one of the finest natural harbors on the Aegean Sea." the boy said.

"The Thessalonians were the first Europeans to accept the gospel of Christ," Yesac said and opened Paul's letter.

'Paul, Silas, and Timothy, to the church of the Thessalonians in God the Father and the Lord Jesus Christ, Grace be unto you and peace, and imitators of us and of the Lord, in whom ye have been instructed with the joy of the Holy Ghost in many tribulations. For we have been absent from you for a little while, brethren, in the face, but not in the heart: but we have zealously endeavored the more to see your faces for the will of God is this, that ye be holy, that is, that ye put away fornication;

that every man take his wife in holiness and honor; that ye be not after lusts, as the heathen are, who know not God; that ye be not unequallyyoked together, and that ye harm not a brother over against a brother. Brethren, be ye not in darkness, that the day may not come upon you as a thief: for ye are all sons of light, sons of the day: we are not of the night, neither of the darkness: therefore, let us not sleep as others sleep, but let us watch and do sober duty.'

"It is God's will that you should be sanctified." the boy said.

"We are all sons of light and day, not of darkness, so let us be vigilant and strive for holiness in the likeness of Jesus," Yesac said.

"St. Paul says that it is not for us to write concerning the day or the hour, for the day of the Lord will come like a thief in the night." The boy spoke freely.

"The enlightened one is always ready, so the time and place, which only God knows, is of no consequence." Yesac, the old man, spoke calmly and with resolve.

"Yes." The boy replied with a look of realization.

'Do not repay evil for evil to anyone, but always seek to do good, whether in dealing with one another or all men. Rejoice always; pray without ceasing; give thanks in all circumstances. For this is the will of God in Christ Jesus for you. Quench not the Spirit, despise not prophecy, give thanks in all things, abstain from all manner of evil, and reject every appearance of evil. And the God of peace himself will sanctify you completely in all holiness, and will present you blameless in spirit and soul and body at the coming of our Lord Jesus Christ. For he that hath called you is faithful and will also do it.'

"The letter from Paul, sweeter than honey, how beautiful it is," said the boy as he reflected on the note the old man had handed him. It was a piece of sacred poetry, a divine gift.

'Be patient with everyone; admonish those who are idle and disruptive; encourage the discouraged; help the weak; always strive for good. Warn those who are idle and disruptive, encourage the disheartened, help the weak. Reject every kind of evil in all its forms.'

The boy read and wrote Bible verses in English, Korean, and Chinese over and over again, until the words became muscle memory—etched into his heart, always with him.

'Rejoice always, pray continually, give thanks in all circumstances.'

During the 5.16 Revolution in South Korea, there lived a man in Daejeon—called 'Hang Shi Bum'—
whose very name echoed the verse from 1 Thessalonians:
Rejoice always, pray continually, give thanks in all circumstances.
That verse became a living mantra of truth, which Yesac passed on to the boy.
"This is God's will for us:
to rejoice, to pray, and to give thanks always in Christ Jesus.
This is God's will for you in Christ Jesus."
Then, the old man Yesac gently opened the first chapter of 2 Thessalonians and began to speak.

SJCB Dialogue - 1 Thessalonians

"1 Thessalonians delivers a message of blazing love and a prophetic warning, urging humanity to live as children of light, even in the midst of trials and persecution. The gospel is not merely words—it is a living, breathing power. Our thoughts, speech, and actions must reflect that life. That is the true fragrance of Christ's love." Buddha Siddhartha spoke with the scent of love.

"The people of Thessalonica received the gospel with joy from the Holy Spirit, even in the midst of suffering. The gospel is not mere talk; it reveals itself through fruits and joy. As James said, 'By your deeds, show love to your neighbor'—this is the fragrance of Christ. If one goes to church or temple but gives off the scent of hatred, it is because their faith has already died." Socrates spoke with the fragrant philosophy of love.

"God's will for us is holiness. The goal of faith is not just salvation, but sanctification and distinction in life. All humanity must awaken as children of light through the truth and the Word. We must not ask for seasons or signs, but remain awakened through Scripture beyond time and space." Confucius spoke in wakefulness.

"Look at the birds of the sky and the wildflowers of the field. They thrive without worry or care. Rejoice always, pray without ceasing, give thanks in all things—this is the reason why. Buddha said, 'There is no need to worry in life.' Worry and anxiety are illusions born from our own minds. We need a discerning faith—not blind belief or disbelief—but the courage to live the Word amidst the world. To guard a kind heart and pure thoughts is to put on the full armor of God. 1 Thessalonians is not merely a letter Paul wrote to the Thessalonians, but a living epistle sent to all of humanity, urging us to stay awake and be holy in the truth of the Word." The voice of Jesus swept by like a wind, faster than light.

Buddha Siddhartha, moved by the voice of Jesus, opened the next book—2 Thessalonians.

Volume 14: 2 Thessalonians

"The second letter Paul sent to the people of the Thessalonian church begins," the old man said.

"Second Thessalonians is a short letter from Paul, consisting of only three chapters," the boy said as he began to meditate on the words.

'Paul, Silas and Timothy, to the church of the Thessalonians, in God our Father and the Lord Jesus Christ, Grace be to you and peace from God our Father and the Lord Jesus Christ... Our beloved brethren, for whom we always give thanks, because God hath chosen you from the beginning, that you should be saved through sanctification of the Holy Ghost and faith in the truth.

For we would not have any of you to eat from any man for nothing, but to labor and toil day and night, that no man should be oppressed: For even when we were with you, we commanded you, saying, if any man will not labor, let him not eat. If anyone does not obey our words in this letter, let him be named, and let him have no association with me, and let him be ashamed of me; but do not think as enemies, but as brethren.'

"Praise be to God, who leads us all to be saved through the sanctifying work of the Spirit and through faith in the truth." The boy spoke with gratitude and praise.

"It is important that we take responsibility for our lives, not being lazy but diligent, not taking food from anyone without paying for it," the old man spoke neatly.

"We should not be a burden to anyone in our neighborhood," the boy said.

"Paul's letter, 'The one who is unwilling to work shall not eat,' is a good reminder to live an upright and responsible life." The old man spoke coldly.

The boy reflected once more on the stern old man who had raised two daughters to become professional golfers, despite being born in a remote village without electricity and having no money, yet never begging for $1 or accumulating debt. The story was a tear-jerking drama, a movie in itself. Of course, God sent people to help the two daughters. Among the most grateful were the president and his wife of Seoul Institute of the Arts, Mr. Lee Heung-gu, the president of Fineus Co., Ltd., Mr. Yoon Ui-guk, thechairman of Korea Credit Information Co., Ltd., and Mr. Lee Byung-sang, the president of Hansoo Chemical Co., Ltd. The old man often mentioned them, hoping to meet them in person one day.

"Here the nine letters Paul sent to the church's saints come to an end," said the boy.

"Now, it continues with the four letters sent to the church's pastors," the old man said.

"So, Paul's 13 letters were messages of the gospel, lovingly addressed to the scattered Jewish believers and pastors," The boy said as he opened Paul's letter to Timothy.

SJCB Dialogue - 2 Thessalonians

"*2 Thessalonians is a spiritual training guide urging us to practice the gospel through our lives rather than just with words. It teaches that the muscle of faith is strengthened through daily responsibility. The gospel is both faith and attitude of life. True faith is not just in words but must be revealed in action and life.*" Buddha Siddhartha spoke through the doing of truth.

"*Living diligently without burdening others, and living faithfully—this life itself is the fruit of the gospel. Indeed, one must not eat without working. No one should become a burden to others. We must each live taking responsibility for our own lives.*" Socrates spoke with the faith of a diligent philosophy.

"*The saying, 'Those who do not work shall not eat,' means that laziness is a sin and diligence is evidence of the gospel. This is not just about employment but a spiritual warning regarding our life responsibility before God. It also gives comfort and encouragement to not grow weary or lose heart because of people while doing good. If the left hand does not know what the right hand is doing, then there is no reason to grow discouraged. Persistent goodness eventually leads to awakening and maturity in faith.*" Confucius spoke with enduring kindness.

"*This great teaching emphasizes the balance of love: Do not exclude the disobedient in the community, but rather admonish them as brothers. Loving others as they are, without judging those who think differently from us— This is the vast love of God. Let us not lose thankfulness in all things, and Hold on to the truth of the Word. Gratitude guards our hearts, And truth is the compass that sets our path straight in life.*" As Jesus spoke with a heart that embraced all humanity, Socrates quietly opened the book of 1 Timothy.

Volume 15: 1 Timothy

"Nine of Paul's thirteen letters are titled with names of places. The remaining four letters, beginning with this one, are titled with the names of people, and the first shepherd is Timothy." The old man spoke very simply.

The boy also receives mysterious teachings from the old man. The old man pointed out that the titles of the nine letters Paul sent earlier all end with "ans." For example, the letter just finished, 2 Thessalonians, ends with "ans." This is evidence that those letters were sent to the people of that region, meaning many believers.

"Paul is sending a letter to his fellow worker and disciple, Timothy, who is serving the church in Ephesus."

The boy opened the letter that Paul sent to Timothy.

'For the purpose of vigilance is love in a pure heart and a goodconscience, faith without deceit. Knowing this, that the law is notmade for the upright, but for the lawless, for the insubordinate, and for those who resist good instruction. For everything that God hath made is good, and if we receive it with thanksgiving, there is nothing to be cast away...

Casting off vanity and vain myths, and practicing godliness. For the practice of the flesh profiteth little: but godliness profiteth the whole world: for it hath promise in this life, and in the life to come. This is the wordthat is trustworthy, and worthy of all men.'

"Love comes from a pure heart, good conscience, and sincere faith. It's a truly precious teaching."

'Leaders are clear! Leaders are straightforward and clear,'

theboy said, recalling a phrase the old man had once taught him. Thishonesty from a pure heart is the only common trait amongsuccessful and happy people, reassuring us and instilling confidence in their leadership.

"Healthy people don't seek a physician, just as the law isn't necessary for those with faith and a good conscience. All there is is love for God and one's neighbor." In truth, the old man Yesac's expression was as clear as the sky without a single cloud, as innocent as a lamb.

"Paul says that everything in this world that God has made is good, so nothing should be rejected if received thanksgiving," the boy said with a desire to always live according to the Word of God, walking with Christ.

"Looking at this world from the next, everything is so precious that there's nothing to throw away," Yesac said, recalling his out-of-body experience (OBE), where he experienced the world outside his body. Seeing this world from the next, this world was perfect in every way.

'It would be more accurate to describe it as heaven, just as Christ said, 'The kingdom of God is within you.' The words of the Holy Spirit, conveyed to Moses, 'The place where you stand is holy ground,' and Christ's words, 'What is loosed on earth is loosed in heaven,' gave Yesac great enlightenment. What is the remarkable message that God has given to the old man Yesac? Those with ears to hear will find the answer through this journey with the sacred scriptures.'

The boy's gaze stopped at a small note from Yesac.

'For everything God created is good, and nothing is to be rejected if it is received with thanksgiving, because the word of God and prayer consecrates it.'

"Myths and old wives' tales must not mislead you but train yourself to be godly. It has nothing to do with godless myths and old wives' tales; instead, train yourself to be godly."

Suddenly, the thought that something was vexing flashed through the boy's mind faster than light. Why had so many precious lives been lost in Korea due to religious issues such as the Salvation Sect? How many misguided teachings had arisen from translation errors in the English scriptures? These false teachings had become the root cause of idolatry. The boy prayed with the compassion, mercy, and love of the old man Yesac, hoping that these pains would be cleansed entirely through this journey with the sacred scriptures and that enlightenment would lead to eternal happiness.

The cool afternoon weather in Dallas, Texas, and the license plate for the used car the boy had recently purchased arrived. The boy attached the license plate to the front and rear of the vehicle outside the real estate office.

"Godliness has value for all things," the old man said as he turned the pages of Paul's letter to Timothy.

> *'Do not rebuke an older man harshly but exhort him as if he were your father. Treat younger men as brothers, older women as mothers, and younger women as sisters, with absolute purity. Anyone who does not provide for their relatives, and especially for their household, has denied the faith and is worse than an unbeliever... Do not be hasty in the laying on of hands, and do not share in the sins of others.*
>
> *Keep yourself pure. Stop drinking only water, and use a little wine because of your stomach and your frequent illnesses... We brought nothing into the world and can take nothing out of it. But if we have food and clothing, we will be content with that. Those who want to get rich fall into temptation, a trap, and many foolish and harmful desires that plunge people into ruin and destruction.'*

"Paul tells Timothy to use wine to guard against sour stomachs and frequent illnesses." The boy pointed out.

"Wine or alcohol, when used appropriately according to one's own capacity, can be useful." Yesac agreed.

The boy looked at Yesac's little notebook and saw that Paul's letter was written in Chinese, English, and Korean. There, the phrase 'GongSuRaeGongSuGeo' (공수래공수거, 空手來空手去), a line known from a poem in the Buddhist 'Lotus Sutra', was clearly written in Paul's letter to Timothy.

> *'For we brought nothing into the world, and we can take nothing out of it ; GongSuRaeGongSuGeo (공수래공수거, 空手來空手去)'*

"Who is Master Yesac, who is content to have nothing to eat and nothing to wear, who needs nothing, who lives his life as the flow of the wind? Can I be like him?" The boy asked himself, scratching his head.

"Excess is as bad as deficiency. The more you desire and possess, the heavier the burden of protecting and fearing the loss becomes. A life without the need for anything is always light and abundant," Yesac said.

Indeed, the old man lived a life of abundance without needing anything. It was a life that prioritized words over bread and focused on being rather than possessing.

"Yes. The desire to have more becomes a snare, and it makes life a struggle, and you waste your life in pursuit of more than you need." the boy said.

Due to an injury, Yesac, who has just become goalie recently, was packing his soccer bag to participate in a soccer game.

'For the love of money is the root of all evil: and they that love it have been deceived, and have fallen away from the faith, and have pierced themselves through many sorrows. But flee these things, O man of God, and pursue righteousness, godliness, faith, love, patience, gentleness; fight the good fight of faith, lay hold of eternal life: for to this cause, thou hast been called, and hast borne a good witness before many witnesses.

'Command those who are rich in this generation, that they do not exalt their hearts, nor set their hope on earthly goods, which are unfruitful, but on God, who gives us all things abundantly, that they be rich in good works, generous in giving, cheerful, and compassionate; for this is how they lay up a good foundation for themselves in the future, and partake of the true life.'

"Paul writes that the love of money is the root of all evil, causing people to pierce themselves with many griefs," the boy said.

"We should aim to live in harmony, pursuing the fruits of the Spirit." the old man Yesac said.

The boy liked Yesac's words, which emphasized the harmony between material wealth and the mind without completely disregarding money or material things. The problem lay in an excessive focus on material wealth, which amounted to idolatry of material things. Idolatry inevitably led to corruption and destruction.

A note in Yesac's small notebook caught the boy's eye, and he began to read it aloud.

'Retirement Plan for True Life'
Do not place your hope in uncertain wealth.
Do not be arrogant toward the rich,
but sympathize with the poor.
Do not lift up your heart toward the rich,
but sympathize with the poor.
Have hope in the Word,
do good deeds, and be willing to give.

SJCB Dialogue - 1 Timothy

"Love comes from a pure heart, a good conscience, and sincere faith. True love is not about appearances or emotions—it is the fruit of the Spirit that grows within a pure heart. The law is not for the righteous, but for the lawless and rebellious. The righteous follow truth even without the law. That is the love of Christ toward our neighbors." The Buddha Siddhartha spoke these words of truth.

"We must hold on to faith and a good conscience. True religion is built on a clean conscience and never loses peace of heart. External beauty is not true beauty; it is acts of goodness and reverence that create genuine inner beauty." Socrates spoke with a philosophy of inner harmony.

"Godliness requires continual training. Just as physical muscles grow through consistent exercise, godliness and holiness grow through repeated training in the Word. Everything God created is good, and all existence in the world is sacred when received with gratitude. That is why God loved the world so much He gave His only Son, Christ. That's the reason we must revere God, truth, and the Word." Confucius said, gazing upon the small notebook of the Buddha where the words were written.

'For everything God created is good, and nothing is to be rejected if it is received with thanksgiving.' - 1 Timothy 4

"We brought nothing into the world, and we can take nothing out. So let us focus not on possessions but on being. Wealth is not the goal, only a tool. Do not place your hope in uncertain riches, but live a life of generosity and compassion. Fight the good fight of the faith. The journey toward eternal life is a battlefield of faith, requiring a heart that never gives up. The true retirement plan for life is godliness and sharing. Those who are rich before God are not the ones who possess much wealth, but those who place their hope in the Word and live a good and righteous life." When Jesus finished reading from Confucius's small notebook, the Buddha opened the book of 2 Timothy.

'For we brought nothing into the world, and we can take nothing out of it. ; GongSuRaeGongSuGeo 空手來空手去' - 1 Timothy 6

Volume 16: 2 Timothy

"Paul is writing his second letter to Timothy, the Roman prisoner-turned-pastor of the Ephesian church. Paul's faithfulness in instilling in Timothy a sense of mission and adopting the attitude of a student who is willing to learn." Yesac instructed.

"Yes." The boy replied briefly before flipping to 2 Timothy.

'Paul, an apostle of Christ Jesus according to the promise of life in Christ Jesus, by the will of God, to Timothy, my beloved son, Grace be unto thee, and mercy, and peace, from God the Father and Christ Jesus our Lord.

For in my night and day prayers, I have not ceased to think of thee, and to give thanks unto God, whom thou hast served from thy fathers with a pure conscience; and I have thought of thy tears, and longed to see thee, that my joy might be full, because of the faith that is in thee, which is not in vain: for God hath not given us a spirit of fear, but of power, and of love, and of diligence: therefore be not thou ashamed of the testimony of our Lord, or of me that am a prisoner for thy sake, but suffer with the gospel, according to the power of God, considering what I say.

For the Lord will give thee understanding in all things. Behold, if we are dead with thee, we shall also live with thee. Put away foolish and ignorant arguments. For I know that out of these come contentions.'

"It was Timothy's clear conscience and sincere faith in God that brought Paul to tears and made him miss him." The boy remarked

"Like Timothy, we should go forward fearlessly with the power, love, and self-discipline that God has given us," Yesac said.

"The gospel brings hardship, but we must overcome it with God-given insight," the boy said, more understanding now about Paul.

"The enlightened man has no fear, for God has taught him the secret of facing every situation in life. If we died with Christ, we will also live with him, for we have been honored," The old man spoke with a calm expression, free of fear.

"Above all, as Christ's apostles, we must put away all vain andgodless chatter and pursue righteousness, faith, love, and peacein a pure heart." The boy said.

"Don't have anything to do with foolish and stupid arguments because you know they produce quarrels, but only with the fruit of the Spirit, embroidering your life with love for your neighbor," Yesac advised.

The alarm went off, and he hurried out of the office to make his appointment. As was his custom, Yesac arrived at his appointment half an hour early, taking time to read the boy's notebook.

The old man, having returned, turned the page of Paul'sletter.

'And from a child thou hast known the Holy Scriptures, which are able to make thee wise unto salvation through faith which is in Christ Jesus: for all scripture is given by inspiration of God, andis profitable for doctrine, for reproof, for correction, for instruction in righteousness: that the man of God may be perfect, thoroughly furnished unto all good works: that the Lord may deliver me from all evil, and may preserve me to enter into his kingdom: to whom be glory forever and ever. Amen.'

"The teaching that a soldier, or righteous man, does not quarrel reappears in Paul's letters." The boy noted.

"Just by keeping a heart of gentleness and patience and avoiding useless quarrels, we can live an improved life." Yesac nodded.

Yesac's face glistened as he emerged from his morning workout and shower. Was the Master reborn through the waterin his early morning shower? The boy thought to himself, remembering Yesac's words about reciting the Lord's Prayer and the Apostles' Creed in the shower.

"God delivered Paul from all persecutions and sufferings in Antioch, Iconium, and Lystra." the boy said.

"Paul realized the mystery of the Scriptures, which is the wisdom that is made perfect unto salvation through faith which is in Christ Jesus." the old man said.

"The Bible is the biggest bestseller in human history, with more than six billion copies sold." Yesac mused.

Yesac's eyes stopped on the boy's small notebook. It was Paul's letter to Timothy.

> *'All Scripture is God-breathed and is useful for teaching, rebuking, correcting, and training in righteousness,'*

"We can do every good work by reading, meditating on, and practicing the Bible, which is also the kingdom of heaven with Christ." The boy agreed.

"That's God's will." the old man Yesac said.

The boy closed the last chapter of 2 Timothy and opened the first chapter of Titus.

SJCB Dialogue - 2 Timothy

"The Second Letter to Timothy is like Paul's final will and testament, written from prison to his beloved son in the faith. This letter delivers a powerful message to all humanity: Keep your faith to the end and follow the truth. Even facing death, Paul confesses, 'I have kept the faith.'" The Buddha spoke with a sincere heart for all of humanity.

"Choose power, love, and self-discipline over fear. Indeed, God has not given us a spirit of fear, but of power, of love, and of self-control. Faith begins in the heart, and pure, sincere faith is true strength." Socrates spoke from the depth of his heart.

"The Bible is the Word of God, inspired and holy—over 6 billion copies sold, it is the greatest book of truth in history. We must not engage in foolish arguments, but overcome life's hardships through the power of the Word, truth, and love. Suffering is not something to avoid but a school of grace we pass through to learn." Confucius said with a patient expression.

"Paul's final words were full of love—he called each person by name and sent his greetings." Jesus spoke briefly while gazing at Confucius's notebook, where the verse was written.

'Grace be with you all. Amen.' - 2 Timothy 4

Volume 17: Titus

"Paul, who is in Corinth, writes to Titus, who is living in Crete," Thinking of Crete, the most famous island in Greek territory, the boy said.

"Crete is the most famous of the Greek islands." Yesac opened the first page of Paul's letter to Titus and said.

"Wild and full of confusion, Crete is the largest island in the Mediterranean." Yesac opened the first page of Paul's letter to Titus and said.

'The bishop is to be a steward of God, unreproachable, not selfish, not quick to anger, not a winebibber, not a striker, not covetous of uncleanness, but hospitable to strangers, a lover of goodness, diligent, righteous, holy, temperate, with the teaching of the word of God, which can exhort with sound doctrine, to reprove those who speak against it.

And bring us up in such a way that we may remember to deny all ungodliness and the lusts of this world, and to live in this world in soberness, righteousness, and godliness, not to disturb anyone, not to quarrel, to be forbearing, to show meekness to all men in all things.

For according to the gracious mercy of God our Savior, and the love of man, He saved us, not according to our works of righteousness, but according to His compassion, by the washing of regeneration and renewing of the Holy Ghost, after admonishing a heretic once or twice, put him away.'

"How beautiful is the household of God, as in Paul's letter, hospitable to strangers, lovers of goodness, sober, righteous, holy, temperate, adhering to the teaching of the beautiful word." The boy exclaimed.

"How fresh and faithful is Paul's letter to Titus, to exhort him with sound doctrine and to rebuke those who speak backwardly," Yesac said.

"The short letter Paul sent to Titus revealed God's mercy through the washing of rebirth and the renewal by the Holy Spirit."

SJCB Dialogue - Titus

"The Book of Titus teaches that a steward of God must be blameless, not self-willed, but self-controlled and gentle. Only those who stand firm on sound doctrine and trustworthy words can rebuke false teachings and build up souls. The gospel is fulfilled through the washing of rebirth and the renewal by the Holy Spirit." The Buddha spoke as a faithful steward for all humanity.

"Indeed. Salvation comes through the washing of rebirth and the renewal by the Holy Spirit. One must cast away worldly passions and ungodliness. True faith means severing ties with earthly desires and living a life of godliness and righteousness." Socrates spoke with a spirit renewed in reverence.

"Truth must be testified not just in words or knowledge, but in life itself. Gentleness, self-control, temperance, and good deeds are the greatest evidence of the gospel. A true Christian does not quarrel or slander, but responds to all with kindness and humility." Confucius spoke with a gentle and virtuous heart.

"The grace of God, who is the Word and the Truth, is open equally to all of humanity. Beyond nations, races, and religions—Jews and Gentiles, slaves and free—the same grace is given. Trustworthy teachings restore both home and society. Right instruction in the Word, truth, and faith restores individuals, strengthens families, and builds healthy communities. If someone refuses to listen even after two or three warnings, do not argue further—let wisdom lead you to step away. This world is too beautiful and precious for endless strife. Titus may be a short letter, but it is a rare gem, boldly declaring that the Word is human dignity, and action is the fragrance of the gospel." Jesus's words struck the backs of both the old man and the boy like thunder.

As the old man closed the Book of Titus, the boy, now grown into a young man (Sonyun 少年) opened the pages of Philemon.

Volume 18: Philemon

"Tell me about the Epistle to Philemon," the old man said as he sipped his green tea.

"The Epistle to Philemon deals with slavery and is the shortest letter of Paul's writings. It is also one of Paul's prison letters." The boy looked out the window at the carefree and free-roaming squirrel and said.

"Philemon was a man who became a Christian after hearing Paul preach while traveling," Yesac said, opening Paul's letter to Philemon.

'Paul, a prisoner for Christ's Jesus' sake, and Timothy, our brother, and Philemon, our beloved and fellow laborer, and Apphia, our sister, and Archippus, who is a soldier with us, and the church at your house, Grace to you and peace from God our Father and the Lord Jesus Christ. For... The fellowship of your faith worketh in you to know the good that is among us, and to come unto Christ... No longer as a slave, but better than a slave, but as a beloved brother; no longer as a slave, but as a dear brother.'

"Philemon offered his home as a meeting place for the church and had a slave, Onesimus, who stole some of Philemon's things and ran away to Rome," the boy said.

"Onesimus met Paul and became a Christian, and Paul wrote a letter to Philemon urging him to leave his slavery and accept Onesimus as a brother in Christ." The old man, thinking of Onesimus, Paul, and Philemon all at once, said.

"The covenant of grace through the Lord Jesus brings master and slave into loving fellowship on an equal footing in the body of Christ." The boy said with dignity and depth.

"Onesimus, who left as a chained slave, returned in a new status as a brother in Christ's love." The old man said as he thought of Christ, who transforms all things.

Onesimus, a former slave, is later transformed into a pastor serving the church in Ephesus.

SJCB - Philemon

"Onesimus, once a slave, was restored as a beloved brother. No longer as a slave, but as a dear brother. Love has the almighty power to transform relationships—it is omnipotent (MooSoBoolNeung 무소불능 無所不能). In Christ, master and slave, all social distinctions are transcended, and all are equal." The Buddha spoke with peace and equality.

"Paul embraces the runaway Onesimus and appeals to Philemon for forgiveness. Repentance and forgiveness restore the fabric of society. True transformation comes from a change of heart through the gospel. Not by forced submission, but by voluntary forgiveness through love." Socrates spoke with a heart of love and reconciliation.

"Christianity is built upon the respect for human dignity. Paul did not treat Onesimus as a slave, but as a person of worth. He volunteered to take upon himself all of Onesimus's debts—an act of sacrificial love. Paul became a mediator between Philemon and Onesimus to bring reconciliation. Though it is the shortest letter in the New Testament, Philemon is a beautiful letter that encapsulates the gospel, love, and freedom from slavery." Confucius spoke with the gentle heart of a beautiful letter.

"Through the transformation of a single man—Onesimus—an entire community was changed. The power of love is greater than that of command. Paul did not demand by authority, but appealed in love: 'I appeal to you on the basis of love.' Philemon is a short letter, but it moves the soul." Jesus spoke, embracing Paul's heartfelt letter. As the old man closed the Book of Philemon, the boy turned the page and opened the Book of Hebrews.

Volume 19: Hebrews

"Tell me about Hebrews." Rather than speaking first, Yesac's teaching method was to ask questions, encouraging the learner to discover and make the knowledge their own. This approach was similar to the Socratic method of education.

"Hebrews is the only book in the New Testament with an unknown author and is characterized by its heavy use of Old Testament references." The boy recalled when he studied the Old Testament with Yesac, said.

"It's also a unique aspect of the Book of Hebrews that frequently uses metaphors related to various fields, such as education, discipline, farming, construction, navigation, and even sports competitions." the old man said.

"The author of Hebrews' preference for stylistic and rhetorical flourishes suggests that he was not only familiar with ancient cultures but also a sophisticated literary figure." Turning the first page of Hebrews, the boy said.

'Wherefore hath any man testified, saying, what is man, that thou considerest me, and what is the son of man, that thou counsellest me?

For he hath made me less than the angels for a little while, and crowned me with glory and honor, and put all things in subjection under his feet: for he hath put all things in subjection unto me, and there is not one thing that is not subjected: but now we see not that all things are yet subjected unto him; but we see him whom he hath made less than the angels for a little while, even Jesus, whom he hath crowned with glory and honor, even the suffering of death, that he might taste death for every man, according to the grace of God, for he is able to help them that are tempted, because he himself has been tempted, who is able to suffer with them that are tempted.

That he may be faithful to him that set him up, as Moses was in all the house of God; for I am more worthy of honor than Moses, as the builder of a house is more honorable than the house; for every house has a builder, and it is God that made all things.'

"Of course, Moses and Aaron were good sons who fulfilled their God-given mission, but we are being urged to know, believe in, and rely on Christ, the fulfillment of the law in love." Recalling Moses, Aaron, the Law, and the freedom given by Jesus Christ, the boy said.

"Christ is better than the angels and Joshua, and is the pattern of faith who fulfilled the old covenant with the new," the boy said.

"Yes. There is only one righteous man, Christ Jesus, who died on the cross to pay for the sins of mankind and went to God forgiving all." The sound of the boy's voice resonated in Yesac's ears as if the entire Bible were speaking.

"God loved humanity so much that He sent His only Son, Jesus, with the truth." Yesac sipped his warm green tea and said.

'And Moses was faithful as an ambassador in all the house of God for a testimony of things to come, and Christ was faithful as a son of his house; and if we hold fast the boldness and boasting of our hope to the end, we are his house... and if we hold fast that which we began surely to the end, we shall be made partakers with Christ. For the word of...

God is living and active, and sharper than any two-edged sword, piercing even to the dividing asunder of soul and spirit, and of the joints and marrow, and is a discerner of the thoughts and intents of the heart; and nothing that is made is hidden from him but is laid bare as naked before the eyes of him that apprehendeth us.

We earnestly desire that each one of you should manifest the same diligence, that ye may be imitators of them that receive the promises as an inheritance, not slothful unto the end, but faithful and long-suffering, not slothful unto the riches of hope: for when God promised Abraham, he had none greater than himself to swear by, saying, I will surely bless thee, and make thee fruitful, and multiply thee, and increase thee: and he received the promise by long-suffering.'

Yesac looked deep in contemplation as his keen eyes pierced the words written in English on the boy's little notebook.

'For the word of God is alive and active. Sharper than any double-edged sword, it penetrates even to dividing soul and spirit, joints and marrow; it judges the thoughts and attitudes of the heart. Nothing in all creation is hidden from God's sight. Everything is uncovered and laid bare before the eyes of him to whom we must give account.'

"Of all the books in the world, there are few that can be read more than once, but the Bible can be read over and over again, and yet the secrets of its words are always new and never-ending." Yesac stared off into space.

"That's because the Bible is eternal truth and life. It's all there is," the boy said.

"One book of the Bible is enough for life," Yesac said.

The 100-degree summer days were long gone, and it was now fall in October, which felt a little chilly. Instead of bright, cool clothes, the boy wore black pants and a red top to work, like how Tiger Woods dresses on the last day of a golf tournament. Together, he and his teacher continued their lessons.

'This Melchizedek is the king of Salem and a priest of the Most High God. He met Abraham on his return from slaying many kings and blessed him. And Abraham gave him a tenth part of all, which is the translation of his name: The king of the first righteousness, and the king of Salem, and the king of peace: without father, and without mother, and without genealogy, and without beginning of days, and without end of life: a priest everlasting, like unto the Son of God.

For Levi was yet in his father's loins when Melchizedek met Abraham: and this is more evident from the fact that there was raised up a priest like unto Melchizedek, whowas not after the law of the commandments which pertain unto the flesh, but after the power of the inexhaustible life. And this isthe covenant that I will establish with the house of Israel after those days, saith the Lord, and they shall put my laws in their minds, and write them in their hearts: and I will be to them a God, and they shall be a people unto me...

The censer, and the ark of the covenant overlaid with gold on all sides, and the golden jars of manna therein, and the rod of Aaron's bud, and the tables of the covenant. How shall the blood of Christ, who offered himself without blemish to God by the eternal Spirit, purify your consciences from dead works, to serve the living God, if the blood of Christ is not shed to cleanse you from all unrighteousness... For without shedding of blood, there is no remission.'

"Melchizedek was a priest who did not follow the ordinances of his ancestors, but only the power of an indestructible life." the boy said.

"The law requires almost everything to be purified by blood, and without the shedding of Christ's blood, there is no remission of sins," Yesac said, remembering his father's tombstone.

"Just as Moses was with the Israelites in the wilderness for 40 years, just as Joshua led the Israelites into the Promised Land, so Christ will lead our humanity into God's eternal resting place." the boy said.

"Christ is the eternal truth, sinless and unchanging," Yesac said.

"God sent the prophets, angels, Moses, Joshua, the law, and all the priests first to prepare the way for the sending of Christ." the boy said.

There was a break in the lesson then. The boy felt hungry and went to H Mart, which was located next to the office, to buy something to eat. Once he came back, the lesson continued.

'For it is written above, Sacrifices and offerings and whole burnt offerings and sin offerings He hath no desire nor pleasure in, (for they are all offered according to the law) ... but by the offering of the body of Jesus Christ once for all, according to the will of God, we have obtained sanctification...

Therefore, brethren, we have boldness to enter into the holy place by the blood of Jesus. And he that hath promised is faithful; and let us hold fast the hope of the profession of our faith, without wavering: not forsaking the assembling of ourselves together, not as is the habit of some, but exhorting one another to love and good works, and all the more so as we see the day approaching.

For this is of great reward: for patience is necessary unto you, that ye may receive the promise, after ye have done the will of God: For as he saith, the just shall live by faith: so, shall my heart have no pleasure in me, if I go backward. For we are not of them that turn backward and fall into error; but of them that have faith unto the saving of the soul.'

"For the practices of Judaism and the sacrifices, offerings, burnt offerings, and sin offerings under the old covenant, the law, were imperfect and limited." The boy noted.

"Therefore, to achieve perfection, Christ offered Himself, in His perfect divinity and humanity, as a spotless sacrifice to God to set mankind free from sin," Yesac said.

"Yes. We are to hold fast the hope of the faith with boldness, caring for one another, and encouraging love and good works." the boy agreed.

"We can receive the promises of God when we persevere and do the will of Christ." Yesac continued.

After watching an early morning soccer match between South Korea and Vietnam, he seems a little rushed to get to work. The boy was ticketed by the police for driving 30 mph in a school zone on the 20th. Unlike other times, he received the ticket with a cheerful expression, wishing the cop, "Have a nice day". The boy was learning to live by the Word, remembering to always rejoice, but he chastised himself for being impatient and rushing.

'Now faith is the substance of things hoped for, the evidence of things not seen, so that the advanced have been convinced of them. By faith, we know that the worlds were created by the word of God, so that the things that are seen are not made of things that are made.

But without faith it is impossible to please him, for he that cometh to God must believe that he is, and that he is a rewarder of them that seek him. By faith Noah, being warned of things not yet seen, through fear prepared an ark, and saved his house: by which he condemned the world, and became the author of righteousness after the faith.'

"Strive for the Way of Christ, so that in your life you may realize that the visible world was built by the invisible Word of God, so that you may have the mind's eye to see the invisible."

Yesac said, and his gaze rested on the boy's small notebook.

'Faith is confidence in what we hope for and assurance about what we do not see.'

"Yes. Noah received the ark by faith, Abraham received Isaac at the age of 100 by faith, and Isaac and Jacob inherited a great deal of land by faith," the boy said.

Yesac and the boy flipped through the book of Hebrews while sipping orange juice at Taco Bell for the first time in a long time.

'By faith Moses, when he was born, seeing that his parents were beautiful, hid him for three months, not fearing the king's command; and by faith Moses, when he grew up, refused to be called the son of Pharaoh's princess, preferring rather to suffer

with the people of God than to enjoy for a little while the reward of iniquity; and counting the reproach that was suffered for Christ's sake as a greater riches than all the treasures of Egypt, because he looked unto the presence of God.

By faith they left Egypt, not fearing the king's wrath, but endured it as though they were seeing him that is not seen; by faith they appointed the Passover and the sprinkling of blood, that he that destroyeth the firstborn might not touch them; by faith they crossed the Red Seaas by land, and the Egyptians were drowned in the testing of it; by faith they walked about Jericho seven days, and the city fell; by faith Rahab the prostitute received the spies in peace, that she might not perish with them that disobeyed.

What more shall I say, to tell you of the works of Gideon, Barak, Samson, Jephthah, David, Samuel, and the prophets, for there is not enough time for me?'

"By faith Moses refused to be the son of a princess; by faith he crossed the Red Sea; by faith he suffered in the wilderness with the Israelites; by faith he counted the suffering for Christ's sake greater riches and honor than the treasures of Egypt," the boy said reverently.

"Moses' steadfast faith gave him the eyes of his heart to see the invisible Christ." Yesac said, smiling.

Yesac and the boy continued to meditate on the faith of prophets and kings such as Gideon, Barak, Samson, Jephthah, David, and Samuel.

'Therefore, since we are surrounded by so great a cloud of witnesses, let us lay aside every weight, and the sin which so easily ensnares, and let us run with patience the race that is set before us, let us look unto Jesus the author and perfecter of our faith, who for the joy that was set before him endured the cross, despising the shame, and is set down at the right hand of the throne of God, for whom the Lord chastens whom he loves, and scourges every son whom he receives: for if ye endure, ye are chastened. For God dealeth with you as with sons: for what son hath a father that chasteneth him not, and he receiveth all chastening: but if ye be not chastened, ye are not sons of God.

For chastening seemeth not pleasant at the time, but grievous: but afterward it bringeth forth the peaceable fruit of righteousness unto them that endure it: therefore, let weary hands be lifted up, and feeble knees made firm; let straight paths be made for your feet, that they may not stumble, but be healed; and let all men pursue peace and holiness with one another: for without these no man shall see the Lord.

Fear lest ye look back and see that any fall short of the grace of God; fear lest there be a bitter root, which grieveth, and many are defiled by it: but fear not lest ye rebel against him that hath spoken against it, that ye may serve God with reverence and fear, pleasing to him: for our God is a consuming fire.'

"Jesus endured the cross and now sits at the right hand of God's throne," The boy said, thinking of the cross.

"The way we can escape from all the heavy burdens of life and the sins that bind us is to walk boldly in doing good, fixing our eyes on Christ who makes us perfect." the old man Yesac said.

"The hardships or trials we face in our walk will later produce the fruits of love, joy, and peace," the boy said.

"Lift our tired hands and strengthen our weak knees, and together with our neighbors, we must pursue peace and holiness," Yesac said.

"We cannot see Christ our Lord unless we serve him acceptably with reverence and fear. We cannot see Christ our Lord unless we serve him acceptably with reverence and fear." His teacher responded.

Yesac and the boy turned to the last page of the book of Hebrews as they talked back and forth.

'Keep on loving your brothers, and do not forget to be hospitable to guests, for some among you have hospitality to angels. For as you are in prison, so are they in prison with you; and as you have a body, so do they that are mistreated.

Do not love money, but count your goods for what they are; for he himself hath said, I will never forsake you, neither will I leave you; therefore, let us be bold, saying, The Lord is my helper; I will not be afraid. Be not carried away with divers precepts: for the heart is beautiful to be hardened by grace, and not by the works of the flesh: for no man hath profited by the works of the flesh.

Do this with cheerfulness, and not with anxiety, for otherwise it profits you nothing; for they watch for your souls, as if they were to give an account. Pray for us. For I am persuaded that we have a good conscience, because we will do good in all things: and I desire your prayers the more, that I may return unto you more speedily.'

"Since God, who is unchanging, will never leave us or forsake us, we should not love money, but be content with what we have, and never cease to serve and love our neighbors," the boy said.

"What will anyone who loves the Lord worry about or fear?" Yesac said.

"What is it that pleases God?" the boy asked.

"To beautify the heart with grace, to keep on sharing, to do good works with joyfulness." Yesac's expression was holy as he looked up at the blue sky.

SJCB Dialogue - Hebrews

"Jesus Christ, surpassing the shadows of sacrifices and the Law, offered Himself once for all as the perfect atonement—the true and complete High Priest. Faith is the power that turns the unseen into reality. By faith, our ancestors gained approval, and by faith, humanity walks the path of salvation. The Law is a shadow; Christ is the substance." The Buddha spoke with firm conviction, but within that firmness was compassion for all humanity.

"The sacrifices under the Law could not make us perfect, but Christ's sacrifice makes all people whole. Jesus is the same yesterday, today, and forever. Our faith remains unshaken in the unchanging Word of the Lord. Jesus is the unchanging Word—He is Truth itself." Socrates spoke as if singing a song of devotion to Truth.

"Suffering is the discipline of love, a training that leads to awakening and righteousness. God's discipline is an expression of His love—guiding us to the fruits of righteousness and peace. Like Abraham, Moses, David, and the prophets, we too must live by faith. Love and good deeds are the natural fruit of faith. True faith is a life of encouragement, sharing, and mutual help." Confucius spoke with a heart full of love for others.

"Beyond the trials and persecution of this world, eternal rest and our heavenly home await. Let us serve the living God—who is the Word and the Truth—with reverence and awe. To fear God is the root of love, and the true attitude of service. Loving our neighbors is the fruit of that root." Jesus spoke through the nine fruits of the Spirit. As the boy closed the Book of Hebrews, the old man opened the Book of James.

Volume 20: James

"James, the brother of Jesus Christ, is writing to the twelve tribes scattered abroad. He is teaching them the importance of doing as the Master did, emphasizing the importance of practice." The boy said.

"The motto of South Korean President Kim Dae-Jung in 2000, 'Conscience in Action,' is also said to have been influenced by James' writings from Jerusalem." Yesac, recalling the prison letters of Kim Dae-jung, the 15th President of the Republic of Korea, said.

"James is a short letter, only five chapters, but it's a really great book that shows how a Christian should live." The boy spoke with an expectant and flushed expression.

Yesac flipped to the first chapter of James.

'James, a servant of God and of the Lord Jesus Christ, greetings to the twelve tribes that are scattered abroad. Consider it all joy, my brethren, when ye meet with divers temptations because ye know that the testing of your faith produces patience.

Make patience perfect, that ye may be perfect and complete, lacking nothing: and if any of you lack wisdom, let him ask of God, who giveth to all men liberally, and rebuketh not, and it shall be given him. But let him ask in faith, and let him not doubt in the least. For he that doubts is like the waves of the sea tossed and tossed by the wind; and such a man thinketh not to obtain anything of the Lord.

A double-minded man is undecided in all things. The lowly brother shall boast of his exaltation, and the rich brother of his lowliness: for they pass away as the flower of the grass. When the sun riseth, and a hot wind bloweth, and driesthe grass, it fadeth away, and the beauty of its form is gone: so shall the rich man also fade in his works.'

"It is not unusual to be taught to rejoice in trials from the beginning," the boy said.

"A person who can rejoice in the trials and tribulations of life is a true Christian of good works," Yesac said.

"Yes. Rejoicing in suffering is a great unseen work.

Ordinarily, when we are faced with difficulties, we grieve rather than rejoice," the boy said.

"Because they do not know that the testing of their faith produces patience so that they lack nothing," the old man said.

"Yes. Knowing is not knowing unless you do." Yesac nodded.

The boy's small notebook contained James' teaching about trials and perseverance leading to perfection.

'Let perseverance finish its work so that you may be mature and complete, not lacking anything.'

"The only thing that increases a Christian's happiness quotient is doing, act!" Old man Yesac's words carried strength.

The boy gazed at the distant mountains and thought to himself, Will I be a hearer of God's word or a doer of the word?

'Blessed is the man who endures temptation. Let no man say when he is tempted, I am tempted by God; for God cannot be tempted by evil, neither does he tempt anyone with evil. My dear brothers, be not deceived. Every good gift and every perfect gift is everywhere given from above, coming down from the father of lights: with whom is no variableness, neither shifting shadows:

who hath begotten us, according to his own will, by the word of truth, that we should be the first fruits of his creatures. My beloved brethren, ye know that every man is swift to hear, slow to speak, slow to become angry; for the anger of man fulfilleth not the righteousness of God.'

"James' teaching that God, who does not change like shifting shadows, tempts no one and is tempted by no one, is very enlightening." The boy spoke fluently.

"The mind creates everything, but forgetting Solomon's teaching, people deceive themselves by thinking that the trials come from the outside." The old man was momentarily lost in thought due to the boy's words. He was confused whether it was God's voice or the boy speaking. Moreover, the boy's small notebook contained Solomon's teachings that bring enlightenment.

'IlCheYuSimJo 一切唯心造 일체유심조 ;
Everything you do flows from your heart.'

"We should recognize that temptation comes from our own greed and overcome it to obtain the crown of life that God gives as a gift." Yesac tried to hide his surprised heart as he said.

Yesac's little notebook contained a great teaching that was sweeter than James' honey.

'Each person is tempted when they are dragged away by their own evil desire and enticed. Then, after desire has conceived,

it gives birth to sin; and sin, when it is full-grown, gives birth to death.'

"God has begotten us by the word of truth, so we should live by the word, the Bible," the boy said. As the journey with the novel scriptures came to an end, the boy's enlightenment only deepened.

"As if we had two ears and one mouth, we would be quick to hear, slow to speak, and slow to anger, for this is how we live as the Word." The old man's words sounded sacred to the boy's ears.

"Anger is a hindrance to fulfilling God's righteousness." Yesac cautioned.

The screen of the computer laptop where they were studying the Word suddenly went dark. The battery was dead. Thirsty for the Word, Yesac pulled the cord out of his bag with quick fingers and began charging it.

'Therefore lay aside all filthiness and all abundance of wickedness, and receive with meekness the instruction of the heart, which is able to save your souls. Be ye doers of the word, and not hearers only, deceiving yourselves.

For if any man hear the word of God, and do not fulfill it, he is like a man looking into a mirror at his own face, and seeing his own likeness, and going away and forgetting what it is: but he that looketh into the whole law, which maketh free, he is not a hearer and forgetter, but a doer, and shall be blessed in his deeds.

For if any man thinketh himself godly, and gaggeth not his tongue, but deceiveth his own heart, his godliness is vain. For godliness that is pure and undefiled before God the Father is this: to visit the fatherless and widows in their affliction, and to keep oneself from the world.'

"James speaks of the word that will save us as 'the word planted in your heart,' the Tao (Do 道 도)," the boy said.

"The Bible, the Word of God, is the Tao of Christ, which guardsand protects us." The old man Yesac spoke in the way of the Tao(Do 道 도).

"You use the phrase save and protect instead of salvation," the boy said.

"The correct translation of save should be guarded and protected rather than salvation. The word save has been translated as salvation so many times that it has led to false teachings and misunderstandings about salvation throughout history. Salvation is never given by anyone, but only by God as a gift to each person according to his or her own measure, so we should realize this for ourselves and be free from being deceived."

The boy fell silent, a look of realization on his face.
"Salvation doesn't begin when we die; it began when we werewith Christ." The boy finally broke the silence.

Yesac smiled compassionately as he stared off into the distant mountains, hiding his surprise at the boy's realization. With gratitude and compassion for the boy. The boy had grasped the secret of the Word and was already walking on his own in the world of enlightenment, between heaven and hell, life and death.

"A word that appears quite a lot in the Bible is meekness, which is the eighth fruit of the Holy Spirit. James says to receive the word with meekness."

"The first law of riches is meekness, right?" Yesac said.

"What?" The boy's eyes widened in surprise.

"In the Sermon on the Mount, Jesus said that the meek shall inherit the earth, which is immovable property. Real estate has been the golden rule of getting rich since the beginning of time." Yesac explained.

The boy recited the Sermon on the Mount with graceful movements. "Blessed are the meek, for they will inherit the earth. Blessed are the meek, for they will inherit the earth."

In fact, the people in the Bible were able to become rich because of the real estate on the land that God had given them. Just like the Jews got rich from real estate in New York, USA.

'Be doers of the way, and not hearers only, deceiving yourselves. For whosoever heareth the way, and does not do, he is like a man that looketh in a mirror and sees his own face: and he that looketh upon himself, and goes, and immediately forgeteth what his likeness is: but he that looketh into the whole law which hath set him free, is not he that heareth and forgeteth, but he that doeth, and this man shall be blessed in what he doeth.'

"James is telling us that if we just listen to God's word and don't do it, we are deceiving ourselves," the boy said wisely.

"A religion that only hears and looks at the Word is close to superstition, like the totemism of ancient society. Even now, when we live in the age of civilization, if we do not have enlightenment, it is no different from idolatry." Yesac said.

"Yes, true faith and good works are inseparable. Our thoughts, words, and deeds with our neighbors are a mirror of our own faith." The boy agreed.

The boy's little note contained James' letter on the "acting faith." It was Jacob's message to mankind.

'Do not merely listen to the word, and so deceive yourself. Do what it says. Anyone who listens to the word but does not do what it says is like someone who looks at his face in a mirror.'

Late in the night, Yesac and the boy entered the H Mart next to the office to stop the departure. The Mexican staff were delighted to say hi to Yesac, and some of his friends offered him some delicious food. Yesac wondered what kind of person could be a brother or friend to anybody. The boy walked out of the market with a jealous look. Yes, my thoughts, my words, and my actions with my neighbor are my faith. The boy thought again.

'My brothers, you have received faith in the Lord of glory, our Lord Jesus Christ. Don't take men for an appearance. If you keep the supreme law of loving your neighbor as your own body, as it is written in the book, it is good to do it; but if you take men by appearance, you sin. The law will make you sinners. He who doesn't do mercy will have a judgment without mercy.

The merciful triumphs over judgment and boasts. What profit, my brothers, if a man says, "I have faith," and doesn't have works? Is his faith able to save himself? If a brother or a sister is naked and has no bread to eat, and any of you says to him, "Go in peace, warm him up, and satisfy him," and doesn't give him anything to eat. Thus, faith without works is dead in itself.'

"James teaches that the royal law in Scripture is to love your neighbor as your own body, as you always emphasize," the boy said.

"'Love your neighbor as yourself(AeIn 愛人애인)' is the greatest teaching of Jesus Christ appearing simultaneously in your Gospels," Yesac said.

The boy's little note contained a beautiful letter James sent to the Jews.

'Judgment without mercy will be shown to anyone who has not been merciful.'

"Mercy before judgment is another doctrine of Christ which must be studied and enlightened separately." the old man said.

"Christ?" The boy asked.

"One of the Beatitudes (Eight Blessings) is mercy (compassion)." Yesac said.

"Isn't the sermon on the mountain the teaching of Jesus?" he questioned.

The boy agilely moved to extend the mountain instruction in the Gospel of Matthew. Mercy is the heart of mercy that loves and is compassionate.

'Blessed are the merciful, for they will be shown mercy.'

"The poor in spirit, the mourners, the meek, the hunger and thirst for righteousness, the pure in heart, the peacemakers, the persecuted for rightness, all are merciful servants."

Yesac remained silent at the boy's words because the boy seemed admirable.

"Here comes also the great teaching of James, which gives understanding to mankind." He spoke.

The boy then spread his little note and began to read. 'Faith by itself, if it is not accompanied by action, is dead.' Yesac was silent.

'Or say, you have faith, and I have works. Show me your faith without works. I will show you my faith by works." Do you believe that God is one? Do you do well? Even the demons believe and depart. Do you want to know, you deceitful man, that faith *without works is vanity? Wasn't our father Abraham justified by his deeds when he offered his son Isaac on the altar?*

You see that faith works with his works, and faith is perfected by his works. Behold, man is justified by works, and not by faith alone. Isn't it not by his deeds that the priest Rahab was justified, when he received the angel, and sent him out by another way? Faith without works is dead, as the body without a soul is dead.'

"It is also a faith with works that we treat the very least, not by appearance, but as Christ." The boy said.

"It is a great faith to do the small things with Christ's heart rather than only looking at the big things," Yesac admitted, turning to James' letter.

'People are considered righteous by what they do and not by faith alone. In the same way, was not even Rahab, the prostitute, considered righteous for what she did when she gave lodging to the spies and sent them off in a different direction? The body without the spirit is dead, so faith without deeds is dead.'

The man is considered righteous by what they do and not by faith alone. And he moved it into his little note. Thinking of Rahab the prostitute, the brother and sister of the boy who was justified by her deeds. Because we are all brothers and sisters in Christ.

'Who teach will be judged more strictly, my brothers, knowing that we are taught, don't be many teachers. We all make many mistakes, and we are perfect if we have no mistakes in words. Behold, the boat is so great, that it drives the things that are driven by the wind, with a very small height, according to the will of the man: even so the tongue is a small part, but boasts of great things. See how a small fire burns a lot of trees. The tongue is a fire, a world of injustice.

The tongue defiles the whole body in our members, and burns the wheels of life. Their burning comes out of the fire of hell. The tongue is full of deadly poison. By this, we praise the Lord the Father, and by this we curse him who was made in the image of God. With one mouth, we sing praise and curse. My brothers, this is not worth it. How can a seed bring forth fat and sprinkled water with a single hole? My brethren, how can the fig tree bear its fruit, and the vine its fruit?

Thus, the water of the flesh can't produce the fruit. But wisdom from above is first holy, and then peaceful, and tolerant, and gentle, and full of mercy and good fruit, and without sidewalls and falsehood. Those who make peace sow peace with peace, and reap the fruit of righteousness.'

"No matter how big the car is, what moves it is a tiny key, just as in our body, a tiny part, the tongue, can create a heaven of love or a hell of hatred. The letter of James teaches us that anyone who is never at fault in what they say is perfect. This is indeed a great teaching," the boy said without restraint.

"The tongue also is a fire, a world of evil; praising God with one mouth while cursing people with the same is hypocrisy (contradiction)," Yesac said with a kind heart.

"We must bear the fruits of righteousness and the Holy Spirit from the seeds of holiness, peace, considerate, submissive and mercy that God gives us," the boy responded.

Instead of answering, Yesac turned the page to James' letter.

'For you don't ask for what you do not have, but you ask for it, and you don't receive it, to misuse it for lusts. Brothers, do not blaspheme one another. He who reproaches his brother, or judges his brothers, reproves the law and judges the law. One is the Lawyer and the Judge. He is able to save and to destroy. Who do you judge your neighbor? You don't know what tomorrow will be. What is your life? Brothers, do not reproach one another. That way, you will be exempt from judgment. Behold, the Judge stands at the door.
Brothers, be examples of affliction and long- suffering to the prophets who spoke in your name. Behold, we are blessed with those who are patient, because you have heard of Job's patience, and have seen the end of the Lord, who is most merciful and merciful. Nevertheless, my brothers, do not swear by the heavens, nor by the earth, neither by any other thing; but if you say yes, you will not do, but you will say yes. Pray one to another, for the petitions of the righteous have much power to work.'

"Because they don't answer their prayers, James answers why. God doesn't listen to an unrighteous prayer," the boy declared.

"God does not listen to prayer for receipt, but to the prayer of offerings and sacrifices." the old man said.

"James also advises our neighbors not to blaspheme or reproach one another." the boy spoke in the face of peace.

Then Yesac began to speak. "There is only one who makes the law and judges."

"Yes. He is the one God who protects us and destroys us."

"We are only the dew on the grass and the mist in the air that appears momentarily and then disappears, so we should carry the word in our hearts and live poetically," Yesac said softly, likedew.

"The loving and merciful God will have mercy on us," the boysaid with relief.

Boys may experience some conflict in the process of doing real estate work. It is life that we hope for a world in which all love all, but that we cannot receive perfection from all, just as Christ without sin was crucified. The answer is Christ's love, mercy, wisdom, and forgiveness.

"Conflict in human relationships is the best opportunity to defeat evil with goodness. If you are hated for no reason, you must have mercy on him and love him as good. It is the best way to overcome good and evil by patience." Yesac's words were powerless.

The boy listened to the teacher and realized there was nothing to throw away from James' eyes, just as God had created everything in this world. The boy read and meditated quietly on the five chapters of the book of James, which was the same size as that of Christ on the Mount. The Mount Reminder was a noble letter from James to almost the same quantity of mankind as James, chapter 5, verses 111 and 108.

Yesac broke his silence and opened the book of Peter.

SJCB Dialogue – James

"True faith is proven through action. It must appear not only in words but in life itself. Words are vessels of the soul—one word can create heaven or unleash hell. 'Be quick to listen and slow to speak.' Speak less and act more. This is the secret to a healthy and long life. Let us not speak lightly, but speak with harmony and virtue toward our neighbors. Such faith is faith in action. One's words reflect one's character." The Buddha spoke with compassion for all humanity.

"Trials are a blessing that refines the soul, and suffering is the teacher of life. Suffering gives birth to endurance, and endurance leads us to completion. Consider it pure joy when you face various trials. Love and mercy are greater than any law. To love your neighbor is the royal law. God's entire law is fulfilled in love." Socrates spoke with enlightenment and love for humanity.

"Prayer is answered when it rises from a sincere heart. Rather than praying to receive, pray to give. Unanswered prayers often stem from selfish desires. Like Solomon, let us seek not riches, but wisdom and understanding. In humility, we draw near to the kingdom of heaven." Confucius spoke with a spirit of simplicity and humility.

"We are called to discern and love, but not to judge. Judgment belongs not to us. Life's suffering often stems from judging those who are different. Love others as they are. Just as I differ from others, others need not be the same as me. We are a shared destiny, bound in diversity. Wisdom comes from living out these truths." Jesus spoke with the fruits of the Holy Spirit.

*As Jesus spoke of the fruits of the Spirit,
the the old man closed the book of James,
and the boy opened the book of 1 Peter.*

Volume 21: 1 Peter

"Tell me about 1 Peter," the old man said.

"The Apostle Peter, a disciple of Jesus Christ, wrote this letter to encourage the early Christian community and to guide them on how to live as Christians," the boy answered.

"Peter teaches that we should keep our faith not only in good times but also in times of suffering and trials. He encourages believers to follow Christ, live as strangers, and glorify God with their good deeds, even when they face persecution," Yesac continued.

The Apostle Peter, like James, traveled between Rome and Babylon and wrote letters to Jewish Christians scattered across the world.

"Peter advises us not to be surprised by suffering in life but to accept it calmly and overcome it with the strength and wisdom given by God," the boy said.

"The attitude of accepting suffering as a natural part of life is a sign that a person is close to enlightenment," the old man said.

"When did this story of Peter take place?"

"It was around 65 AD, about 1959 years ago from now," the old man said, turning the first page of Peter's letter.

'Peter, an apostle of Jesus Christ, to the exiles who are scattered abroad in Pontus, Galatia, Cappadocia, Asia, and Bithynia, who were chosen according to the foreknowledge of God the Father to obedience and the sprinkling of the blood of Jesus Christ on you by the sanctification of the Holy Spirit according to the foreknowledge of God the Father, Grace be unto you and peace be more abundant.

That the trial of your faith, though it be tried with fire, though it perish, being more precious than gold that perisheth, may be found unto praise and honor and glory at the appearing of Jesus Christ. Jesus whom ye have not seen, but whom ye love. And now, though ye have not seen him, yet believing, ye rejoice with unspeakable and glorious joy: for the end of your faith is the salvation of your souls. Be ye holy in all manner of conversation, even as he that hath called you is holy.

For it is written, Be ye holy, because I am holy. But with the precious blood of Christ, as of a lamb without blemish and without spot, whom he foreknew before the foundation of the world, but was manifested for you in these last days... having purified your souls by the obedience of the truth, that ye might love your brethren without deceit; and that ye might love them with a fervent heart.

For ye were not born again of corruptible seed, but of incorruptible, by the living and everlasting word of God; wherefore all flesh is as grass, and all its glory as the flower of the field: the grass withereth, and the flower falleth away; but the word of the Lord abideth for ever: which is the gospel which was preached unto you.'

"How does the boy think we are chosen by God?" Yesac questioned.

"By the foreknowledge of God the Father, who foreknew our needs and chose us, through the sanctifying work of the Spirit, to be obedient to Jesus Christ and sprinkled with his blood," the boy answered.

Speaking in a mixture of Korean and English, the boy was becoming an eloquent speaker.

"We should thank Peter for his good letter and pray for much grace and peace to all mankind," Yesac said.

"Yes. As Peter says, we should be holy in all our behavior, just as the holy God who called us is holy." the boy agreed.

"Christ, who was foreknown before the creation of the world, shed his precious blood for us, like a lamb without blemish and without spot," Yesac said in the holy form and then began to preach.

"We have purified our souls by obeying Christ, who is the truth, so that we may love one another without deceit," the boy said.

"We should heed Peter's plaintive letter, 'Love one another deeply from the heart.'" Yesac said.

"We must leave the flesh, which is like flowers that fade and grass that dries up and withers, and live by the word of God, which endures forever and will not decay," the boy said.

The boy ordered a big breakfast at McDonald's for the first time in a long time. It cost $6.54, a price he felt bad about paying for a long sit and study of the Word. The playground inside the restaurant was noisy, with children running around, but to the boy's ears, it sounded precious and beautiful, like a beautiful melody.

'Therefore, lay aside all malice and all guile, and all deceit, andall envy, and all slanderous talk, and as newborn children, desirethe pure and divine milk of the word. For by it ye are brought upunto salvation: but ye are a chosen race, a royal priesthood, a holy nation, a peculiar people, his own possession, that ye may declare the praises of him that hath called you out of darkness into his marvelous light.

For ye were not then a people, but noware the people of God; ye were not having compassion, but noware having compassion. Beloved, I exhort you, as strangers and passers-by, to control the passions of the body, which war against the soul. Honor your father, love your brother, fear God,and honor your king. For if we suffer for God's sake, we are beautiful; but if we suffer for sin's sake, what praise is there in it;but if we suffer for doing good, we are beautiful in the sight of God.

He himself bore our sins in his own body on the tree, that we should die to sin and live to righteousness. And by his stripesye are healed; for ye were once like sheep going astray, but nowye are returned unto the Shepherd and Overseer of your souls.'

"How can we be saved alive?" the boy asked.

"Peter teaches, 'Like newborn babies, crave pure and divine milk, so that by it you may grow up in your salvation.'" Yesac saidwith childlike innocence.

"We are all God's chosen people, a royal priesthood, a holy nation, a people who are living out the beautiful virtues of Jesus Christ." The boy spoke as if he were living the Word himself.

"Christ has called us out of darkness into his marvelous light." The old man spoke with his face shining, and it was the light of Christ.

"If we endure suffering for the sake of the word of Christ, which destroys sin and makes righteousness alive, we will be found commendable before God by doing good." The boy said with a kind face.

Saturday morning, which is a bit of a slow day, was laundry day. Yesac's face was unusually cheerful as he did his laundry at the laundromat located right next to the fitness center. He used the waiting time to work out and catch up on the news, killing two birds with one stone, and Yesac has always had a habit of doing multiple things at once. This is what Paul meant when he wrote to the Ephesians about redeeming the time: making the most of every opportunity. The boy was also learning from Yesac, who was always living the Word. When the boy finished doing the laundry and returned, the old man handed him Peter's letter.

'But if you suffer for righteousness' sake, blessed are those who suffer for righteousness' sake: fear not, be not troubled; sanctify and hallow Christ in your hearts; and always be ready to give an answer to every man that asketh you a reason of the hope that is in you: but do it with meekness and fear, and have a good conscience: that they which revile your good works in Christ may be ashamed of their slander.

For it is better to suffer for doing good, if it be the will of God, than to suffer for doing evil: for Christ also hath once suffered for sins, the righteous for the unrighteous, that he might bring us to God: being put to death in the flesh, but quickened in the spirit, he also preacheth in the spirit to the spirits in prison.

For they were disobedient in the longsuffering of God in the days of Noah, in the preparation of the ark: and there were but few saved by water in the ark, even eight: and water is now the pledge of your salvation by the resurrection of Jesus Christ from the dead: which is baptism, which is the putting away of the filthiness of the flesh, which is not the putting away of the sins of the flesh, but the searching of a good conscience toward God. For I am seated at the right hand of God in heavenly places, and angels, and powers, and authorities, and might, are made subject unto me.'

"By our words, by our speech, we are both graced and offended," said the boy with love.

"SaUnHang(思言行 사언행), each person's thoughts, words, and actions are the vessel, character, and proof of their faith. You should live as a person who exudes the aroma of Christ to your neighbors by carefully observing these three greatest guidelines."

Indeed, the boy could sense the aroma of Christ emanating from Yesac. It was the love of God toward humanity.

"Yes. Words spoken at the right time bring good days. Like the eight who survived the Noachian deluge." The boy recalled Noah, his wife, Noah's three sons Shem, Ham, and Japheth, and their wives.

"Everyone has trials and tribulations in life. But if we face them with a clear conscience, with a clear conscience that is positive and not negative, that is the way to Christ. The reward from God will be a world of difference." Yesac instructed.

Saturday was also the day Yesac went for acupuncture. As Yesac walked out the office door to heal a soccer injury, he texted, "O Elder, thank you for the acupuncture of grace today, and thank you for my daily bread." Yesac then texted, thanking the church for living out the words of Christ... giving their gifts to their neighbors, just as James wrote.

Yesac, who had returned after finishing his treatment, turned over Peter's letter.

'For the time is fulfilled in which ye walked after the lusts of the Gentiles, in lewdness, lusts, drunkenness, revelries, uncleanness, and lawless idolatries; but the end of the age is at hand: be sober, be vigilant, be prayerful. Above all, love one another with all fervor, for love covers a multitude of sins. Be hospitable to one another, without resentment, serving one another as good stewards of God's manifold grace, as each one has received a gift.

And if any man speak, let him speak as the word of God; and if any man serve, let him serve as the power of God supplyeth: that in all things God may be glorified through Jesus Christ: to whom be glory and power unto the ages of ages, amen. Beloved, count it all joy when ye encounter temptations, which come to try you, as strange things: but count it all joy when ye partake of the sufferings of Christ, that ye may be glad and rejoice with exceeding joy when he shall be revealed in his glory.

Younger men, be subject unto the elders, and bow yourselves one to another in lowliness of mind: for God opposeth the proud, but giveth grace to the humble: humble yourselves therefore under the mighty hand of God, that he may exalt you in due time. Cast all your cares upon the Lord, for he counsels you.'

"Christ is love, and Peter is exhorting us above all things to love one another generously." The boy spoke in love.

"Love forgives a multitude of sins, so we should love and serve one another with the mind of Christ, just as God does," Yesac said with a heart of service.

The boy considered Peter's advice and wondered if his master Yesac had cast all his worries upon the Lord. Reflecting on Yesac, who lived a life free from any worries or concerns, the boy thought about how Yesac embodied both the visible and invisible, a life requiring nothing from either side. This image of the old man Yesac reminded the boy of the teachings in Paul's letter to the Philippians about finding peace and contentment in poverty, which means AnBinNakDo(安貧樂道안빈낙도) in Korean and chinese.

SJCB Dialogue - 1 Peter

*"Rejoice even in suffering. It is the refining of your faith, like pure gold.
The trials of our belief are more precious than gold that perishes in fire. Within suffering lies the hidden truth of life. In due time, God lifts up those who remain with Him through patience and humility."*
Siddhartha(Buddha), spoke on the treasure of suffering.

"Each of us must serve one another with the gifts we've been given, as faithful stewards of God's goodness. We are called to holiness by modeling after Jesus. As we think, speak, and act through the truth of His Word, we walk closer with Christ, and so we draw near to holiness." Socrates spoke with a heart of holiness.

"Long for the pure spiritual milk like newborns do. God walks with those who seek such sincerity. Do not repay evil for evil, nor insult for insult—instead, bless others. That is when the Word becomes you, and truth begins to live through you." Confucius spoke with an innocent face.

"Trials are the fire of faith. They qualify us to share in His glory. Roaring lions, unfair pain, and persecution cannot destroy us— they only refine us. Because we are a love that cannot perish."
Jesus spoke through the power of love.

"Suffering and refinement are not flames that destroy us, but fire that shapes us into pure gold. Love never fails. Truth does not fall. And the Word always blooms." The Old Man spoke like gold refined, and the Boy opened the book of 2 Peter... in love.

Volume 22: 2 Peter

"Peter is writing his second letter from Rome to the Jews who are scattered throughout the world." The boy thought of Augustus, the first emperor of the Roman Empire, and said.

"He is exhorting them not to be deceived by false shepherds who have arisen since the death and resurrection of Jesus Christ. False shepherds were in the past and are in the present, so you must keep yourself informed by the Word." As Yesac spoke, he opened Peter's second letter.

'For by his divine power he has given us all things that pertain to life and godliness, through the knowledge of him who called us by his own glory and virtue. Whereunto he hath given us precious and exceeding great promises, that by them ye should escape the corruption that is in the world through lust, and should be conformed to the divine nature; wherefore, with all diligence, let your faith supply virtue, and virtue supply knowledge, and knowledge supply temperance, and temperance supply patience, and patience supply godliness, and godliness supply brotherly charity, and brotherly charity supply love.

And we have a more sure prophecy, which is as a lamp that shineth in a dark place, till the day dawneth, and the daystar ariseth in your hearts, that ye may give heed unto it. First know this, that all the prophecies of the scriptures are not given in secret: for the prophecy did not come at any time by the will of man, but men spoke as they were moved by the Holy Ghost, as they received it from God. Beloved, remember this one thing, that with the Lord, a day is as a thousand years, and a thousand years as a day.

The promise of the Lord is not slack concerning you, as some suppose slowness, but is longsuffering toward you, not willing that any should perish, but that all should come to repentance; but the day of the Lord will come as a thief in the night, in which the heavens shall pass away with a great noise, the elements shall roast, and the elements shall be dissolved in fervent fire, and the works of the earth and all that is therein shall be revealed.

And all these things shall be revealed, what manner of men ought ye to be. In holy conduct and godliness, looking for and eagerly desiring the coming of the day of God. For in that day the heavens shall be burned up, the elements shall be dissolved, and the furnace shall melt with fervent heat; and we shall see new heavens and a new earth, wherein dwelleth righteousness according to his promise.'

In the boy's little notebook, he had written down Peter's teaching to protect himself from false shepherds. He began to read them aloud.

'For this very reason, make every effort to add to your faith goodness; and to goodness, knowledge; and to knowledge, self-control; and to self-control, perseverance; and to perseverance, godliness; and to godliness, mutual affection; and to mutual affection, love.'

"With holy conduct and godliness (holy and godly life), those who are with Christ have nothing to fear," Yesac said with an unblinking expression.

"Yes. A person who is open to the enlightenment of the Word is always free from everything because he is not limited by time and space." The boy said and closed the last volume of 2 Peter.

SICB Dialogue – 2 Peter

"2 Peter is short yet powerful. It weaves holy living, warnings against falsehood, and hope for the end into one message. It speaks of judgment and love, truth and mercy. The call to add godly virtues to faith is a magnificent teaching." Siddhartha (Buddha) said this while gazing at words carefully written in Socrates' small notebook.

'Add to your faith goodness, and to goodness, knowledge; and to knowledge, self-control; and to self-control, perseverance; and to perseverance, godliness; and to godliness, mutual affection; and to mutual affection, love.' – 2 Peter Chapter 1

"We must take seriously the words warning us against false teachers. No man, no priest, no sage is someone to rely on—only to love. One must awaken and reflect the divine nature within, but relying on people causes confusion and delays true awakening. This is the tragic error of misguided religion." Socrates spoke with enlightening clarity.

"The Lord's promise is not delayed—it is long-suffering toward humanity. We must live not with lives where one day feels like a thousand years, but with joy where a thousand years feel like a single day. God does not wish any to perish, but for all to turn back through truth and the Word." Confucius spoke with gratitude.

"God wants us to live in holiness and reverence. There is a new heaven and new earth where the righteousness of truth dwells. His patience is salvation. 2 Peter is not a warning of terror but an invitation to holiness. If falsehood is darkness, the Word is the lamp. The Day of the Lord is not fear—it is reunion in joy." Jesus spoke with joy.

"The new heaven and new earth open first within the soul of the holy. When the morning star rises in your heart, you are no longer in darkness. This Word is light, freedom, and love toward one another." The Young Man, So-Nyeon (蘇年), spoke like his name—revived each year.

Volume 23: 1 John

The old man said, "Tell me about 1 John."

The boy, recalling the Gospel of John he studied in Ephesus, currently located in modern-day Turkey, said, "John is writing his first epistle following the Gospel."

"John is writing from Ephesus, the first letter after the Gospels. God is love, and John was the apostle who best expressed who God is to us." Yesac said with love.

"He wrote five books and letters: the Gospel of John, 1 John, 2 John, 3 John, and Revelation," Yesac instructed.

"John's first letter had five purposes: fellowship in Christ, joy, eternal life, avoiding sin, and not being led astray.'"

The boy opened the first chapter of John's letter.

'If we say that we have fellowship with God, and walk in the darkness, we lie, and do not do the truth; but if we walk in the light, as he is in the light, we have fellowship with one another, and the blood of Jesus Christ his Son cleanseth us from all sin, He that saith he abideth in him, even so walketh he also, even as he walketh... in the light: he that hateth his brother is so far in darkness: he that loveth his brother abideth in the light, and hath no stumbling in him: but he that hateth his brother is in darkness, and walketh in darkness, and knoweth not whither he goeth, because the darkness hath blinded his eyes.

For if any man love the world, the love of the Father is not in him: and the world passeth away, and the lust thereof: but he that doeth the will of God abideth forever. We know that we have passed from death unto life because we love the brother: but he that loveth not abideth in death.'

"Praise be to God, who is light; in him is no darkness at all." The boy said as if praising.

"Just as not to love one another is to abide in darkness, so the cessation of love is the cessation of life," The old man said of eternal life.

"In this world, we have nothing to boast of but love." The boy spoke with love and humility.

"All things pass away, but the word of Christ, which is truth, is an everlasting law." The old man spoke with truth.

The boy's gaze paused for a moment on John's letter,

'Do not be surprised, my brothers and sisters, if the world hates you.'

'Everyone who hates his brother is a murderer. Everyone who kills knows that eternal life does not dwell in him. Because he gave his life for us, we know that we are worthy to give our life for our brothers. How can the love of God dwell in him, if he sees his brother's need with the riches of this world, and refuses his heart to help him? Children, let us not love with words and tongues, but with deeds and truth. Beloved, love is of God, that we may love one another. Everyone who loves is from God, and he who knows God and doesn't love him, he does not know God, for God is love. Here is the love, because we didn't love God, but God loved us, and sent his Son as a sacrifice of atonement for our sins. Beloved, because God has so loved us, we are worthy to love one another.

'For no man has ever seen God; but if we love one another, God dwells in us, and his love is perfect in us. Because he has given us his Holy Spirit, we know that we dwell in him, and that he dwells in us. We have seen and testify that the Father has sent his Son to be the Savior of the world. Whoever confesses that Jesus is the Son of God, God dwells in him, and he also in God. For we know and believe that God loves us. God is love. He who remains in love dwells in God, and God in him. Thus is the love made perfect in us, that we may have confidence in the day of judgment, even as you are in the world.'

"John says that hatred of one's neighbor is murder." The boy noted after he finished reading.

"Hate is the extinction of love; without love, there is no life." The old man said with enlightenment.

"Yes. We need to know how to see what is invisible to the eyes of our hearts." The boy said with the eyes of the heart.

"John's letter appeals not only to love with words and tongues but to love in deeds and in truth." The boy said with action and sincerity.

"Those who don't believe in an invisible God love their loversor their families. John's great teaching, "God is love," is making itclear to those who do not believe that God is alive. Otherwise, we cannot say that it is invisible love." The boy said with love.

"If we love one another in Christ, God dwells in us."

Both Yesac and the boy's faces were the loving faces of Christ.

'For in love there is no fear, but perfect love drives out fear, and in fear, there is punishment, for he who fears is not perfected in love. He who loves God must also love his brother. We love him because he loved us first. If anyone says that he loves God and hates his brother, he is a liar.

Behold, he who doesn't love hisbrothers cannot love God without seeing him. We have receivedthis commandment from the Lord, that he who loves God shouldalso love his brother, for everyone who is born of God overcomesthe world. This is the victory over the world: our faith. Who is hewho overcomes the world unless he believes that he is the Son of God? This is the one who came by water and blood, Jesus Christ. He came not by water only, but by blood and water. The Holy Spirit testifies, and the Spirit is the truth.

'There are three witnesses: the Spirit, the water, and the blood. And these three together are one. He who has the Son haslife, and he who doesn't have the Son of God has no life. I wrotethese things to you who believe in the name of the Son of God, that you might know that you have eternal life.

This is what we have for him. Whatever he asks, according to his will, he hears. He doesn't know that he hears what we ask, nor that we have obtained what we asked of him. And we know that the Son of God has come to give us understanding, that we may know the true One, and that we are in the truthful One, Jesus Christ, his Son, who is the true God, and eternal life.'

"Through John's letter, we learn a lot. The statement that fear comes from a lack of love is heard with a great echo that awakens us." The boy said as if he were a person without fear.

"Fear is the creation of one's own heart, and a man who lives in love is not cruel." The old man said with an open heart. In Yesac's words, there was always no fear or cruelty.

"Love makes all things perfect. God, the Holy Spirit, and Jesusare one, testifying to us of their love." The boy spoke with a holyface.

"For we are in the true One, Jesus Christ, the Son of God." The old man said with freedom and holiness.

"John clearly testifies that Jesus is the true God and eternal life. The letter from John, which reveals that Jesus is the true God, is a great gift that leads humanity to enlightenment." the boy said.

"If Jesus had not come, we would not have been able to see God forever and ever." The old man Yesac said with a heart that is always with Christ.

"So God and Jesus dwell in us."

Yesac and the boy opened 2 John with the fullness of the Holy Spirit face.

SICB Dialogue – 1 John

"God is light, and in Him there is no darkness at all. Truth cannot be hidden, and hatred blinds the eyes. Whoever hates a brother or sister still walks in darkness. Hatred is the seed of murder, but love is the key to life." Siddhartha (Buddha) said this as he looked at the Scriptures neatly laid beside the Buddhist texts.

"The desires of the world will pass away, but the will of God endures forever. Love, which is truth and the Word, is eternally indestructible. To believe in eternal life is to awaken and become the truth, to live as the Word. For the awakened, there is no death. Even our living soul does not belong to us but to Christ—so what death remains?" Socrates spoke with awakening.

"Love must not be in word or tongue, but in action and in truth. Love cannot be hidden. It shines on the face with the fragrance of Christ. God is love, and whoever loves is born of God. Whoever loves others dwells in God." Confucius spoke with the fragrance of Christ.

"There is no fear in perfect love. Love drives out fear, and even on the day of judgment, gives us boldness. God's command is neither burdensome nor complex. Love God, who is the Word and Truth, and love your brothers and sisters—how simple and pure this teaching is." Jesus spoke simply and clearly.

"1 John is not merely a simple letter—it is a secret code of love that restores humanity." The Boy said this, and the Old Man opened John's second letter with joy.

Volume 24: 2 John

"John in Ephesus is writing to the elect man and his children, emphasizing the importance of harmony." the boy said.

"He's commending them for standing firm in the love of Christ," Yesac said as he opened John's second letter.

'I, the elder, write to the elect woman and her children, whomI truly love, and not only I, but all who know the truth, because of the truth that abides in us and will be with us forever. Grace be with you, and mercy, and peace, from God the Father, and from his Son Jesus Christ, in truth and love.

I am well pleased to see that thy children walk in truth, according to the commandment which we have received of the Father. And this Ibeseech you now, Married women, love one another. This is notwritten unto you as a new commandment, but as we have had from the beginning.'

"It is not a new commandment to love one another, for our God, who is alpha and omega, the beginning and the end, is love." The boy said with love.

"Fear God and love your neighbor is the bottom line of the Bible," Yesac said and opened the book of 3 John.

SICB Dialogue – 2 John

*"Though brief, 2 John is a densely packed revelation of truth and love
among the chosen. Truth dwells within us and remains with us forever.
Truth is not external information, but the One who abides within, as
the Word and as love."* Siddhartha (Buddha) spoke, quoting
'All is created by the mind' just as Solomon once spoke in Proverbs.

*"Grace, mercy, and peace come through truth and love.
God's blessings do not flow from emotions, but from truth.
It brings joy to witness those who live out the truth,
for faith delights when it becomes action.
The command to love one another is not new,
but given from the beginning. Love is not a choice—it is truth."*
Socrates spoke as the Word became truth within him.

*"To love is to walk in His commandment,
and that commandment is the will of God.
We must love not with knowledge or words, but with life itself.
To discern the deceivers in the world,
we do not rely on people—but on staying awake in the Word."*
Confucius spoke from wakefulness.

*"No matter how religious one may appear,
without the Word, it is all empty.
For God is the Word.
Though 2 John seems like a brief love letter,
the love within it is a blessing reserved
for those who stand upon truth."*
Jesus spoke, becoming the Word and the Truth.

*"Love boldly, but do not be deceived.
Stand firm on truth, and walk like the horn of a mighty ox—undaunted."*
The Boy declared with courage as Truth itself,
and the old man Yesac turned the page to 3 John with a loving smile.

Volume 25: 3 John

"Ninety years after Jesus was born, John is writing a letter of praise to Gaius and Demetrius in Ephesus." The boy spoke as he opened John's letter.

"He's also rebuking Diotrephes for his pride," Yesac said.

The Third Epistle of John was a short letter consisting of a single chapter.

'The elder writes to you, my beloved Gaius, my true beloved. I pray thee, my beloved, that thou mayest be well and strong in all things, even as thy soul is well, for I rejoice greatly that thou walkest in the truth, even as thy soul is in thee.

For I have no greater pleasure than to hear that my children walk in the truth... beloved, imitate not evil, but what is good: for he that doeth good is of God, and he that doeth evil hath not seen God.'

In the boy's little notebook, he had written a letter from John that was commonplace in the world.

'Dear friend, I pray that you may enjoy good health and that all may go well with you, even as your soul is getting along well.'

"We have no greater joy than to do all things in the love of Christ, who is the truth." The boy's voice was firm.

"When the soul prospers, everything else will prosper, so we must cherish the truth and live by the word."

Yesac opened the book of Jude with a compassionate smile.

SICB Dialogue – 3 John

"Though 3 John is a single letter, it encapsulates the essence of the gospel—a life where the prosperity of the soul and the health of the body walk hand in hand. Those who dwell in truth value not outward success first, but the well-being of the soul as the true blessing."
Buddha spoke, blessing humanity from the depth of his heart.

"Indeed, John's third letter may be short, but the truth it holds, the prosperity of the soul, the leadership of the community, love, and warnings—all are remarkably deep and sharp. Only when our soul prospers by the Word will all things prosper as well." Socrates spoke with a clear and awakened spirit.

"More than knowledge, it is practice. More than preaching, it is life. God delights when we walk in the truth. Truth is not merely knowledge, but a way of life walked according to the Word.
Truth becomes alive only when lived." Confucius spoke through action.

"The one who does good with a joyful heart belongs to God. Holiness is proven through the fruits of a life lived. One who is praised like Demetrius is, in and of himself, a testimony of truth."
Jesus spoke in praise of Demetrius.

"God rejoices over those who walk in truth. Though 3 John may seem like a brief letter, it holds profound insight, warnings, and encouragement for the church—which must be a vessel of inner reflection, communal leadership, and the flow of love and truth."
As the Boy spoke like flowing water,
the old man opened the book of Jude.

Volume 26: Jude

"Tell me about the book of Jude," Yesac said.

"Of the 27 books in the New Testament, almost 80% are letters. Specifically, 21 out of the 27 are letters, which is 77.78%. The last of these letters is the book of Jude," the boy's approach to the Bible was refreshing.

"Jude, the brother of James, wrote this letter to combat the heresy of Gnosticism, which claims to possess special spiritual knowledge about the origins of the universe." Yesac thought of Jude's brother, James, and said,

"The Church's efforts to reject heresy and promote the correct faith are ongoing even today." The boy opened his short letter to Jude and said.

'Judas, the servant of Jesus Christ, the brother of James, writes to those who have been called, who have received love in God the Father and have been preserved for Jesus Christ. May mercy, peace, and love be more abundant in you. Sodom and Gomorrah and their neighboring cities have also committed adultery in their likeness; they have followed another color and have become a mirror of the punishment of eternal fire.

Beloved, build on your most holy faith, pray in the Holy Spirit, and wait for the mercy of our Lord Jesus Christ to preserve you in the love of God and to attain eternal life. Have mercy on those who doubt. You shall save some of them out of the fire. You shall have compassion in fear of anyone who hates his clothes that are defiled with his flesh.

May the glory, the majesty, the power, and the authority be with you through our Lord Jesus Christ, our only Savior, God, who is able to preserve you without blemish and to make you stand before his glory with joy without fault, from now on and forever and ever. Amen.'

"We must pray in the Holy Spirit and establish ourselves on the holy faith." The boy said with a prayerful heart.

"In God's love, we must strive to keep ourselves in the truth of His word and reach eternal life." Yesac, grateful for Christ's compassion, said with an expression of mercy.

"God will protect us and make us stand without blemish before His glory with joy without fault." The boy said with a joyfulface and opened the first chapter of Revelation, the last book ofthe Bible.

"As discussed in the beginning, Epistles provides valuable resources on theology, spiritual guidance, and religious wisdom.These resources help Christians navigate their faith and life." The old man spoke with love for humanity.

"It also dives deep into the diversity in the early church as well as the struggles and triumphs experienced by early Christians." The boy, reflecting on the suffering and triumph of the Christians, spoke—and the old man opened the final book of the 66 canonical Scriptures, the Book of Revelation.

SJCB Dialogue - Jude

"Jude is a letter filled with a remarkable balance of warning and comfort, judgment and mercy. It is a sacred cry sent to the soldiers of faith, like the resolve of a general before the final battle."
Buddha, speaking with interest.

"It's like the battle declaration of the New Testament. Though short, every sentence is ablaze with love and judgment, warning and mercy, the Holy Spirit and truth. It is the final cry of the canon."
Socrates, speaking eloquently.

"We live the eternal life of mercy by keeping ourselves in the love of God. Those who endure to the end are the ones who have practiced love within themselves. God will keep us to the end and make us stand before His glory."
Confucius, speaking with reverence toward God and love for neighbors.

"Jude is the final shield of truth, a trumpet of warning crying out for the last chance of mercy. In this age of heresy and corruption, cover with love, stay awake by the Holy Spirit, and arm yourself with the Word. That is the earnest cry of Jude." Jesus, speaking with love, mercy, and urgency for all of humanity.

As Jesus closed the Book of Jude,
Buddha opened the final book of the canon,
the Book of Revelation.

Chapter 4: Prophecy

"This is the final book of the Christian Bible. It talks about prophetic visions and the messages provided by God to John, who was in exile on Patmos." The boy spoke with a sense of freedom born from enlightenment.

"It further talks about letters writtento the seven churches, the four horsemen, and the throne room.Moreover, there is a discussion on the fall of Babylon and the riseof the beast. Lastly, it talks about the final judgment, Jesus' return, and the new creation." The old man spoke with a heart full of love for humanity.

With a face shining like the Dawn Star, the boy opened the final scroll—the Book of Revelation.

Volume 27: Revelation

"Tell me about the Book of Revelation," the old man Yesac said with a look of nostalgia, reflecting on the long journey with the 'Novel Scriptures.'

"John is in exile to him on the island of Bithmos of the sea, writing a book about the coming of Christ and the creation of the new heavens and the new earth through the Revelation." the boy said.

"Writing and living in exile on the island? It's very romantic." Yesac said with a smile.

"Revelation is also the most difficult book to understand." The boy admitted.

"A good teacher or student is one who can teach or learn something difficult in an easy way," Yesac said with a light face.

"It also contains the hope that Christ will conquer the world captured by the forces of evil, judge the evil forces, and open a new world." The boy opened the first chapter of Revelation and said.

The Revelation of Jesus Christ.
For God has given him an angel and sent him to his servant John
to show his servants what must soon take place.
Behold, he will come in the clouds.
Everyone's eyes will see him,
and those who pierced him will mourn.
All the families of the earth will mourn for him.
Amen.

The Lord God said:
"I am the Alpha and the Omega.
I am the Almighty.

I, John, am your brother,
who shares in the tribulations,
the kingdom,
and the sufferings of Jesus.

*I was on the island of Patmos
because of the word of God
and the testimony of Jesus."*

*On the Lord's day,
I was moved by the Holy Spirit,
and I heard behind me a loud voice like a trumpet, saying:*

*"Write in a book what you see,
and send it to the seven churches:
Ephesus, Smyrna, Pergamum, Thyatira, Sardis, Philadelphia, and
Laodicea."*

*His feet were like burning bronze,
and his voice like the sound of rushing waters.
He held seven stars in his right hand,
and from his mouth came a sharp two-edged sword.
His face was like the sun shining in full strength.*

*When I saw him,
I fell at his feet as though dead.*

*But he laid his right hand on me and said:
"Do not be afraid.
I am the First and the Last.*

*You have seen in my right hand
the mystery of the seven stars
and the seven golden candlesticks.*

*The seven stars are the angels of the seven churches,
and the seven lampstands are the seven churches."*

"The people say that the voice, which came upon John through the Holy Spirit and sounded like a trumpet, cannot be deciphered or understood," the boy said, with a heart longing to resemble the glowing bronze refined in a furnace.

"We cannot know all the mysterious works of God," Yesac said, his voice as clear as running water.

"The complexity is that there are more than 300 symbols." the boy said.

"It can be seen by one's symbols, and the illusion cannot be recognized by itself, but it can be reached by anyone." The old man said calmly yet with a steely resolve.

"The seven stars and the candlestick are merely seven churches and angels. The boy also said calmly.

"The Alpha and Omega, God, with feet like glowing bronze refined in a furnace and a voice like the sound of rushing waters, says, 'Do not be afraid,' so what is so complex and difficult to understand about that?" The old man responded with composure as if asking a question in return.

"How holy and magnificent is the face of the sun that shines so brightly." The boy spoke with an expression that radiated light.

After that, he uncovered a laptop brought by Yesac after a football match. The result was a 4:2 victory, and the same team, the D team, used the time in the game to open the record for two goals. A BBQ party was scheduled after the match.

'He who has an ear, let him hear what the Spirit says to the assemblies. To him who overcomes, I will give to eat the fruit of the tree of life in God's paradise. To the angel of the assembly of Sumer, the first and the last, he who was dead and was raised from the dead, said, "I know your affliction and your need, for you are rich. I know the reproach of those who call themselves Jews.

They are not Jews, but the congregation of Satan. Don't be afraid of the suffering you will suffer. Behold, the devil will cast some of you into prison to be tried, and you will be afflicted for ten days. Be faithful to death, and I will give you the throne of life. Let him who has an ear hear what the Spirit says to the assemblies. Whoever wins will not receive a second death. But hold fast that which is with you until I come.

To him who overcomes and keeps my works to the end, I will give authority over all the nations; and he will rule over them with a rod of iron, as he breaks a vessel of iron. I also have received from my Father. I will also give him the morning star. He who has an ear, let him hear what the Spirit says to the assemblies.'

"We are indeed rich compared to Jesus' tribulation and needy, and the resurrected Jesus gives us to eat the fruit of the tree of life in God's paradise. What is so complicated about Revelation?" The boy also reflected on the words and asked himself a question.

"Compared to the suffering and poverty of Jesus, we are wealthy. Moreover, the resurrected Jesus grants us the fruit of the tree of life in God's paradise, so why do people find the Book of Revelation so complex and difficult to understand?" The boy reflected on the words and asked himself the question.

"If you are faithful unto death, you will receive the crown of life, so how grateful and beautiful is the Book of Revelation that tells us not to fear the sufferings we may face?" the boy said, expressing his beautiful heart.

"Faithful unto death means living according to the Word," Yesac said.

"The truth is not complex but simple," the boy realized, his eyes gazing at the sky with an enlightened expression. "The Book of Revelation is not a subject of fear but of love, for God is love," he whispered, his expression signifying eternal happiness.

"Jesus says to hold firmly to the truth until He comes and that the second death will not hurt those who overcome. So, what is there to fear?" Yesac said with a face free from any worries.

"We were crucified with Christ and died with Him, so our livesare not our own. How then can death have any power over us?"the boy said with eternal freedom.

"Jesus promises to give the authority to rule over all nations to those who keep the works of Christ to the end and overcome," the boy said with a free expression.

"He even promises to give the morning star, so those who have ears will hear what the Spirit says to the churches," the old man said with composure.

At the BBQ grill table at the soccer court, he was studying the words. Ed, a friend of Yesac's from Puerto Rico, was the first to finish a football match. He and Yesac were very good friends. After some time, Yesac recovered from the wind.

'To the angel of the church in Sardis, said one who had the seven spirits of God and the seven stars, I know your works. He who overcomes will be clothed with white garments, and I will not erase his name from the Book of Life, but I will confess his name before my Father and before his angels. Let him who has an ear hear what the Spirit says to the assemblies.

To the apostle of the church in Philadelphia, who is holy and true and has the key of David, he says, When he opens, no one shuts, and when he closes, there are not ten. Because you have kept the word of my patience, I will also keep you from the time of trial, which is to come on all the earth to test those who dwell on the earth.

Let him who has an ear hear what the Spirit says to the assemblies. 'To the apostle of the church in Laodicea, Amen, the faithful and true witness, the foundation of God's creation, says, "I know your works: you are neither cold nor hot. I want you to be cold or hot."

Thus you shall be unclean, neither hot nor cold; and I will pluck you out of my mouth. Behold, I stand outside the gate and knock. If anyone hears my voice and opens the door, I will come into him, and I will eat with him, and he shall eat with me. To him who overcomes, I will make him sit with me on my throne, as I overcame and sat with my Father on the throne.'

"The Holy Spirit is speaking to the churches." said the boy.

"What he opens, no one can shut, and what he shuts, nobody can open," Yesac said with an open mind.

"Jesus is the Holy Spirit and the Truth," the boy responded.

"Christ is the Amen, the faithful and true witness, the ruler of God's creation," Yesac said, praising Christ.

"Yes. We must keep the word of Christ's patience to the end." The boy said thoughtfully.

"Jesus wants us to be clear and clear apostles, whether cold or warm." Yesac nodded.

"When we hear the voice of Christ knocking at the door and open the doors of our hearts, we eat and live with Christ." The boy said with a warm heart.

"If we always keep the word of truth, we shall enjoy the same glory as Christ sits on the throne of God," said Yesac, finishing the lesson.

Unlike any other day, after finishing his early morning workout and showering, Yesac's face shone even brighter today. Over the past six months, he had changed his diet, reducing his three meals to two and eating with great wisdom. As a result, Yesac's physique had reached its peak, with his triceps and well-proportioned muscles drawing admiration from those who saw him. Moreover, his body had become as sleek as a flying tiger, resembling an ageless figure transcending time, space, and generations, not the appearance of a 63-year-old man. Yesac was born in the year of the tiger in 1962.

> *'And the throne was surrounded by twenty-four thrones, and on the thrones were sitting twenty and four elders, clothed in white clothing, and with gold vessels on their heads. From the throne came lightning, and voice, and sound, and seven lamps burned before the Throne: these are the seven spirits of God."You are worthy, O Lord our God, to receive glory, honor, and power, for you have made all things.*
>
> *All things were according to your will and were made." He took the book, and the four living creatures and the twenty-four elders fell down before the Lamb, each with a vessel of gold full of incense and perfume, which are the prayers of the saints. He said with a loudvoice, "The Lamb who was slain is worthy of power, wealth, wisdom, power, honor, glory, and praise," He said, "Don't harm the earth, nor the sea, or the trees until we have put a thumb onthe foreheads of our God's servants."*
>
> *I heard the number of those who were sealed: one hundred and forty-four thousand ofthe tribes of the children of Israel, one and twenty-two thousandfrom the tribe of Judah, one thousand and two thousand out of the Tribe of Reuben, and one and twelve thousand Out of the Tribes of Gad, and two hundred thousand From the Tribes of Asher, and twentieth and two Thousand Out from the Tribal of Naphtali, and a thousand And twenty Thousand Out of Manasseh, Out of Simeon, and ten thousand In Levi, And ten thousand In the Middle of Issachar, And one thousand Out of Zebulun, And the thousand Outside of Jephun.*
>
> *For the Lamb whois in the midst of the throne will be their shepherd, and will lead them to the spring of the water of life, and God will wipe away every tear from their eyes.'*

"From the throne, lightning, voice, and noise..." Yesac whispered alone, staring at him.

It was a reminder of the moment when Jesus came to Him in the Holy Spirit. "All that you seek and hope for is in you from the beginning." Yesac received a flash of lightning, rumblings, and peals of thunder from the Holy Spirit Jesus on the Big Bear Mountain.

"Christ, our shepherd, will lead us to the fountain of living water, and God will wipe away every tear from our eyes." The boy spoke as he turned the final page of the Book of Revelation, the last book of the 66 books of the Bible.

'He who takes captivity shall be taken captive,
and he who kills by the sword shall surely die by the sword.
Here is the patience and faith of the saints.
There is wisdom. He who has understanding,
let him count the number of the beast.
The number of a man was six hundred sixty lakhs.

I heard a voice from heaven, saying,
"Write. Blessed are those who die in the Lord after the money."
The Holy Spirit said,
"Thus will they cease their labor and rest;
for according to the work they have done."

And he saw another sign, great and strange, in heaven:
and the seven angels had seven plagues—the last plague;
and the wrath of God would be finished in this.

The song of Moses the servant of God, and the song of the Lamb:
"Great and marvelous is your work, Lord God Almighty.
O King of the nations, your ways are righteous and true."

There was a smoke in the temple because of the glory and the power of God, and no one could enter into it until the seven plagues of the seven angels were accomplished.
Here is the meaning of wisdom:
The seven heads are the seven mountains on which the woman sits.

I am the Alpha and the Omega, the First and the Last,
the Beginning and the End.
I, Jesus, have sent my messenger for the churches,
to bear witness to these things to you.
I am the Root and the Seed of David, the Bright Morning Star.

The Holy Spirit and the bride say, "Come!"
He who hears will say, "Come!" He who is thirsty will come.
He who desires, let him "get free the water of life."

May the grace of the Lord Jesus be on all. Amen.'

"I thank Jesus, the Root, and Offspring of David, the bright Morning Star, for freely giving us the water of life," the boy said like the bright Morning Star.

"May the grace of the Lord Jesus be with all humanity. Amen." Yesac prayed.

The old man and the boy, grateful for having found the answers to life through their long journey with the 'Novel Scriptures,' embraced each other with Christ's love.

The faces of the boy and Yesac, having completed the 66 books of the Scriptures, shone like Moses descending from Mount Sinai with the tablets of the Ten Commandments. Their appearance was the light of Christ, the light of the world. The miraculous and mysterious event occurred when the boy closed the final page of the Scriptures: the sound of clear water turned into a thunderous roar, uniting the world through the Word and humanity through love. Thus, humankind attained enlightenment and eternal happiness.

SJCB Dialogue - Revelation

"In the Old Testament, Habakkuk protested to God about how the wicked seemed to prosper. But in the history of humanity, injustice and greed ultimately collapse, and though God's justice may seem delayed, it never disappears. The wicked will surely be judged, and the punishment can even extend to the third and fourth generation — we must awaken to this truth." Buddha Siddhartha spoke firmly, filled with love for humanity.

"Those who hold onto faith in truth and the Word until the end will be victorious. This world is not eternal, but God wipes away every tear. When we walk with the Word and truth, the world of pain and tears comes to an end, and the eternal kingdom of comfort opens." Socrates spoke with serene detachment.

"The Book of Revelation is a message of hope. It proclaims God's final victory over the forces of evil. It gives us courage to stand firm and persevere through trials. It also reminds us to wait for the return of Christ and deeply inscribes in us the sovereignty, mercy, and grace of God." Confucius spoke with grace and hope.

"Falsehood and greed collapse on their own, while a life centered on God leads to restoration. Without love, we are nothing. Revelation is not a book of fear, but an invitation to the restoration of love and holiness." Jesus spoke as love itself.

"'The Root and Offspring of David, the Bright Morning Star' — our Christ — We give infinite thanks to Jesus, who gave us the water of life freely to us all." The boy prayed with a face shining like the morning star.

"May the grace of the Lord Jesus be with all mankind. Amen." The old man Yesac prayed with a reverent heart.

After finishing all 66 books of the Scriptures,
the faces of the boy and Yesac shone,
just like Moses' face did
when he came down from Mount Sinai
with the tablets of the Ten Commandments.
Their faces radiated the light of Christ
and became the salt of the world.
The old man and the boy,
having completed their long journey
through the "Novel Scriptures,"
embraced each other in gratitude for having found
the answer to life —embracing one another with the love
and mercy of Christ.
As the boy closed the final page,
the sound of clear water thundered like a roar,
and the world was united by the Word,
a new world opened —
one in which humanity became one through love.
Thus, all humankind reached enlightenment
and eternal happiness.

🌐 The End.

The Author's Poem

— A love story between God, me, and you
The final chapter, yet the journey goes on.

Here I am,
At the place where I've just finished novelizing all 66 books of the Scriptures,
And when I close my eyes, my heart still beats.

I hear the voices of the boy and Yesac,
Socrates, Confucius, Buddha, and Jesus
Whisper to me gently, smiling beyond language and time.

"You're on the right path. Now, it's your turn to share this dialogue with the world."

Enlightenment and Eternal Happiness
Is no longer one man's story.
This book penetrates the truths of millennia
And becomes a flame of love and enlightenment
Given to each of us who live in this very moment.

I am no longer a wandering man of nothing.
Now I walk with humanity's hope on my back,
The lead of a mobile concert that breaks down every wall,
A foolish pilgrim walking from nothing toward everything.

To you who read this book,
You too have now become part of this journey.
Our story knows no pause.
Until the final step of life is taken,
I will keep writing — laughing and crying
With those I love.

This is the offering of my life,
My purpose, and my mission.
And I believe
These stories will surely
Shine into the deepest part of your life,
As Enlightenment and Eternal Happiness.

Now That All Stories Have Been Told,
I Finally Understand
This book was not simply words —
It was a prayer.
It was not a confession —
It was destiny.

The boy and Yesac,
Socrates and Jesus, Confucius and Buddha —
In the end, they all dwelled within me.
The time I lived with them,
That itself became this book.

I was, merely,
A beggar, sick, and alone.
But now,
I am a writer who embraces the Kingdom of Heaven,
A foolish man who still dreams of love,
And half of a blazing couple
Piercing through the world with love for our neighbors.

To you who have read this book,
This is not simply a reading.
It is an invitation sent to you by Heaven.

Now it is your turn.
Awaken. Love. Be happy.
And proclaim to the world:

"At this moment, I judge no one by what they've done.
I love everyone just as they are.
And when I finally placed others above myself,
I stood at the threshold of enlightenment
And entered eternal happiness."

Even in this very moment,
The author breathes with your tears, your laughter, your trembling.
Just like the first page we shared,
This last chapter... is the beginning of a new night.

I quietly close my eyes.
Every word was written in blood from my chest,
Every sentence was born, risking my life, to reach you.

The boy's gaze,
The old man's smile,
The silence of Socrates,
The tears of Confucius,
The embrace of Jesus,
The breath of the Buddha—

They were all our stories,
A love letter from Heaven whispered to your soul.
I did not write this book—
This book rewrote me.

To you who have read this book,
You are no longer who you once were.
Now, a fire has been lit within you.

The fire of awakening,
The fire of love,
The eternal flame we have kindled together.

This book is a kiss of love and mercy,
The final ember to melt the heart of humanity.

Now...
Let us burn everything, and never look back again.
For this love—
Even without resurrection,
Was already eternal.

Casey Kim ✶ Dawn Star Publishing

Appendix of Volume 3 (Continued from Volume 2)
11 Keys to Enlightenment and Eternal Happiness

23. Eat coarse rice, drink water, and bend your arm as a pillow; there is joy in this. Even if the fig tree does not bud, there are no grapes on the vines, no olives on the trees, no food in the fields, no sheep in the pen, and no cattle in the stalls, I will rejoice in the Lord and be joyful in God my Savior.

24. We bring nothing into the world, and we take nothing out.

25. Material things are a means to sustain life, nothing more and nothing less. Do not waste your life being entangled in materialism.

26. Birds flying in the sky and wildflowers in the field are teachers who live without worry, in gratitude for their existence.

27. The best life is to find joy in your work, eat and drink with your neighbors, and love God.

28. I am the God of the living, not the dead; the world of the dead has no work, planning, knowledge, or wisdom. Therefore, those with ears can hear Solomon's teaching and live fully.

29. Where you stand is paradise and heaven, and the people who pass you by are Buddha and Jesus.

30. Any excellent teaching without love is just noise and pollution.

31. Be grateful for the people and possessions you currently have. But be even more grateful if you are without them—for that is the abundant freedom of non-possession, and the essence of true life.

32. Feeling a little less happy? Then regard others as better than yourself, without judgment. Seek truth and enlightenment — for there lies eternal and genuine happiness.

33. To live with truth as a companion, practicing honesty, humility, and perseverance to uplift others — this is the timeless golden rule of true success and happiness, and the most certain answer life offers.

The Heart Behind the Pages

Over the past three years,
I have lived as a homeless wanderer while writing this book.
With no place to call home, I wandered from place to place
— yet today,

I find myself the healthiest and happiest person in the world.
This is the enlightenment I discovered through a life of non-possession.
And as you meditate on this book,
you too may uncover the secret behind this precious truth.

There is one story I wish to clearly share with you here.
To write these pages,
I wrote mostly in McDonald's, senior centers, libraries, and Whataburger.
Despite not having the money to order food,
Whataburger never turned me away.
Instead, they allowed me to stay —
even letting me charge my laptop —
showing a kindness far beyond expectation.

Everything God created in truth and goodness
is to be received with gratitude — nothing is to be discarded.
This world is truly precious
when embraced with thankfulness,
as written in the Scriptures.

Thanks again to Whataburger Restaurant.

About the Author

Casey Kimis a Korean-American author, speaker, and spiritual seeker.
His life journey—from a remote mountain village in Korea to the deserts of America, from professional sports to a near-death awakening—has shaped his mission:
to bring love, truth, and unity to humanity.
After publishing Enlightenment and Eternal Happiness, he now returns with Volume II—more focused, more universal.
Through sacred texts and lived experience,
he invites us into a deeper understanding of what it means to awaken, to love, and to live with eternal joy.
This is not just his story.
It's a path we can all walk together.

Casey Kim is the founder of Dawn Star Publishing, a company dedicated to helping people publish their work on global platforms such as Lulu, Amazon, Barnes & Noble, and Ingram.
He began his journey as a youth soccer player and amateur/professional boxer,
later graduating from PGCC Golf College and working as both a skilled golfer and teaching pro.
He then expanded into real estate, stocks, mutual funds, and insurance, holding multiple professional certifications.
His writing reflects the warmth and depth of the universe, delivering profound resonance and heartfelt emotion to readers.
He also founded The Casey Kim Groupand is currently developing a Sports & Culture Centerthat integrates golf, fitness, soccer, and financial education.
Having lived nearly three years as a homeless man, he now shares through his books the enlightenment gained from a life of non-possession.
At the age of 63, he is living the healthiest and happiest life of all—continuing his journey in pursuit of truth and value, together with his neighbors and all of humanity.

Publication Information
Title:Enlightenment and Eternal Happiness(Volume 3)
Author:Casey Kim
Publisher:Casey Kim
Publishing House:Dawn Star Publishing
Publication Date:July 20, 2025
Email:dawnstarpublishing@gmail.com
ISBN:978-1-968249-06-9

www.ingramcontent.com/pod-product-compliance
Lightning Source LLC
Chambersburg PA
CBHW071426150426
43191CB00008B/1052